GRAMMAR OF ETULO

Grammar of Etulo

A Niger-Congo (Idomoid) Language

Chikelu I. Ezenwafor-Afuecheta

https://www.openbookpublishers.com

©2025 Chikelu I. Ezenwafor-Afuecheta

This work is licensed under the Creative Commons Attribution-NonCommercial 4.0 International (CC BY-NC 4.0). This license allows you to share, copy, distribute and transmit the text; to adapt the text for non-commercial purposes of the text providing attribution is made to the authors (but not in any way that suggests that they endorse you or your use of the work). Attribution should include the following information:

Chikelu I. Ezenwafor-Afuecheta, *Grammar of Etulo: A Niger-Congo (Idomoid) Language*. Cambridge, UK: Open Book Publishers, 2025, https://doi.org/10.11647/OBP.0467

Further details about CC BY-NC licenses are available at
https://creativecommons.org/licenses/by-nc/4.0/

All external links were active at the time of publication unless otherwise stated and have been archived via the Internet Archive Wayback Machine at
https://archive.org/web

Digital material and resources associated with this volume are available at
https://doi.org/10.11647/OBP.0467#resources

This volume is part of a long-lasting series which can be accessed at
https://philsoc.org.uk/Monographs

Publications of the Philological Society, vol. 1
ISSN Print: 0265-0649 | ISSN Digital: 2977-845X

ISBN Paperback: 978-1-80511-597-7
ISBN Hardback: 978-1-80511-598-4
ISBN Digital (PDF): 978-1-80511-599-1
ISBN HTML: 978-1-80511-601-1
ISBN Digital ebook (epub): 978-1-80511-600-4

DOI: 10.11647/OBP.0467

Cover image: Photo by Chikelu I. Ezenwafor-Afuecheta, 'The Etulo land, Buruku Local Government Area of Benue State, Nigeria', June 2014
Cover design: Jeevanjot Kaur Nagpal

Table of Contents

ACKNOWLEDGEMENTS — xv
ABBREVIATIONS — xvii
LIST OF TABLES — xxi
LIST OF FIGURES — xxiii

1. GENERAL INTRODUCTION — 1
1.0 An overview — 1
1.1 The sociolinguistic background of the Etulo speaking community in the Benue state — 1
   1.1.1 The Etulo language and its dialects — 1
   1.1.2 Estimated number of speakers — 2
   1.1.3 Geographical location of Etulo speakers — 2
   1.1.4 Linguistic classification of Etulo — 4
   1.1.5 Sociolinguistic situation of the Etulo speech communities in the Benue state — 4
   1.1.6 The historical origin of the Etulo people — 4
   1.1.7 Religion, culture and tradition of the Etulo people — 5
1.2. Fieldwork, logistics and data representation — 6
1.3 Previous research on Etulo — 7
1.4 Scope of this work — 7

2. THE PHONOLOGY OF ETULO — 9
2.0 Introduction — 9
2.1 An overview of previous works on Etulo phonology — 9
2.2 Phoneme inventory of Etulo — 10
   2.2.2 Distribution of Etulo consonant phonemes — 12
   2.2.3 Etulo vowel phonemes — 14
   2.2.4 Allophonic realization of Etulo vowels — 15
   2.2.5 Nasalized vowels — 16

2.3 Vowel lengthening and sequence	17
2.4 Tone and intonation	19
2.4.1 The high tone [´]	19
2.4.2. The low tone [`]	20
2.4.3 The mid tone [-]	20
2.4.4 The falling tone [ˆ]	21
2.4.5 The rising tone [ˇ]	21
2.4.6 Functions of tone	21
2.4.8 Tonal change	23
2.4.9 Tone polarity	23
2.5 Etulo syllable structure and phonotactics	24
2.5.1 V syllable structure	25
2.5.2 CV syllable structure	25
2.5.3 Ṇ syllable structure	25
2.5.4 CCV syllable structure	26
2.5.5 CVN syllable structure	26
2.5.6 Implication of NC sequences for Etulo syllable structure	26
2.6 Phonological processes in Etulo	27
2.6.1 Elision	27
2.6.2 Consonant elision	29
2.6.3 Assimilation	29
2.6.4 Vowel coalescence	31
2.6.5 Vowel insertion	31
2.6.6 Glide formation	32
2.6.7 Vowel harmony	33
2.7 Conclusion	35
3. MORPHOLOGICAL PROCESSES	**37**
3.0 Introduction	37
3.1 Derivational morphology	37
3.1.1 Unproductive derivation (deverbal nouns)	38
3.2 The nominalizing ò- vowel prefix	38
3.2.1 The infinitive verb	38
3.2.2 Gerundive nominals	39
3.2.3 Derived agentive nominals	41
3.2.4 Adjectives derived from ideophones	41

3.3 The -*lu* suffix 42
3.4 Reduplication 43
   3.4.1 Reduplication of ideophones and nouns 43
3.5 Compounding 44
   3.5.1 Nominal compound 44
      3.5.1.1 Genitive compound 44
      3.5.1.2 Amalgamated compound 45
      3.5.1.3 Synthetic compound 47
   3.5.2 Nominal compounds vs associative constructions 47
   3.5.3 Verbal Compound 48
3.6 Conclusion 50

4. WORD CLASSES 51

4.0 Introduction 51
4.1 The pronominal system 51
   4.1.1 Personal pronouns 51
      4.1.1.1 Subject pronouns 53
      4.1.1.2 Object pronouns 55
      4.1.1.3 A note on free and bound forms 56
   4.1.2 Possessives 59
   4.1.3 Reflexive pronouns 61
   4.1.4 Anaphoric and logophoric reference 64
   4.1.5 Interrogative pronouns 66
   4.1.6 Relative pronouns 67
   4.1.7 Demonstratives 67
   4.1.8 A note on the indefinite pronoun quantifiers 71
   4.1.9 Conclusion 72
4.2. The noun category and noun phrase 72
   4.2.1 Theoretical backdrop 73
   4.2.2 Phonological structure of Etulo nouns 74
   4.2.3 Morpho-syntactic characterizations of nouns 74
   4.2.4 A class of determiners 75
      4.2.4.1 The category of definiteness 76
      4.2.4.2 Interrogative determiners 76
      4.2.4.3 Quantificational determiners 77
   4.2.5 The noun phrase 77
   4.2.6 Associative constructions 79

4.2.7 Distinguishing nouns from adjectives	81
4.2.8 Semantic classification of nouns	82
4.2.9 Conclusion	82
4.3 The verb category	**83**
4.3.1 Phonological structure of verb roots	83
4.3.2 Verb classification	85
4.3.2.1 Obligatory complement verbs (OCVs)	86
4.3.2.2 Non-obligatory complement verbs (NCVs)	90
4.3.3 Simple vs complex predicates	90
4.3.4. Selectional restriction	91
4.3.5 Conclusion	91
4.4 Qualificatives	**92**
4.4.1 Typological criteria	92
4.4.2 The adjective class	93
4.4.3 Verbs as qualificatives (adjectival verbs)	96
4.4.3.1 Verbs in attributive function	98
4.4.4 Other means of expressing property concepts	98
4.4.5 Semantic characterization of qualificatives	100
4.4.6 Differentiating between adjectives and adjectival verbs	100
4.4.7 Expression of degree	101
4.4.8. Use of the intensifier *sáān* with qualificatives	102
4.4.9 Conclusion	103
4.5 The adverb category	**103**
4.5.1 The classification of adverbs	103
4.5.1.1 The morphological classification of adverbs	104
4.5.1.1.1 Simple adverbs	104
4.5.1.1.2 Complex adverbs	104
4.5.1.1.2.1 Phrasal adverbials	104
4.5.1.1.2.2 Adverbs formed by reduplication	105
4.5.1.2 The functional classification of adverbs	105
4.5.1.2.1 Manner adverbs	105
4.5.1.2.2 Temporal adverbs	106
4.5.1.2.3 Place adverbs	108
4.5.1.2.4 Frequency adverbs	110
4.5.1.2.5 Adverbs of magnitude	111
4.5.2 The relative order of adverbs	112
4.5.3 Conclusion	113

4.6 The preposition category	113
4.6.1 Etulo prepositions	114
4.6.1.1 The preposition *mì*	114
4.6.1.2 The preposition *jì*	115
4.6.1.3 The preposition *m̀bí*	116
4.6.1.4 The preposition *ŋátāā*	116
4.6.2 Derived prepositions	117
4.6.3 Phonological features of prepositions	118
4.6.4 The syntactic distribution of prepositions	118
4.6.5 Other means to express locative and related meanings	119
4.6.5.1 The existential copula as a locative marker	120
4.6.5.2 The kìè verb as a preposition marker	120
4.6.5.3 Preposition markers in complex predicates: the verb *kɛ*, and the existential copula	121
4.6.6 Conclusion	122
4.7 The status of Etulo ideophones	122
4.7.1 Towards a definition	123
4.7.2 The Etulo ideophone	123
4.7.2.1 The phonological characterization of Etulo ideophones	124
4.7.2.2 The morphological characterization of Etulo ideophones	124
4.7.3 Towards a semantic classification of Etulo ideophones	126
4.7.4 Syntactic characterization of Etulo ideophones	126
4.7.5 The categorial status of Etulo ideophones	129
4.7.6 Conclusion	130
4.8 The numeral system	130
4.8.1 Cardinal numerals	131
4.8.1.1 Cardinal numerals formed by compounding	131
4.8.1.2 Cardinal numerals formed by addition	132
4.8.1.3 Cardinal numerals formed by compounding and addition	133
4.8.2 Ordinal numerals	134
4.8.3 Cardinal and ordinal numerals as modifiers	136
4.8.4 Distributive numerals	137
4.8.5 Arithmetic operations	137
4.8.5.1 Addition	137
4.8.5.2 Subtraction	138
4.8.5.3 Division	138
4.8.5.4 Multiplication	138
4.8.5.5 Fractions	139
4.8.6 Conclusion	139

5. ASPECTS OF ETULO SYNTAX — 141

5.0 Introduction — 141
5.1 Negation — 141
    5.1.1 Negation of basic declarative constructions — 142
    5.1.2 Negation of imperatives — 143
    5.1.3 Negation of interrogatives (polar questions) — 144
    5.1.4 Negation of complex clauses — 145
    5.1.5 Negative words — 146
    5.1.6 Conclusion — 147
5.2 Interrogatives — 147
    5.2.1 Polar questions — 147
    5.2.2 Content questions — 148
        5.2.2.1 Syntactic distribution of interrogative words — 149
        5.2.2.2 Interrogative words in simple clauses — 149
    5.2.3 Interrogative complex clauses — 151
    5.2.4 Conclusion — 152
5.3 Coordination — 152
    5.3.1 Coordination types — 153
    5.3.2 Conjunction markers — 154
        5.3.2.1 The coordinator *jì* — 154
        5.3.2.2 The coordinator *dí* — 155
        5.3.2.3 The coordinators *mà/mân* — 156
    5.3.3 Disjunction markers — 157
    5.3.4 Adversative marker — 157
    5.3.5 Single vs multiple coordinate marking — 158
    5.3.6 Conclusion — 158
5.4 Subordination — 159
    5.4.1 Complement clause — 159
        5.4.1.1 The complementizer *dĩ* — 160
        5.4.1.2 The complementizer *gbɛ̌ɛ̄* — 160
        5.4.1.3 The pairing of *gbɛ̌ɛ̄* and *dí* — 161
        5.4.1.4 Pairing of *gbɛ̌ɛ̄* and *nì* — 161
        5.4.1.5 The complementizer *dàfí* — 161
        5.4.1.6 Complement clause in the subject argument position — 162
        5.4.1.7 Speech verbs — 163
    5.4.2 The relative clause — 164
        5.4.2.1 Syntactic and semantic functions of the relativizers — 164

5.4.2.2 Position of the relative clause	165
5.4.2.3 A note on the relative pronoun	165
5.4.2.4 The relative clause-final morphemes	166
5.4.3 The adverbial clause	167
5.4.3.1 The causal clause	167
5.4.3.2 Time adverbial clause	167
5.4.3.3 The conditional clause	169
5.4.3.4 The purpose clause	170
5.4.3.5 Adverbial clause of manner	171
5.4.3.6 The concessive clause	171
5.4.4 Conclusion	172
5.5 The copula construction	172
5.5.1 The copula *lì*	173
5.5.2 The semi copula *dzè*	174
5.5.3 The copula *lè*	177
5.5.4 Conclusion	177
5.6 Constituent order	177
5.6.1 Basic order of subject, object and verb	178
5.6.2 Order of tense-aspect particles relative tothe verb	180
5.6.3 Order of copula and predicate	181
5.6.4 Order of adposition	181
5.6.5 Order within a noun phrase	182
5.6.5.1 Article and noun	184
5.6.5.2 Plural word and noun	184
5.6.6 Order in possessive/genitive constructions	185
5.6.7 Order of the relative clause and noun	185
5.6.8 Order in comparative constructions	186
5.6.9 Correlation with cross-linguistic generalizations	186
5.6.10 Conclusion	188
6. VALENCY, TRANSITIVITY AND SERIALIZATION	**189**
6.0 Introduction	189
6.1 A definition of valence	189
6.1.1 Intransitive verbs	190
6.1.2 Intransitive OCVs	191
6.1.3 Transitive verbs	193
6.1.4 OCVs and transitivity	193

6.1.5 Ditransitive verbs	195
6.1.5.1 Double object construction	196
6.1.5.2 Applicative construction	196
6.1.6 Ambitransitive verbs	197
6.1.7 Argument marking	198
6.1.7.1 Word order	198
6.1.8 Symmetrical verbs	200
6.1.9 Conclusion	201
6.2 Valence-adjusting operations	201
6.2.1 Valence-increasing operation	201
6.2.1.1 Causative	202
6.2.1.2 Applicatives and object alternation (dative shift)	203
6.2.2. Valence-decreasing operations	204
6.2.2.1 Absence of passivization	204
6.2.2.2 The reflexive construction	205
6.2.2.3 The reciprocal construction	206
6.2.2.4 The anticausative	206
6.2.3 The valence pattern of serial verbs	207
6.2.4 Conclusion	207
6.3 Verb serialization	208
6.3.1 The typological criteria	208
6.3.2 The functional properties of SVCs	210
6.3.2.1 Comparative and superlative meaning	211
6.3.2.2 Completive aspect	211
6.3.2.3 SVCs and grammaticalization	211
6.3.3 Monoclausality	213
6.3.4 Optional and obligatory SVCs	213
6.3.5 The asymmetric and symmetric divide	214
6.3.6 Wordhood and contiguity	216
6.3.7 Argument sharing	217
6.3.7.1 Subject sharing	217
6.3.7.2 Object sharing (same subject-same object)	217
6.3.7.3 Arguments and switch function	218
6.3.8 Differentiating SVCs from consecutive constructions	218
6.3.8.1 TAM values of SVCs and consecutive constructions	219
6.3.9 Conclusion	221

7. TENSE, ASPECT AND MODALITY — 223

7.0 Introduction — 223
7.1 An overview of tense and aspect — 223
7.2 Etulo tense and aspect system — 225
    7.2.1 The non-future — 225
    7.2.2 The future — 226
7.3 Aspectual distinction — 227
    7.3.1 The progressive — 227
    7.3.2 The habitual — 231
    7.3.3 The compatibility of statives with progressive and habitual markers — 234
    7.3.4 The perfectal — 234
7.4 Modality in Etulo — 236
    7.4.1 The imperative — 236
    7.4.2 The hortative — 237
    7.4.3 The obligative — 238
    7.4.4 The counterfactual modality — 239
    7.4.5 The hypothetical modality — 239
    7.4.6 The potential/permissive modality — 240
    7.4.7 The probability modality — 240
7.5 Conclusion — 241

8. GENERAL CONCLUSION — 243

APPENDIX — 245

Text 1. A story of the king, the hare and other animals — 245
    Translation — 249
Text 2. How we plant yams — 251
    Translation — 252
Text 3. What I did yesterday — 252
    Translation — 253
Text 4. What I do every day — 253
    Translation — 254
Audio recordings — 255
REFERENCES — 257
INDEX — 265

Acknowledgements

This work is an improved version of my PhD dissertation 'A grammatical sketch of Etulo' submitted to the Department of Linguistics, Scuola Normale Superiore, Pisa, Italy.

The list of individuals who contributed toward the success of this work is endless. My heartfelt gratitude goes to Prof. Emeritus Pier Marco Bertinetto under whose tutelage the original draft of this grammar was written. He painstakingly read through this work, asked questions that made me dig a little deeper, gave insightful suggestions and consistently encouraged me to rework the dissertation for publication. I am indebted to Prof. Felix Ameka and Dr. Melanie Green for their invaluable role in the drafting of this grammar book, and particularly thankful for their constructive criticisms and helpful suggestions that aided me in its production. I am also grateful to my colleagues at the Department of Linguistics, Nnamdi Azikiwe University, Awka, Nigeria for their immense support.

I appreciate my invaluable Etulo language informants: Mr Morro Akanya for welcoming me to his home, being patient with my endless probing, crosschecking of data and incessant calls, the late Mr Clement Ingyu Agyo for all the folk tales, and Ms Inyani Adams for being not only an informant but a friend and sister, for making me very comfortable in her home, for allowing her mother and siblings (Ishe and Owaita) answer my numerous questions. I am in awe of your kindness and hospitality. I am also thankful to Mr Benjamin Jukwe who was of great help to me.

I am grateful to my parents Mr Samuel and Mrs Irene Ezenwafor, and my siblings (Onyema, Chibunma, Sopulu, Chiaghanam and Chiazom) for their love, support, encouragement and prayers. To my loving husband, Emmanuel Afuecheta, I say thank you for always being there for me, for your persistent prodding on the progress of my work and for your overall support. I am thankful for my little ones, Nkasiobi, Chimadika and Ihuoma who could neither fully comprehend why mom had to lock herself away many times nor why she stayed awake on many nights.

Above all, I am grateful to God almighty for the grace to multitask. I alone take responsibility for any shortcomings in this work.

Abbreviations

ADJ	adjective
ADV	adverb
ATR	advanced tongue root
AUX	auxiliary
C	complement
CONS	consonant
COP	copula
COMP	complementizer
COND	conditional
CONJ	conjunction
CONN	connective
DEM	demonstrative
DET	determiner
EXCLM	exclamation
F	falling tone
FUT	future
GEN	genitive
GN	genitive-noun
H	high tone
HAB	habitual
IMP	imperative
IDEO	ideophone
INF	infinitive
INT	intensifier
IPA	international phonetic alphabet

L	low tone
LOC	locative
LOC.COP	locative copula
M	mid tone
MOD	modal
N	nasal
Ṇ	syllabic nasal
N1	1st noun
N2	2nd noun
NCV	non-obligatory complement verb
NEG	negation
NOM	nominalization
NUM	numeral
NG	noun-genitive
NP	noun phrase
OBJ	object
OC	obligatory complement
OCV	obligatory complement verb
PST	past
PL	plural
POSS	possessive
PP	preposition phrase
PFV	perfective
PRF	perfect
PREF	prefix
PROG	progressive
PTCL	particle
Q	question
R	rising tone
RECP	reciprocal
RED	reduplicative
REFL	reflexive

REL	relative
REL.P	relative pronoun
SUBR	subordinator
SUFF	suffix
SG	singular
SUBJ	subject
SVC	serial verb construction
SVO	subject-verb-object
SYMV	symmetric verb
V	vowel
Ṽ	nasalized vowel
VP	verb phrase
VH	vowel harmony
1SG	first person singular
2SG	second person singular
3SG	third person singular
1PL	first person plural
2PL	second person plural
3PL	third person plural

List of Tables

2.1	The Etulo phonemic inventory proposed by Armstrong (1968: 67)	p. 9
2.2	Etulo consonant phonemes	p. 10
2.3	Distribution of consonant phonemes	p. 13
2.4	Distribution of Etulo vowels	p. 16
3.1	Features of associative constructions and nominal compounds	p. 48
4.1	Etulo personal pronouns	p. 52
4.2	Reflexive pronouns	p. 64
4.3	Demonstratives	p. 71
4.4	Syllable structure of the Etulo noun	p. 74
4.5	Number marking	p. 75
4.6	Semantic classification of nouns	p. 82
4.7	Phonological structure of the Etulo verb	p. 83
4.8	Contracted verb + noun forms	p. 86
4.9	Selectional restriction	p. 91
4.10	Etulo adjectives	p. 94
4.11	Adjectival verbs	p. 96
4.12	Corresponding adjectives and adjectival verbs	p. 100
4.13	Summarized features of adjectives and adjectival verbs	p. 101
4.14	Categorial status of ideophones	p. 129
4.15	Cardinal numerals 11–39	p. 132
4.16	Traditional vs modern counting system	p. 134
4.17	Ordinal numerals	p. 135
5.1	Constituent order of the Etulo NP	p. 183

5.2	Correlating vs non correlating patterns	p. 187
6.1	Valence features	p. 202
6.2	Distinguishing SVCs from consecutives	p. 221
7.1	Tense-aspect distinctions	p. 225
7.2	Aspectual compatibility with stative verbs	p. 234

List of Figures

1.1	Map of Etulo land in the Benue valley. Extracted from Katsina Ala Sheet 272 SE (Scale 1:50,000) (Adapted from Tabe 2007: 24)	p. 2
1.2	Etulo language family tree. Drawn by the author (2025)	p. 3
2.1	Etulo vowel chart. Drawn by the author (2025)	p. 14
2.2	Etulo syllable structure. Drawn by the author (2025)	p. 24
5.1	A summary of the semantics of *dzè*. Drawn by the author (2025)	p. 176

1. General Introduction

1.0 An overview

This work offers a grammatical description of Etulo, an Idomoid language spoken in Nigeria by a minority group in the Benue and Taraba states respectively. It focuses on the variety spoken in the Etulo community of the Benue state and serves as the bedrock for further description of the Etulo grammar and for providing pedagogical materials needed in Etulo language teaching. It also serves as a reference point for linguists interested in language typology. This chapter gives an overview of the sociolinguistic background of the Etulo speaking community, their history and cultural practices. It reviews previous works done on aspects of Etulo grammar. It explains the fieldwork technique used, and other conventions relevant for this work.

1.1 The sociolinguistic background of the Etulo speaking community in the Benue state

The name 'Etulo' simultaneously refers to the language, the land and the people. Historically, the Etulo were wrongly called Turu and Utur respectively by their neighbours, the Tiv and Hausa peoples. It was not until 1976 that the correct version of the name 'Etulo' was adopted with the help and support of the Benue state military government under the then Military Governor, Colonel Abdulahi Shelleng (Tabe 2007). Etulo is made up of 14 clans. Nine of these (Agbatala, Oglazi, Agbɔ, Ugiɛ, Agia, Ogbulube, Oʃafu, Okpaʃila and Ingwadʒɛ) fall into the Buruku Local Government Area, while the remaining five clans (Otsazi, Otanga, Okadiɲa, ʃɛwɛ and Aʃitanakwu) belong to the Katsina Ala Local Government Area of the Benue state. The map in Fig. 1 below shows the Etulo land and highlights some of its clans.

1.1.1 The Etulo language and its dialects

It is assumed that every speech community has dialects prompted by sociological stratification (sociolect) or individualism (idiolect) and Etulo is no exception.

However, in purely geographical terms, no dialectical variations are observed except for minor phonological differences associated with the speech of Etulos belonging to different clans in the Etulo land. Perhaps one may find dialectical variation when the varieties spoken in Benue state and Taraba state are compared.

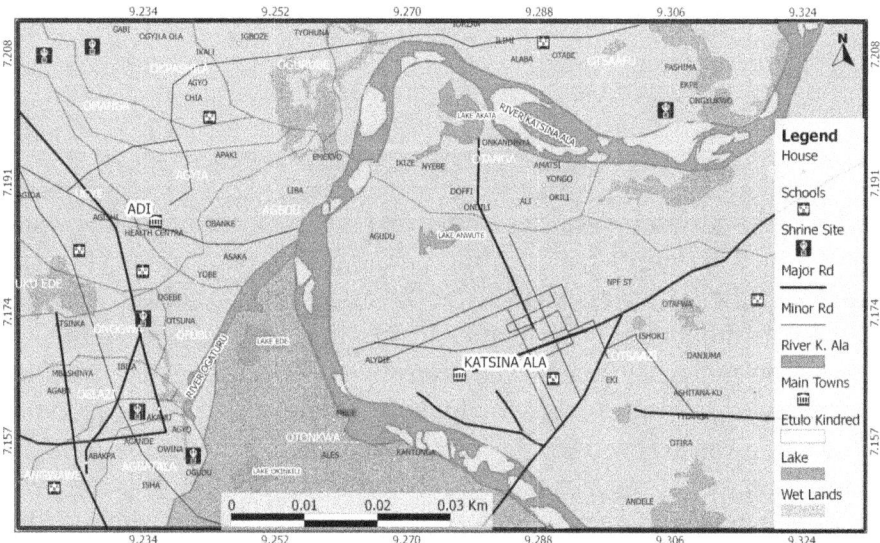

Fig. 1.1 Map of Etulo land in the Benue valley. Extracted from Katsina Ala Sheet 272 SE (Scale 1:50,000) (Adapted from Tabe 2007: 24)

1.1.2 Estimated number of speakers

The estimated number of Etulo speakers varies from one source to another, ranging from 10,000–100,000 speakers. According to the 1988 census as recorded in Shain (1988), Etulo has about 10,000 speakers. The Joshua Project, a US evangelical Christian organization coordinating missionary work globally (2015), records about twenty thousand Etulo language speakers. In Tabe (2007), the projected population of Etulo speakers based on tax assessment over a period of seventy years is about 100,000 at the growth rate of 2.5%.

1.1.3 Geographical location of Etulo speakers

Etulo people are found in two states (Benue and Taraba) of the North-Central geopolitical zone in Nigeria. In the Benue state, they are located in Buruku and Katsina Ala Local Government Area (LGA) respectively. In the Taraba state, Etulos are found in Wukari LGA. This work investigates Etulo as spoken in Buruku and Katsina Ala LGA. The speakers live on both banks of the Katsina

Ala River, about 136 kilometres east of Makurdi, the Benue state capital. The Etulo land (Ikpese Etulo) in the Benue state stretches from 70N to 90N latitudes and 110E to 130E longitude (Tabe 2007). Based on oral accounts, some Etulo natives claim that the division of the Etulo people into two different LGAs was orchestrated by the majority and governing ethnic group, Tiv, to further reduce the numerical strength of Etulo as a minority group. The Etulo land situated in Buruku LGA hosts a popular market called Adi, named after a famous Etulo man. The market has become so widely recognized that its name is gradually overshadowing the original name of the area, Etulo.

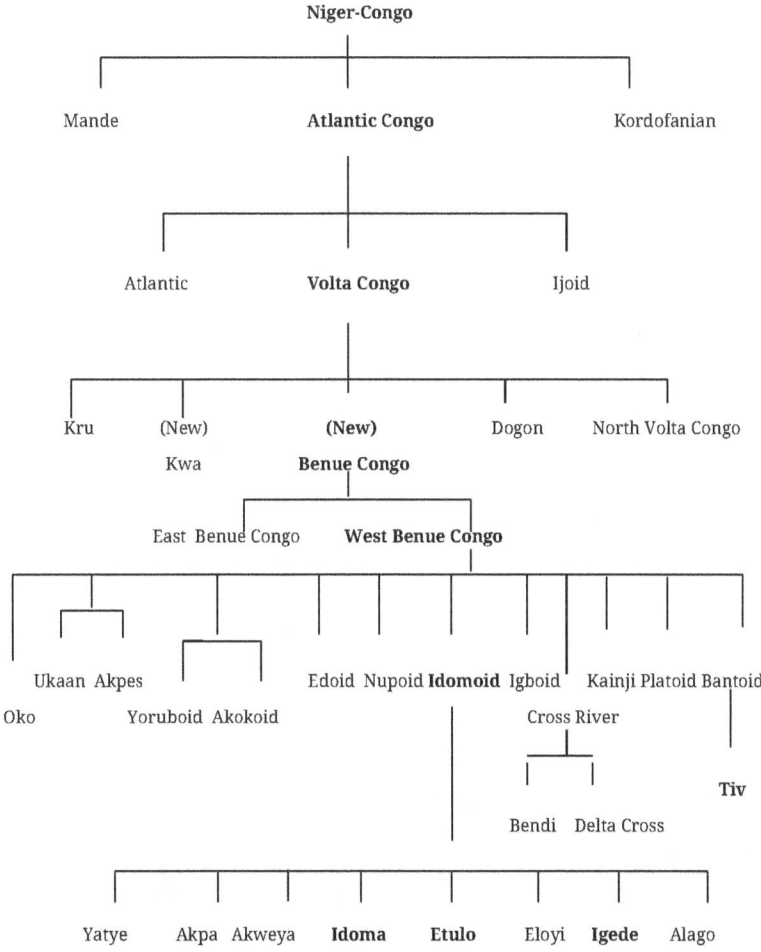

Fig. 1.2 The Etulo language family tree. Drawn by the author (2025)

1.1.4 Linguistic classification of Etulo

Armstrong (1989) classifies Etulo as an Idomoid language of the Benue Congo subgroup of the Niger Congo language family. This classification is maintained in Williamson and Blench (2000) and Gordon (2005). Tabe (2007) considers Etulo to be closely related to some Jukunoid languages of the Platoid subgroup of the Niger Congo language. This could be traced to the fact that Etulo has strong historical and cultural ties with the Jukun people, with whom they migrated from the old Kwararafa Kingdom.

Fig. 1.2 shows the internal articulation of the Etulo language group, as adapted from Williamson (1989) and Williamson and Blench (2000) with slight modifications.

1.1.5 Sociolinguistic situation of the Etulo speech communities in the Benue state

The Etulo speech community is multilingual. In the Benue state, Etulo exists alongside some other indigenous languages like Tiv, Hausa, Idoma, Igede etc. Of all these languages, Tiv is the dominant one. Thus, in addition to their native language, most Etulo people also speak Tiv, which is taught in schools to all students and equally serves as the main language of commerce. The use of Etulo is therefore largely restricted to the home domain and markets or church in the Etulo land. This has caused an influx of Tiv words into the Etulo lexicon. Besides Etulo and Tiv, English (being one of the official languages in Nigeria together with Igbo, Hausa and Yoruba) is used as a medium of instruction in schools and other formal sectors. The restricted use of Etulo by native speakers places it on the endangered languages list. In their study of the ethnolinguistic vitality of Etulo, Agbedo and Kwambehar (2013) observe that Etulo is critically endangered and requires urgent, deliberate efforts to revive and save it from total extinction.

1.1.6 The historical origin of the Etulo people

The history of the Etulo people mostly draws from oral accounts passed on from one generation to the next. Tabe (2007) traces the history of the Etulo to one of the Jukunoid groups of people that formed the erstwhile Kwararafa Kingdom in the distant past. As a result of some sociopolitical factors, these groups separated and migrated to different areas for settlement. The groups include Etulo, Idoma, Igbirra, Ogoja, Afo, Nupe and Jukun. The Etulos occupied the land long before the migration of Tivs to Benue. Gbor (1974) recounts that the Etulos had settled on the bank of the Benue River long before the Tiv, who migrated from Swem around the Cameroon hills, settled alongside the Etulos. Gbor claims that it was through conquest that the Tiv people pushed the other segments of the Kwararafa Kingdom (such as the Jukuns and the Idomas) out of the Benue valley and settled where they are today. Hanior (1989) explains that the Etulo people decided to remain on the bank of the Benue River to retain their claim to the land.

The Etulos believe they have a progenitor named Ibagye, from whom they trace their descent. Ibagye is said to have had several children, including Itsikpe, who was known as the leader of his people. Itsikpe had three sons namely: Okakwu the eldest, Ozi and Okwe. History has it that these three sons later became the leaders of their people and consequently established a royal family to rule the Etulos (Tabe 2007). The centre of the old Kwararafa Kingdom is located in Api, Wukari Local Government Area of the Taraba state. The ruler of this kingdom is known as the Aku Uka. Present-day Etulo people still maintain a connection to this ancestral heritage; even today, the enthronement of a new king in Etulo land requires the blessings of the Aku Uka.

1.1.7 Religion, culture and tradition of the Etulo people

Before the advent of Christianity, the Etulo people practiced a form of traditional African religion. According to Tabe (2007), Etulos believed in 'one supreme being' called Mgbasho, who reveals himself through myriad 'minor gods', such as Esekio 'god of the river', Emakpala 'god of thunder' etc. Different families had different shrines. In each family, it is normal to find a sacred enclosure known as Ozoka, which houses the family gods and equally serves as a place for spiritual purposes such as sacred rites. Even after the advent of Christianity in the Etulo land around 1939, many of the fetish practices are still retained today.

In traditional Etulo culture, individuals who had been dedicated to idols were considered taboo. Such individuals and their families were treated as outcasts and avoided, especially in matters of marriage. This practice is, however, no longer prevalent. One of the Etulo cultural practices retained to this day is the age-grade system. Age groups are the pillars of Etulo society, playing important roles in enforcing law and order, settling disputes, and providing defence.

Many festivals, such as Opleka and Agashi, are held among the Etulo people. Opleka features prayers, traditional dances, sacrifices and other rites of passage to Etulo ancestors and gods, while Agashi involves the reincarnation of ancestral spirits. It is performed especially when a man is experiencing hard times. Etulos are predominantly fishermen and farmers. As farmers they are known for the cultivation of crops such as rice, millet and oranges etc. They also work as blacksmiths, wood carvers and herbal practitioners.

1.2. Fieldwork, logistics and data representation

The data for this research was gathered in two field trips. The first field trip was undertaken in the spring of 2014 and lasted eight weeks. I embarked on a second field trip in 2015 for a period of eight weeks. On different occasions, between 2017 and 2020, I invited my Etulo language consultants to my resident state in Nigeria for additional field sessions. I worked with three language consultants: two men, aged forty-six and fifty-five, and one woman, aged thirty. All three have received some formal education and are plurilingual, proficient in Etulo, Tiv, English and Nigerian pidgin. Etulo is, however, their first language. Data elicitaiont was conducted primarily in English, and occasionally in Nigerian pidgin. My male consultants, Mr Moro Akanya (a farmer) and Mr Ingyu Agya (a catechist, photographer and farmer) are members of the Etulo bible translation team working under the Nigerian Bible Translation Trust, Jos. The female consultant, Ms Inyani Adams, holds a BA and MA in Linguistics and was very helpful with the technical aspects of my data collection. Mr Moro Akanya was a particularly valuable consultant, demonstrating strong linguistic intuition about his native language. Both male consultants are born and raised in Etulo land and permanently reside there.

For data elicitation, I adopted the use of different structured questionnaires. On phonology, I used the Swadesh wordlist, the comparative wordlist compiled by Blench (2008) and the 1,700-hundred SIL Comparative African Wordlist (SILCAWL). On morphology, I used a questionnaire on word formation processes proposed by Štekauer (2012). Other relevant questionnaires on syntactic structures were taken from the website of the Max Plank Institute for Evolutionary Anthropology. They include, but are not restricted to, Klamer's (2000) questionnaire on valence, the relative clause questionnaire proposed by the Bantu Psyn project members (University of Berlin, Universite Lyon 2010) and the questionnaire on complement clauses by Hengeveld (2009). Language data on narratives were also gathered. The data used for this work are in field notes and in an electronic corpus and have potential for development into a shared source. The elicited data were audio recorded using an Edirol Roland Wave MP3 recorder.

The Etulo language data is transcribed according to the International Phonetic Alphabet (IPA). Since Etulo currently does not have a generally accepted, official orthography, the IPA serves as an alternative system, without the ambiguity and controversy associated with the use of an unofficial orthography. The suprasegmental feature 'tone' is fully marked. High tones are marked by the acute symbol [′]. Low tones are marked by the grave accent [`]. The mid tone and downstep feature is marked by a macron [¯] and contour tones by the circumflex [ˆ ˇ] (falling and rising tone). Segments enclosed within slant lines are phonemic, while those enclosed within square brackets are phonetic.

It is usually the case that words are pronounced differently in isolation than in connected speech. Etulo, for instance, is characterized by phonological processes such as assimilation and elision which alter the inherent phonemic structure of words in natural speech flow. This can be seen in verb + noun combinations such as *na una* 'sleep', realised in connected speech as *nuna* 'sleep'. One has to decide how to represent these words; as they occur in isolation or as they occur in connected speech. In the data representation (excluding the Appendix), such words (verb-noun combinations) are mostly written fully, as they occur in isolation. In other words, the phonological processes that these words undergo in connected speech are not captured in the data representation for the sake of consistency. An in-depth investigation on the phonological processes concerning words in context needs to be carried out.

1.3 Previous research on Etulo

Besides publications on the history and culture of the Etulo people, and on the sociolinguistic situation of the Etulo language, very little work has been done on the grammar of Etulo. Armstrong (1952) was first to publish on grammatical aspects of Etulo. His work included a working hypothesis on the Etulo sound system, a word list, independent and possessive pronouns etc. This was followed by his publication on Idomoid languages in 1989. Anyanwu (2008) used Etulo as one of the sample languages in exploration of the phonology and tonology of African languages. Ezenwafor, C. A. and Mmadike (2011) published research on the the syllable structure of Etulo. Okoye and Egenti (2015) worked on Etulo ideophones.

Other unpublished works and thesis on Etulo include the following: a proposal for Etulo orthography (Adams 1975), reading and writing in Etulo (a trial edition) proposed by the Nigerian Bible Translation Trust (NBTT) in 2012, a preliminary investigation into the morphology and syntax of Etulo (Okoye, A. 2009), interaction of tone with syntax in Etulo (Ezenwafor, C. A. 2009), and negation in Etulo (Ezenwafor, C. I. 2012).

1.4 Scope of this work

This work outlines the phonological system of Etulo, and describes Etulo word classes and their morphological characterization. Next, it focuses on aspects of derivational morphology, especially the derivation of one lexical category from another, either by reduplication, compounding or affixation. It also examines the tense-aspect features. At the syntactic level, it investigates different sentence types, verb classifications and argument structures of the verb (including verbs that are syntactically transitive but semantically intransitive, and those that take both complements and objects). It also investigates valence-increasing and valence-decreasing mechanisms, word order, negation, complementation, relativization, coordination and subordination.

2. The Phonology of Etulo

2.0 Introduction

This chapter establishes the phonemic inventory of the Etulo sound system. It distinguishes between phonemic sound segments and their allophonic variants. It examines tone as a supra-segmental feature, noting its lexical and grammatical functions. It equally investigates the syllable structure, the phonotactic constraints of phoneme combinations and the phonological adaptation of loan words. Also explored are common phonological processes such as glide formation, vowel harmony, elision, assimilation and coalescence.

2.1 An overview of previous works on Etulo phonology

In the scarce existing literature on the phonology of Etulo, one observes a number of discrepancies in the number of identified sound segments. Armstrong (1968) proposes a working hypothesis on the Etulo phonemic inventory. He identifies a total of thirty-six phonemes; twenty-eight consonants and eight vowels /i e ɛ a ə ɔ o u/. Three of these vowels are nasalized (/ĩ ɛ̃ ɔ̃/). It is not clear from his work how he arrived at this number of phonemes since he does not provide a substantive number of examples of minimal pairs. Excluded in his consonant inventory are voiced and voiceless affricates /tʃ dʒ/ which are attested in Etulo. The consonant chart below shows the proposed consonantal inventory.

Table 2.1 The Etulo phonemic inventory proposed by Armstrong (1968: 67)

Place → Manner ↓	Bilabial	Labio dental	Alveolar		Palatal		Velar		Labialized			Labio velar	
Plosive	b		t	d	ky	gy	k	g	bw	kw	gw	kp	gb
Fricative		f	s	z	ʃ				ɣw				
Affricate			ts	dz									
Roll			r										
Lateral			l										
Nasal	m		n		ɲ		ŋ					ŋm	
Semi vowel	w												

According to Adams (1975), Etulo has a total of twenty-six phonemes. He identifies seven vowels /i e ɛ a ɔ o u/ which roughly correspond to the vowel inventory of Armstrong

(1968) except for the omission of the schwa. He also identifies about nineteen consonants. His consonant inventory excludes about ten consonants proposed in Armstrong (1968). In comparison with the phonemic inventory of Armstrong, the following phonemes are excluded /ts dz ky gy ŋ bw kw gw kp gb/. It seems that Adams (1975) mostly identified consonants which are also attested in English, thereby ignoring other consonant phonemes peculiar to Etulo. Ezenwafor C. A. and Okoye (2009) identify a total of thirty-six sound segments comprising nine vowels /i ɪ e ɛ a u ʊ o ɔ/ with their nasalized and lengthened variants and twenty-seven consonants. Their vowel inventory excludes the schwa sound but includes /ɪ ʊ/ which are absent in Armstrong (1968). The largest phonemic inventory established so far in Etulo is found in Inyani Adams (2010). In her unpublished thesis, Inyani Adams claims that Etulo has a total of forty-one phonemes, comprising thirty-three consonants and eight vowels.

In 2012, the Etulo Language Development and Bible Translation Group in conjunction with NBBT (Nigerian Bible Translation Trust) put forth a proposal for writing the Etulo language. In their manual, they identify seven vowels which may be nasalized or lengthened and twenty-six consonants. They differentiate these twenty-six consonants from what they call 'combined consonants' such as /ky gy fy bw kw gw/.

Despite the disparity, it seems obvious from previous research that Etulo has little or no diphthongs, but has labialized and palatalized sound segments which have been represented differently by various researchers. Notably, all of these accounts characterize Etulo as a tone language with contrastive level tones. In the following section, I establish a phonemic inventory of Etulo using data from my own fieldwork, noting how my findings correspond with or differ from previous postulations.

2.2 Phoneme inventory of Etulo

The consonant phonemes of Etulo are represented in the table below.

Table 2.2 Etulo consonant phonemes

Place of Art → Manner of Art ↓	Bilabial	Labiodental	Alveolar	Palato-Alveolar	Palatal	Velar	Labiovelar	Labialized Velar	Glottal
Plosive	p b		t d			k g	kp gb	kw gw	
Nasal	m		n		ɲ	ŋ		ŋw	
Trill			r						
Fricative		f v	s	ʃ		ɣ			h
Affricate			ts dz	tʃ dʒ					
Lateral			l						
Approximant					j		w		

A total of twenty-nine distinctive consonants are attested in our data. In the following examples, I illustrate phonemic contrasts using these consonants in minimal pairs and near minimal pairs.

(1) a. /p/ ápá 'rib'
　　　　/b/ bâ 'tooth'
　　b. /t/ tó 'sting'
　　　　/d/ dó 'send'
　　c. /m/ má 'mould'
　　　　/n/ ná 'sleep'
　　d. /ts/ tsé 'praise'
　　　　/dz/ dzɛ́ 'cut'
　　e. /s/ sá 'wash'
　　　　/f/ fá 'drive'
　　f. /n/ nū 'give'
　　　　/l/ lú 'resemble'
　　g. /f/ ifú 'stomach'
　　　　/v/ ìvù 'forest'
　　h. /k/ kíé 'take/carry'
　　　　/g/ gíé 'eat'
　　i. /ɲ/ ɲá 'tell'
　　　　/nw/ nwá 'jump'
　　j. /kw/ àkwɔ̀ 'cry'
　　　　/gw/ ágwɔ̀ 'name of clan/village'
　　k. /ɣ/ ɣá 'divide'
　　　　/ŋ/ ŋá 'suck'
　　l. /ʃ/ ʃá 'laugh'
　　　　/s/ sá 'wash'
　　m. /j/ jē̄ 'return'
　　　　/w/ wé 'remember'
　　n. /kp/ kpà 'vomit'
　　　　/gb/ gbá 'scratch'
　　o. /nw/ nwá 'jump'
　　　　/w/ wá 'drink'
　　p. /tʃ/ m̀tʃè 'star'
　　　　/s/ m̀sè 'blessing'
　　q. /h/ hàhàhà 'arrogant (ideophone)'
　　　　/p/ pàpàpà 'depiction of flapping wings (ideophone)'

The occurrence of the three consonant phonemes /ʤ/, /r/ and /h/ is relatively rare. The first two are not found in the minimal pairs or sets identifiable in our recorded data. However, they do occur in some indigenous words. For instance, the /r/ consonant is mostly observed in a specific set of Etulo words, namely ideophones. On the other hand, the /ʤ/ consonant is not only attested in indigenous words but also in loan words. Below are some examples:

(2) a. /r/ trɔ̀ trɔ̀ 'depiction of smoothness'
    b. /r/ trè trè 'depiction of baldness'
(3) a. /ʤ/ ʤúwō 'rub/mix'
    b. /ʤ/ àʤákìlíbí 'dragon fly'
    c. /ʤ/ ìbìrìʤí 'cast net'

2.2.2 Distribution of Etulo consonant phonemes

Plosives: In the production of plosives, the air flow from the lungs is momentarily obstructed by a complete closure of the oral cavity. Voiced and voiceless plosives are attested in Etulo. They occur in word initial and word medial positions. The voiceless plosives include /p t k kw kp/ while the voiced plosives include /b d g gw gb/.

Nasal: In the production of nasals, the velum is lowered. This causes air to flow through the nasal cavity. Five nasals are identified in Etulo. They include /m n ɲ ŋ nw/. The alveolar nasal /n/ may occur in all positions of a word (word initial, medial and final positions). Other nasals are restricted to the word initial and word medial positions. Note that two of these nasals /m n/ have syllabic variants which function as tone bearing units in word initial position.

Trill: In the production of a trill, the tongue is raised in contact with the alveolar, causing a vibration. In Etulo, the occurrence of the voiced trill /r/ is relatively rare.

Fricatives: Fricatives are produced by the forceful passage of air through a narrow constriction caused by two articulators drawn together. Voicing contrast is obtained in some Etulo fricatives. The voiceless fricatives include /f s ʃ h/, while voiced fricatives include /v ɣ/.

Affricates: In the production of affricates, the articulators come together and momentarily obstruct the outflow of air from the vocal tract as with plosives. These articulators then separate, gradually causing a release of air as with fricatives. Four affricates with voicing contrast are identified in Etulo: the voiceless /ts tʃ/ and the voiced /dz ʤ/. The alveolar affricates /ts dz/ are quite common and may occur in word initial and word medial positions while the palato-alveolar affricates /tʃ dʒ/ are relatively rare. Both are found in word initial and word medial positions.

Lateral: In the production of the lateral, the tip of the tongue is raised to the alveolar causing a blockage which allows air to escape around the sides of the tongue. The voiced Etulo lateral /l/ occurs in word initial and word medial positions.

Approximants: Approximants are produced with no turbulent airflow. The articulators come close but allow enough gap for air to escape. Two approximants are attested in Etulo: the voiced labiovelar /w/ and the voiced palatal /j/. Both of them occur in word initial and word medial positions.

The distribution of Etulo consonant phonemes are illustrated in Table 2.3 below.

Table 2.3 Distribution of consonant phonemes

Consonant phonemes	Word initial position	Word medial position	Word final position
/p/	pílí 'rub'	m̀pò 'vulture'	
/b/	bùlù 'fly'	kwòbà 'many'	
/t/	tù 'meet'	átî 'snail'	
/d/	dúrú 'remove/take off'	ùdé 'home'	
/k/	ké 'go'	ékéká 'tomorrow'	
/g/	gíá 'buy'	ìnúngà 'plate/calabash'	
/kp/	kpánē 'lick'	ékpá 'a type of fish'	
/gb/	gbɔ̀ 'talk'	àgbɔ́ʃɔ̃ 'earthworm'	
/kw/	kwú 'call'	òkwɔ̀ 'farm'	
/gw/	gwéé 'few/little'	ágwó 'village'	
/f/	fúé 'sprinkle'	àfɛ̀ 'book/leaf'	
/v/	vlá 'fast'	óvúlè 'first'	
/s/	sá 'wash'	èsó 'message'	
/ʃ/	ʃɛ́ 'pluck'	àʃí 'song'	
/ɣ/	ɣá 'divide'		
/m/	mà 'cry'	ámá 'they'	
/n/	nū 'give'	ɔ̀nɔ̀ 'time'	ègín 'six'
/ɲ/	ɲá 'tell'	ìɲànì 'name of person'	
/ŋ/	ŋá 'suck'	ìkwáŋá 'foolishness'	
/nw/	nwɔ́ 'kill'	ònwè 'child'	
/ts/	tsò 'teach'	òtsé 'medicine'	
/dz/	dzè 'be'	ǹdzì 'bury'	
/tʃ/	tʃâ 'a type of noise'	m̀tʃɛ̀ 'star'	
/dʒ/	dʒúwō 'rub/mix'	àdʒàkìlíbí 'dragon fly'	
/l/	lɔ̀ 'write'	òlá 'fire'	
/r/		trɔ̀ trɔ̀ 'smooth'	
/w/	wā 'sweep'	àwújá 'money'	
/j/	jé 'know'	àjíwĩ 'shame'	
/h/	hàhàhà 'arrogant'		

It is evident from Table 2.3 that Etulo words mostly end in vowels. There are, however, a few instances where the alveolar nasal /n/ seems to occur as a word final consonant (see Section 2.2.5 for further discussion).

2.2.3 Etulo vowel phonemes

Etulo vowels are described using different parameters which include the shape of the lips, position of the tongue (tongue height), and the advanced/non-advanced tongue root feature. Etulo has a total of eight vowels. They are represented in the chart below.

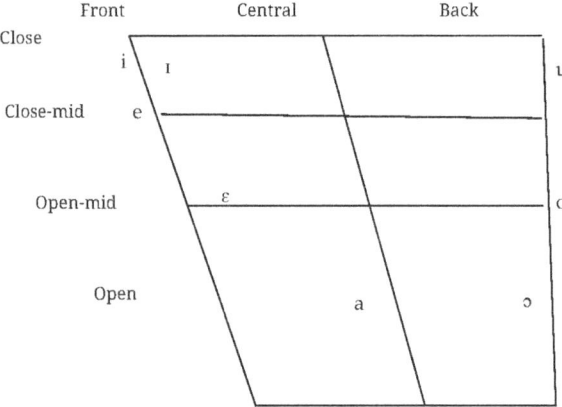

Fig. 2.1 Etulo vowel chart. Drawn by the author (2025)

Using minimal and near minimal pairs, I illustrate the phonemic contrast of oral vowels in Etulo:

(4) a. /i/ ìdê 'relative'
/ɪ/ ìdê 'tongue'
b. /o/ fó 'hear'
/ɔ/ fɔ́ 'clean/wipe'
c. /u/ lú 'resemble'
/a/ lá 'lay'
d. /e/ ʃé 'grow'
/ɛ/ ʃɛ́ 'pluck'
e. /a/ àtsè 'comb'
/i/ ìtsè 'chair'
f. /ɪ/ nwí 'when'
/ɔ/ nwɔ́ 'kill'
g. /a/ bá 'not'
/ɔ/ bɔ́ 'pray'
h. /i/ dí 'see'
/o/ dó 'send'

2.2.4 Allophonic realization of Etulo vowels

All oral vowels in Etulo have their nasalized and lengthened variants. The nasalized variants are realized only as allophones (see Section 2.2.5). The lengthened variants are mostly non-contrastive (see Section 2.3).

/**i**/ is a close front vowel produced with an advanced tongue root. It is realized as /i/, /j/ and /ĩ/. It is realized as the palatal approximant/glide in the environment of non-identical vowel sequences where it precedes other vowels (/ie ia iu io/).[1] It is realized as a nasalized vowel in the environment of the alveolar nasal in word final position. In all other environments, it is realized as /i/. Examples:

(5) a. [i] /ìdà/ [ìdà] 'termite'
    b. [j] /kíé/ [kjé] 'take/carry'
    c. [ĩ] /dín/ [dĩ́] 'see it'

/**ɪ**/ is a close front vowel produced with a retracted tongue root. It is realized as /ɪ/, /j/ and /ɪ̃/ (oral vowel, palatal glide and nasalized vowel). It occurs as a palatal glide when it precedes vowels such as /ɛ ɔ a/. Examples:

(6) a. [ɪ] /ìdɔ́/ [ìdɔ́] 'work'
    b. [j] /kɪ́ɛ̃/ [kjɛ̃] 'be old'

/**e**/ is a close mid front vowel produced with an advanced tongue root as in:

(7) /ènì/ [ènì] 'water'

/**ɛ**/ is an open mid front vowel produced with a retracted tongue root as in:

(8) /ɛ̀mɔ̀/ [ɛ̀mɔ̀] 'mosquito'

/**a**/ is an open central vowel produced with a retracted tongue root as in:

(9) /àdì/ [àdì] 'name of person'

/**u**/ is a closed back vowel produced with an advanced tongue root. It is realized as the labialized approximant [w] when it precedes other vowels such as /ɛ a e o/. Examples:

---

1   What we have here analyzed as the allophones of /i ɪ/ → [j] and /u/ → [w] are represented as features of consonant phonemes in some previous works (Armstrong 1968, NBTT 2012). The consonant phonemes /ky gy fy/ are used for the palatalized and /fw bw/ are used for the labialized. The problem with such an analysis is that it creates additional consonants in Etulo for features which can otherwise be accounted for by phonological rules. Another limitation of this analysis is that it creates stranded tones which should otherwise be realized on the vowels /i ɪ/ and /u/.

(10) a. /u/ /lú/ [lú] 'resemble/ germinate'
　　 b. /w/ /fúé/ [fwé] 'sprinkle'

/o/ is a close mid back vowel produced with an advanced tongue root as in:

(11) /èkìô/ [èkìô] 'river'

/ɔ/ is an open mid back vowel produced with a retracted tongue root as in:

(12) /ɔ̀nɔ́/ [ɔ̀nɔ́] 'time'

All vowels in Etulo may occur word initially, word medially and word finally. Table 2.4 below illustrates the distribution of Etulo vowels in all of these positions.

Table 2.4. Distribution of Etulo vowels

Vowels	Word initial position	Word medial position	Word final position
/i/	ìdà 'termite'	ìdíkà 'soldier ant'	bí 'hold'
/ɪ/	ìtákwɔ̂ 'kite'	ánɪ́nɪ́ 'vein'	nwí 'when'
/e/	èfì 'louse'	ékéká 'tomorrow'	òlé 'which'
/ɛ/	èmɔ̀ 'mosquito'	èdɛ̌dɛ̌ 'yesterday'	ònwɛ̀ 'child'
/a/	àbîì 'faeces'	m̀màfá 'youth'	mìná 'want'
/o/	òtsé 'medicine'	ònòvà 'year'	ìmgbàʃò 'God'
/ɔ/	ɔ̀nɔ́ 'time'	àgbɔ̌ʃɔ̃ 'earthworm'	ùtɔ̀ 'king'
/u/	ùdé 'home'	òbùkúsè 'a type of leaf'	ìfú 'stomach'

2.2.5 Nasalized vowels

As noted in Section 2.2.4, all oral vowels in Etulo have their nasalized variants. These nasalized variants /ĩ/ serve as allophones in complementary distribution with the oral vowels. In other words, they are non-contrastive. They occur in the word final syllable when followed by the alveolar nasal /n/. In most cases, the alveolar nasal consonant is hardly perceived. The nasalized vowels therefore become themselves word final, especially in connected speech. The status of nasalized vowels lends support to the widely held view that the nasalization of vowels historically has been triggered by a neighbouring nasal consonant in many West African languages. Greenberg (1966: 508) argues that the historical development of nasalized vowels spreads from the following nasal consonant to an oral vowel. The second stage involves a deletion of the nasal phoneme which leaves a nasal vowel behind resulting in the sequence VNˇṼNˇṼ. Etulo seems to be in the second stage, i.e. in the process of losing the nasal phoneme that triggers the nasalization of oral vowels. The nasal consonant can only be perceived in a word when it is in isolation but not in connected speech. The phonological rule that derives nasalized vowels is stated as:

[V] → [nasal] /- [nasal cons]

Examples:

(13) a. /dzíkân/ [dzíkã] 'before'
 b. /ègín/ [ègĩ] 'six'
 c. /àgín/ [àgĩ́] 'name of a person'
 d. /íkpén/ [íkpẽ́] 'bottle'

Besides the realization of nasalized vowels in word final position of lexical words, another regular instance of the realization of nasalized vowels is found in the occurrence of verbs with the 3SG pronominal clitic /n/ (see also Section 4.1.1.2). The verb usually hosts this clitic in grammatical constructions. The preceding vowel becomes nasalized in the environment of this pronominal clitic. Consider the following examples:

(14) a. kìɔ̀n → /kìɔ̀n/ [kĩɔ̃̀] 'do it'
 b. gíá-n → /gíán/ [gĩã́] 'buy it'
 c. dɔ́-n → /dɔ́n/ [dɔ̃́n] 'cook it'

Note that oral vowels may precede the nasal consonant in word initial or word medial position, but the latter does not trigger nasalization except in the word final syllable. Excepting this position, oral vowels occur in every other environment.

2.3 Vowel lengthening and sequence

Vowel lengthening in African languages is treated either as a case of allophonic variation represented by adjacent vowels or as a case of long phonemic vowels in contrast with short vowels (cf. Welmers 1978). Lengthening is a feature of all oral vowels in Etulo. These lengthened vowels are here analyzed as vowel sequences realized by two short vowels. Non-contrastive vowel length is observed in words occurring in specific environments or constructions. An example is given with the interrogative construction where the final vowel of the word in sentence final position is always lengthened (see 15 and 16). This lengthening is prompted by a tonal morpheme associated with the interrogative construction (see Section 2.4.8).

(15) a. àdì gíé ḿbúé
        PN   eat meat
        'Adi ate meat.'
     b. àdì gíé ḿbúéé
        PN   eat meat-Q
        'Did Adi eat meat?'
(16) a. àdì kà jágbá nwɔ́ ùndɔ̀
        PN FUT be.able kill goat
        'Adi can kill a goat.'
     b. àdì kà jágbá nwɔ́ ùndɔ̀ɔ̀
        PN FUT be able kill goat-Q
        'Can Adi kill a goat?'

Identical vowel sequences may occur in word medial and word final positions. Each of the vowels in a vowel sequence bears the same or different tone as shown below.

(17) a. àlĩ̀ĩ̀   'fish hook'
     b. gbɛ̌ɛ̄   'say'
     c. lúū   'go'
     d. dúú   'all'

Other vowel sequences attested in Etulo are non-identical. They include /ɪɔ io ɪɛ ie ɪa iu ue uɛ ua ui/. These vowel sequences are not interpreted as a single unit (diphthong) since each vowel may be realized with the same or a different pitch level. The occurrence of these vowel sequences is restricted to the word medial and word final positions. Consider the following examples:

(18) a. /kíɛ̄/   'be old'
     b. /dífĩū/   'notice/observe'
     c. /úkíà/   'trap'
     d. /gíé/   'eat'
     e. /èkìô/   'river'
     f. /kìɔ̀/   'do'
     g. /ìfùà/   'a wound'
     h. /fúé/   'sprinkle'
     i. /íngíú/   'name of person'

2.4 Tone and intonation

Tone is pitch variation that enters as a distinctive factor in the lexical and grammatical level of a language. A language is tonal if it employs tones for meaning distinction at either or both levels. On the other hand, intonation is the contrastive use of pitch variation for the expression of discourse meanings and the marking of phrases. Intonational tones are known to appear on accented syllables or at the edges of prosodic constituents (Gussenhoven 2010). Many African languages are known for their rich and complex tone systems. Etulo is characterized as a register tone language with three contrastive level tones and two contour tones. The level tones comprise the high tone [´] , the low tone [`] and mid tone [̄] while the contour tones include the falling [ˆ] and rising [ˇ] tones. The lexeme's inherent tones may change in grammatical constructions. Two tone bearing units are identified; vowels and syllabic nasals. Etulo is also characterized by intonation as a contrastive feature. In the following sections, I examine the features of tone and intonation in Etulo.

2.4.1 The high tone [´]

The high tone can be realized in every position of a word. Its occurrence is not restricted. When it begins a word, it may be followed by a low tone (L), mid tone (M), another high tone (H) or the gliding tones. The following patterns are obtained with the high tone in disyllabic words: H → HH, HL, HM, HF, HR and LH.

(19)	a.	émé	'bed bug'	HH
	b.	óbá	'sack'	HH
	c.	ítà	'question'	HL
	d.	míò	'fear'	HL
	e.	láfūā	'snatch'	HM
	f.	kpálū	'scrape off'	HM
	g.	ìdó	'work'	LH
	h.	àtsɛ́	'age grade'	LH
	i.	téjî	'already/ before'	HF
	j.	éjî	'we'	HF
	k.	nénǐ	'this'	HR
	l.	nánǐ	'that'	HR

2.4.2. The low tone [ˋ]

The low tone is realized in every position of a word. Just like the high tone, its occurrence is not restricted. It can begin a word and may be followed by another low tone, a high tone and in a few cases, a falling tone. It may equally be preceded by a high tone, or another low tone. Attested tone patterns include L → LL, LH, LF, HL and ML.

(20) a. òkwɔ̀ 'farm' LL
       kàkà 'enter' LL
       bùlù 'fly/jump' LL
    b. ìlú 'gong' LH
       mìná 'want/desire' LH
       ìtó 'insult' LH
    c. èjî 'blood' LF
       ìdû 'market' LF
    d. àlúbāsà 'onions' ML
       ákpékēè 'jaw' ML
    e. ákpà 'root' HL

2.4.3 The mid tone [-]

This distinctive tone is a step lower than the high tone but higher in pitch than a low tone. Unlike the other level tones, it has a restricted distribution. In disyllabic, trisyllabic and polysyllabic words, the mid tone may be preceded by a high tone but not by a low tone. In monosyllabic words, it contrasts with the high and low tones (see Section 2.4.7 (24m) and (24n)). The most common pattern associated with the mid tone is M or HM (high-mid).

(21) a. mámā 'be sour' HM
     b. kpájī 'learn' HM
     c. àtsúbō 'pepper' HM
     d. àjíwī 'shame' HM

In connected speech, it is observed that the inherent high tone of a word may be lowered to a mid when directly preceded by a high tone. For instance, the high tone realized on the 3SG subject pronoun often triggers the lowering of a following high tone realized on monosyllabic verbs (see Section 2.4.9).

2.4.4 The falling tone [ˆ]

The falling tone is a distinctive tone contrasting with the high and low tone. Its occurrence is mostly restricted to the word final syllable/mora of a word. It may be preceded by a high or low tone. The attested tone patterns associated with the falling tone include HF and LF. Examples:

(22) a. ónɔ̂ 'mother' HF
     b. éjî 'we' HF
     c. òfiê 'slave' LLF
     d. èngìâ 'women' LLF

2.4.5 The rising tone [ˇ]

The occurrence of the rising tone is quite rare in Etulo. It is only attested in few words. Unlike other tones, the rising tone has no distinctive function in Etulo. It is restricted to the word final position and is preceded by a high tone. Examples:

(23) a. nénǐ 'this'
     b. nánǐ 'that'

2.4.6 Functions of tone

Tone performs lexical and grammatical functions in Etulo. Two or more lexemes made up of identical segments are differentiated in meaning on the basis of their tonal feature. Many minimal and near minimal pairs are based on their tonal profile. Note that the inherent tones of these lexemes may however change when they enter into grammatical constructions. For instance, the lexical tones of *ènì* 'water' is LL but changes to HF in grammatical constructions such as *m̀búé énî* fish'. In the examples that follow, I illustrate the lexical function of tone in Etulo:

(24) a. dzé 'cut'
        dzè 'be'
     b. bá 'not'
        bā 'come'
     c. ló 'chase'
        lò 'write'
     d. kwó 'stab'
        kwò 'drag'
     e. ná 'sleep'
        nà 'stretch'

	f.	òtú	'night'
		òtuû	'hair'
	g.	dú	'compose'
		dù	'gush'
	h.	nū	'give'
		nù	'leak'
	i.	tò	'dig'
		tó	'sting'
	j.	ábû	'you'
		àbù	'shirt'
	k.	éjî	'we'
		èjî	'blood'
	l.	gbá	'scratch'
		gbà	'chase (goat)'
	m.	wá	'drink'
		wā	'sweep'
		wà	'perfectal marker'
	n.	fíá	'peel'
		fīā	'sweep'
		fìà	'try'

At the grammatical level, tone is used in Etulo to distinguish between the declarative and interrogative constructions. Polar questions are marked by an intonational low tone at the edge of the prosodic constituent in the sentence final position. This results in a lengthening of the sentence final element which is usually a vowel. Consider examples (25a and 26a) in contrast with (25b and 26b).

(25) a. àdì gíé ángwɔ́
    PN eat yam
    'Adi ate yam.'
  b. àdì gíé ángwɔ́ɔ̀
    PN eat yam.Q
    'Did Adi eat yam?'

(26) a. ánî wá énî
    1SG:SUBJ drink water
    'I drank water.'
  b. ánî wá énìì
    1SG:SUBJ drink water.Q
    'Did I drink water?'

In the negated variant of interrogatives, the vowel of the negation particle *lo* is lengthened. The final vowel is assigned a lowered pitch as illustrated in (27a and b) below:

(27) a. íngíú kà jágbá ná úná lóò
      PN FUT be.able sleep sleep NEG.Q
      'Can't Ingiu sleep?'
   b. àdì ŋwɔ́ ùndɔ̀ lóò
      PN kill goat NEG.Q
      'Didn't Adi kill a goat?'

2.4.8 Tonal change

The lexical tone of words may change in grammatical constructions. A systematic pattern of tone change is observed in constructions in which the high tone 3SG subject pronoun directly precedes a monosyllabic high tone verb. The tone of the verb is lowered, giving rise to a mid tone. This change is triggered by the preceding high tone of the pronoun (see 28a and b). In noun compounds, a variety of patterns is observed with tonal change. In (29a), the inherent tone of the N_1 (HL) and N_2 (LH) changes to HM and HH respectively while in (29b), the inherent tone of the N_2 *ùndɔ̀* 'goat' changes from LL to HF tone. Consider the following examples:

(28) a. á nwɔ̄ m̀dà wà
       3SG:SUBJ kill cow PERF
       'They have killed a cow.'
   b. á gīā ájàtù òkwúkwó wà
      3SG:SUBJ buy car big PERF
      'They have bought a big car.'
(29) a. ítsè + èkwɔ́ → ítsē ékwɔ́
       chair tree/wood 'wooden chair'
   b. ìkíé + ùndɔ̀ → ìkíé úndɔ̂
      head goat 'goat head'

2.4.9 Tone polarity

Tone polarity is a pattern where a tone bearing unit (TBU) has a tonal value which is the opposite of that of the immediately adjacent TBU (Meyase 2021). Some Etulo TAM particles are characterized by tone polarity. The future marker *ka* and the progressive marker *le* appear to have no fixed tone. The tonal value assigned to them in constructions is determined by the tone of following TBU.

Both TAM particles are assigned a low tonal value if the adjacent TBU bears a high or mid tone. By contrast, if the adjacent TBU bears a low tone, the TAM particles are assigned a high tonal value. The following examples are illustrative:

(30) a. ánî ká mà àkwɔ̀
        1SG FUT cry cry(N)
        'I will cry.'

    b. ánî kà ʃí áʃí
        1SG FUT sing song
        'I will sing.'

(31) a. àdì lé mà àkwɔ̀
        PN PROG cry cry(N)
        'Adi is crying.'

    b. àdì lè ʃí áʃí
        PN PROG sing song
        'Adi is singing.'

2.5 Etulo syllable structure and phonotactics

A syllable can be defined in terms of the notion of phonotactic constraints restraining the possible phoneme combinations in a specific language. A syllable comprises the onset and rhyme. The onset includes all consonants that precede the nucleus. The rhyme subsumes the nucleus/peak and the coda. The nucleus is typically realized as a vowel and in some languages as a syllabic consonant. The coda includes all elements after the nucleus. All syllables have a nucleus but may or may not have other constituents. In Etulo, the nucleus comprises the vowel and syllabic nasal in conjunction with tone. A sketch of the Etulo syllable structure is given below:

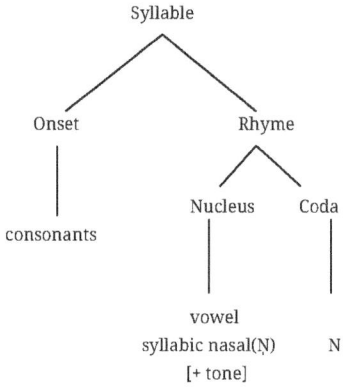

Fig. 2.2 Etulo syllable structure. Drawn by the author (2025)

Etulo mainly presents open syllables except for a few words that end with the alveolar nasal /n/. Three basic syllable types are identified: V, CV, N̩. Other attested but relatively rare syllable types include CVN and CCV. These syllable types are illustrated in the following sections.

2.5.1 V syllable structure

This syllable type comprises just the vowel which serves as the nucleus or peak.

(32) a. [ó]   V   'he/she'
     b. [á]   V   'they'
     c. [ò.kwɔ́] V.CV   'farm'
     d. [á.tí] V.CV   'snail'
     e. [ù.dɛ́] V.CV   'home'
     f. [í.ʃá] V.CV   'laughter'

2.5.2 CV syllable structure

This syllable type comprises an onset and rhyme. The onset is made up of a consonant and the rhyme a vowel.

(33) a. [kè]   CV   'go'
     b. [bá]   CV   'come'
     c. [sá]   CV   'wash'
     d. [dzé] CV   'cut'
     e. [tù]   CV   'meet/find'

2.5.3 N̩ syllable structure

This syllable type involves just the rhyme which is realized as a syllabic nasal. Out of the five nasal consonants identified in Etulo, only three have syllabic variants which may or may not be homorganic with the following consonant. The three nasals that can occur as syllabic are /m n ŋ/.

(34) a. [ŋ̩.kà]   N̩.CV   'venom'
     b. [m̩.tsà] N̩.CV   'mango'
     c. [m̩.dà]   N̩.CV   'cow'
     d. [n̩.dɛ́ɛ̂] N̩.CVV   'be tired'
     e. [n̩.kwɔ́] N̩.CV   'smell'

2.5.4 CCV syllable structure

This syllable type comprises an onset which is realized as a consonant cluster. The occurrence of consonant clusters is restricted to plosive + liquid combinations. The following examples are illustrative:

(35) a. [á.glá.bá]   V.CCV.CV   'cutlass'
     b. [ò.klè.kpá] V.CCV.CV   'bamboo'
     c. [trɔ̀.trɔ̀]   CCV.CCV   'smooth'
     d. [plɛ́]   CCV   'early'
     e. [vlá]   CCV   'fast'

2.5.5 CVN syllable structure

This syllable type comprises an onset and a rhyme. The rhyme consists of nucleus (vowel) and coda (alveolar nasal). As noted earlier, this syllable type is quite rare in Etulo and gives rise to a nasalized nuclear vowel. As previously stated in Section 2.2.5, nasal vowels are purely allophonic, and arise by assimilating the nasal feature of the following /n/. The latter may or may not be pronounced; when it drops in connected speech, the CVN word final syllable turns into CV. In isolation however, the syllable final alveolar nasal may be perceived and the CVN structure is therefore retained as shown in the following examples:

(36) a. [è.gĩ́n]   V.CVN   'six'
     b. [dzí.kãn] CV.CVN   'before'
     c. [àgĩ̂n]   V.CVN   'name of person'

2.5.6 Implication of NC sequences for Etulo syllable structure

NC (nasal-consonant) sequences are not considered as single sound segments or prenasalized consonants. They include combinations which may or may not involve homorganicity. Such sequences include /mb md mgb ms mts nd ndz nts ŋg/. In these combinations, the nasal directly precedes a stop, fricative or affricate. In Etulo, a NC sequence is subject to two different realizations. The nasal is analyzed as syllabic or non-syllabic depending on the context. With regards to syllable structure, the N in a NC sequence is part of a preceding syllable either as a syllabic nasal or a coda, while C serves as the onset of the following syllable.[2] As a syllabic nasal, N is assigned tone and occurs as an independent syllable.

---

2   In some Etulo nouns, the occurrence of a vowel before a nasal in word initial position is optional. The terms for God and person are realized as ḿgbàfò or ímgbàfò 'God', ǹgísè or ìŋgɪsè 'person. When a vowel is introduced, the tone shifts from the nasal to the vowel, otherwise, the syllabic nasal retains the tone.

In a word like m̀tsà 'mango', N is realized a syllabic nasal which forms its own syllable (see 34 above for more examples). As a coda, N is toneless and is directly preceded by a vowel. In a word such as ámgbéká 'some', the /m/ coda is toneless and belongs to the preceding syllable, while /gb/ is the onset of the following syllable. More examples are given below:

(37) a. [ín.dɛ́]   VN.CV   'bundle'
      b. [èm.bì]   VN.CV   'nose'
      c. [ám.gbā   VN.CV   'greeting'
      d. [àn.dzɛ̀]   VN.CV   'sweat'
      e. [ìŋ.giò.gà]   VN.CVV.CV 'guest/visitor'

From the foregoing, the following generalizations emerge for the Etulo syllable structure:

1. Etulo predominantly presents open syllables. A closed syllable is however realized when a nasal serves as a coda of a syllable resulting in VN (word initial position) and CVN (word final position) structures. In the latter case, /n/ is the only admissible nasal.

2. The only type of consonant cluster attested in Etulo consists of stop+liquid. NC sequences are instead heterosyllabic clusters.

3. At the phonological level, non-identical vowel sequences in words like /óngìâ/ 'woman' are best analyzed as CVV rather than CCV since their contrasting tones are preserved, unlike some cases where the tones of adjacent vowels are similar or conditioned. A discussion on glide formation is given in Section 2.6.6.

2.6 Phonological processes in Etulo

In this section, some phonological processes attested in Etulo are discussed. In speech, one observes various sorts of interaction of sound segments in lexemes. Such interactions may result in the influence of the features of one sound on an adjacent sound. In Etulo, the interaction of these sound segments give rise to phonological processes such as assimilation, coalescence, insertion, elision, glide formation and vowel harmony. Most of these processes are mainly linked to the vowel segments.

2.6.1 Elision

Two types of elision are identified in Etulo: vowel and consonant elision. Vowel elision involves the deletion of the first or second of two adjacent vowels at word boundary. The choice of a deleted vowel is unpredictable. In (38–39), one finds the elision of both the word final and the word initial vowel in similar contexts. The phonological rule for elision is written in two ways to reflect the unpredictable nature of the elided vowel.

i) $[V_1] \rightarrow [\emptyset]$ # / – $[V_2]$
ii) $[V_2] \rightarrow [\emptyset]$ # / $[V_1]$ –

Instances of vowel elision are typically found in verb + noun constructions and nominal compounds. In a V+N construction, the noun is usually the complement or object of the verb. In many cases, it is difficult to identify the elided segment. One therefore relies, for instance, on nominalized constructions where the complement or object of the verb is moved to the sentence initial position. The first phonological rule applies to (38), while the second rule applies to (39). [3]

(38) **Verb + Noun**
    a.   /ná/ # /únâ/ → [núnâ] 'sleep'
           sleep   sleep
    b.   /mà/ # /àkwɔ̀/ → [màkwɔ̀] 'cry'
           cry   cry
    c.   /ʃá/ # /íʃá/ → [ʃíʃá] 'laugh'
           laugh   laughter

(39) **Verb + Noun**
    a.   /lɛ́/ # /ólɛ́/ → [lɛ́lɛ̄] 'play'
           play   play
    b.   /lá/ # /èsɛ́/ → [lásɛ́] 'lie down'
           lie   ground
    c.   /jí/ # /ùmî/ → [jímí] 'steal'
           steal   theft

In nominal compounds, only the first deletion rule is applicable. It is always V_1 that is elided at the word boundary.

---

[3] The alternative structures in (38) and (39) suggests that the phonological process of elision may stem from a historical process tending towards lexicalization (at least at the surface level), rather than being a synchronic process. This hypothesis is reinforced by the uniformity and regularity of such elisions among native speakers. Many of them consider these structures as one word. Note however, that they may be easily separated by other constituents in grammatical constructions.

(40) **Noun + Noun**

a. /èkwɔ́/ # /àdê/ → [èkwádēè] 'palm tree'
   tree   palm

b. /ónɔ̂/ # /èkìô/ → [ónékìò] 'sea'
   mother river

c. /ákwɔ̂/ # /àdê/ → [àkwádēè] 'palmnut/palm-kernel'
   seed   palm

d. /ónɔ̂/ # /ògbí/ → [ónógbī] 'hen'
   mother fowl

Vowel elision in Etulo is not restricted to verb-noun or noun-noun constructions. This process may involve words belonging to other categories.

2.6.2 Consonant elision

The elision of a consonant in Etulo is only observed with the alveolar nasal. Consonant elision is word internal. The alveolar nasal is elided in word final position in the environment after a nasalized vowel and is an optional process. The phonological rule for consonant elision is stated as follows:

$$\begin{bmatrix} C \\ +\text{nasal} \end{bmatrix} \rightarrow \emptyset \bigg/ \begin{bmatrix} V \\ +\text{nasal} \end{bmatrix} \underline{\quad}$$

(41) a. /dzíkǎn/ → [dzíkǎ['previously/before'
     b. /ègĩ́n/ → [ègĩ́] 'six'

2.6.3 Assimilation

Assimilation is a process by which a sound takes the features of another by becoming completely or partially similar to it. In most cases, such sound segments are contiguous. Assimilation can be regressive or progressive. In regressive assimilation, the following sound influences the preceding sound, while in progressive assimilation the opposite occurs (X←Y Regressive, X→Y Progressive). In Etulo, only regressive assimilation is found.

Assimilation in Etulo mostly involves vowels and to a smaller extent a nasal consonant of any point of articulation, represented by the archiphoneme /N/. Etulo vowels undergo regressive assimilation at word boundary. The preceding vowel absorbs all the features of the following vowel. Instances of vowel assimilation are found in verb-noun constructions, preposition-noun constructions and nominal compounds. Note that vowel assimilation has no effect on the tone of the assimilated sound segment. The tone on V₁ is retained after taking on the features of V₂. The assimilation rule is represented as [V₁]→[V₂] /# V₂. The following examples are illustrative:

(42) a. /wá/ # /ènì/ → [wé ènì] 'drink water'
 drink water
 /tsò/ # /àbɔ̂/ → [tsà àbɔ̂] 'point hand'
 point hand
 /lɔ̀/ # /àfè/ → [là àfè] 'write book'
 write book
 b. /ònwè/ # /èjéjî/ → [ònwè èjéjî] 'infant'
 child blood
 c. /òwáwá/ # /èkwɔ́/ → [òwáwé ékwɔ̄] 'fruit'
 produce tree
 d. /m̀búé/ # /ènì/ → [m̀búé énî] 'fish'
 meat water
 e. /gíé/ # /ùnwógīē/ → [gìù ùnwógīē] 'eat food'
 eat food

Consonant assimilation in Etulo is of the regressive type. It involves a homorganic nasal whose articulatory feature is conditioned by the features of the following consonant, which is usually a plosive. Unlike vowel assimilation, consonant assimilation is realized word internally. This type of homorganic nasal assimilation occurs in the environment of a plosive, but hardly before a fricative or affricate such as /s/ and /ts/.

(43) a. /aNgbeka/ → [ámgbéká] 'some'
 b. /aNbulu/ → [ámbúlú] 'pieces/particles'
 c. /iNgioga/ → [ìŋgìògà] 'guest/visitor'
 d. /èNga/ → [èŋgá] 'when'
 e. /aNda/ → [ándā] 'a type of fish'
 f. /oNdu/ → [òndû] 'mouth'

2.6.4 Vowel coalescence

Coalescence is the process of merging two different sound segments into a single unit. Coalescence is a feature of vowels in Etulo and occurs at word boundary ($V_1 + V_2 \rightarrow V_3$). The resulting vowel shares one or more features of the input segments. Instances of vowel coalescence are found in verb-noun constructions as illustrated in (44a–c). It is difficult to make any strong generalization on the pattern of vowel coalescence because of insufficient data. However, one generally observes that merging occurs between a rounded and unrounded vowel. The output (resulting vowel) shares a [+/- ATR] feature with at least one of the coalesced vowels. The tone of V_3 may correspond to that of V_1. In some available examples, the resulting vowel bears a high tone which corresponds to the tone of the first vowel of the merged segments (see 44a). These observations are subject to further verification in the light of more language data.

Consider the following examples:

(44) a. /tsé/ # /òɲà/ → [tsíɲà] 'run race'
         run   race

b. /ʃò/ # /èwô/ → [ʃùwô] 'bath'
   bath   body

c. /sɔ̄/ # /èsɛ́/ → [sìsɛ́] 'sit down'
   sit   ground

2.6.5 Vowel insertion

In most languages, borrowed words which are integrated into the lexicon may undergo phonological alterations to conform to the syllable structure or phonotactic constraints of the recipient language. In Etulo, one of the ways of altering the phonological pattern of foreign words (nouns) is by vowel insertion. This is mainly motivated by syllable structure constraints. Vowel insertion may be prothetic or epithetic. It is prothetic when the vowel is inserted at the word initial position and epithetic when inserted in word final position. The Etulo nouns' basic syllable structure is VCV, Ṇ.CV and rarely CVN. Nouns typically begin with a vowel or a syllabic nasal, rarely with a consonant. They also end with a vowel but hardly with a consonant, except for the alveolar nasal /n/. To retain the phonological structure of the noun, a low tone vowel is inserted in borrowed nouns which violate the word boundaries constraint. No systematic pattern of consonant insertion is attested in our data.

The following examples of vowel insertion are based on borrowed words from English and Hausa which begin or end with a consonant. Examples (45a and b) illustrate the prothetic insertion of vowels, while (45c) shows both prothetic and epithetic vowel insertion.

(45) a. **English** **Etulo**
/təmatəʊ/ → /ìtùmátù/ 'tomato'
/wɪndəʊ/ → /ìwéndùlù/ 'window'
/mæθju/ → /ìmátíʊ/ 'Matthew'

b. **Hausa** **Etulo**
/makaranta/ → /ùmákárántá/ 'school'
/makuli/ → /ìmákúlí/ 'key'
/chinkafa/ → /ìtsíkápá/ 'rice'
/rike/ → /àlìkíé/ 'sugar cane'

c. **English** **Etulo**
/bʌkɪt/ → /ìbókótì/ 'bucket'
/baɪbl/ → /ìbíbílò/ 'bible'
/gæs/ → /ìgásì/ 'gas'
/luːk/ → /ìlúkà/ 'Luke'

2.6.6 Glide formation

Glide formation is the process of desyllabification of a vowel in specific environments. It involves a change in the features of some vowels in the environment of a following vowel. In Etulo, the vowels /i ɪ/ and /u/ are realized as the glides /j/ and /w/ in the environment of a following non-identical vowel. This process only occurs in word-medial and word-final positions. Analyzing such vowel sequences as involving glide formation is particularly favourable in contexts where the tone of both vowels is similar or conditioned. However, the hitch that one encounters in analyzing such vowel sequences as a case of glide formation at the phonetic level is tone contrast. The vowels in such sequences may have contrasting tones which are always retained. This is unlike languages such as Ivie and Jukun in which the tone of the palatalized vowel is conditioned, i.e. the tone of the palatalized vowel mirrors that of the following vowel (Welmers 1978).

When glide formation occurs in Etulo, the tone of the affected vowel may be deleted if it is similar or conditioned by that of the following vowel. This is exemplified in (46a). In contrast, (46b) illustrates non-identical vowel sequences with contrasting tones which are not deleted. At the phonological level, such vowel sequences, with or without contrasting tones, are best represented as separate vowels capable of bearing their individual tone. Below are some examples:

(46) a. /fúé/ [fwé] 'sprinkle'
/búá/ [bwá] 'catch'
/m̀mùè/ [m̀mwè] 'respect'
/gíá/ [gjá] 'buy'
/kɪɔ̀/ [kjɔ̀] 'do'
b. /úkɪ́à/ [úkjâ] 'trap'
/óngɪ̀à/ [óngjâ] 'woman'
/kɪ́ɛ̄/ [kjɛ̄] 'be old'
/láfúā/ [láfwā] 'snatch'

2.6.7 Vowel harmony

Vowel harmony describes a situation where all vowels agree in one of their properties within a specific domain. The scope of such process may coincide with the prosodic word or extend beyond it. The features of a stem's vowel may spread leftwards or rightwards to affixes or even pronouns. The shared properties of vowels include roundedness, height and advanced tongue root (ATR). In a language like Igbo, which has a full harmony system, the ATR features of the verb spread leftward to prefixes, the 3SG pronoun and rightward to suffixes (cf. Emenanjo 2015). The vowel of verbal suffixes or prefixes harmonizes with the vowel of the verb root. For instance, the vowel prefix of the Igbo infinitive verb form is realized as /i/ or /ɪ/ depending on the vowel of the verb root. A verb such as *ri* 'eat' takes the /i/ prefix as in *iri* 'to eat' while the verb *sɪ* takes the /ɪ/ prefix as in *ɪsɪ* 'to lie'.

Etulo presents a partial vowel harmony system based on ATR values. Its eight vowels fall into two groups: /i e o u/ [+ATR], /ɪ a ɛ ɔ/ [-ATR]. In what follows, I will call the first group of vowels set I and the second group set II. The scope of vowel harmony is restricted to a prosodic word (a root). This process does not spread leftward to a prefix, pronouns or rightward to a suffix. For instance, the nominalizing low tone vowel prefix *o-* is not subject to the rule of vowel harmony. It occurs with members of both vowel sets: *ò-kɪ́é* 'to take' (set I), *ò-kɪ́ɛ̄* 'to be old' (set II). The harmonic relationship between the members of both groups is illustrated below:

(47) Set I
[+ATR]
a. òbùkúsè 'type of leaf'
b. èkɪ̀ô 'river'
c. ìfú 'stomach'
d. ónwú 'he/she'
e. èwóò 'bee'
f. ìdê 'relative'

(48) Set II
[-ATR]
a. ìdɔ́ 'work'
b. ágbɔ̆ʃɔ̃ 'earthworm'
c. ìtákwɔ̂ 'kite'
d. ètɔ́ 'family'
e. èsɔ́ 'message'
f. ìdɛ̂ 'tongue'

In vowel sequences, /i/ obligatorily co-occurs with members of set I while /ɪ/ co-occurs with members of set II.

(49) /i/
a. kíé 'take'
b. èkìô 'river'
c. íngíú 'name of person'

(50) /ɪ/
a. kíɛ̃ 'be old'
b. kɪ̀ɔ̀ 'do'
c. gɪ́á 'buy'

The two sets of vowels sometimes overlap, for one occasionally finds violations of vowel harmony. For instance, the vowels /u/ and /a/ are compatible with members of both sets except in the environment of non-identical vowel sequences. The co-occurrence of /u/ with members of both sets could be a result of the absence of its -ATR counterpart /ʊ/. The following examples show vowel disharmony in Etulo words:

(51) a. ùtɔ̀ 'king'
b. ùnwɔ̂ 'thing'
c. ònwɛ̀ 'child'
d. ùdé 'home'
e. èsɛ́ 'ground'
f. àdì 'name of person'
g. ámbúlú 'pieces'
h. èngá 'when'

Unlike languages like Igbo and Akan, vowel harmony does not extended to affixes in Etulo. The nominalizing low tone prefix o- is not conditioned by the feature of the vowels of the root. This prefix therefore occurs with vowels of both set I and set II. Examples:

(52) a. òkìɔ̀   'to do'
      b. òndéē   'to be tired'
      c. òfúé   'to sprinkle'
      d. òlúū   'to go'
      e. òlɔ̀   'to write'
      f. ògbó   'to beat'

In nominal compounds/associative constructions, one also observes a violation of vowel harmony. Words comprising vowels of different sets are combined in noun+noun constructions. In an associative construction such as *ikie undɔ* 'goat head', the N_1 comprises vowels from set I while N_2 comprises vowels from both set I and II.

2.7 Conclusion

Etulo is a tone language with three distinctive level tones and two glides. A total of thirty-seven phonemes are established using minimal pairs: twenty-nine consonants and eight vowels. The vowel phonemes have allophones derived from nasalization and lengthening. Etulo has an atypical vowel harmony system. Unlike typical West African languages such as Igbo, Yoruba and Ewe that have full vowel harmony system where there is leftward and rightward spreading to affixes and pronouns, Etulo presents a partial vowel harmony system based on ATR values, albeit with some violations. This process is restricted to the root, i.e. it does not spread to affixes or pronouns. Etulo presents phonological processes such as elision, assimilation, vowel coalescence, vowel insertion and glide formation. It is also characterized by tonal phenomena such as tone polarity.

3. Morphological Processes

3.0 Introduction

In the traditional literature on morphological typology, languages are often classified into different types such as isolating/analytic, agglutinative and fusional, depending on the nature of the relation between their words and morphemes. Though controversial, these terms are largely retained in recent literature with slight modifications to their meaning. As Haspelmath (2009) observes, a language may be agglutinating in one aspect of its morphology and fusional in another. In other words, no language is exclusively characterized as belonging to one language type.

The Etulo language is predominantly an isolating/analytic language with agglutinative features. Most grammatical categories are marked by isolated morphemes rather than affixes. Only two affixes are identified: a derivational vowel prefix, which also has some inflectional properties, and an extensional suffix. Hybrid affixes have been attested in a number of languages. In the study of Zamucoan languages, Bertinetto and Cuicci (2018) report a few cases of deviant or non-prototypical derivational affixes that have nuances of both inflection and derivation.

In this chapter, three word formation processes are examined: affixation, compounding and reduplication, focusing on the function and productivity. The domain of application is as follows: the vowel prefix concerns the verb category and a subset of ideophones; the very productive compounding process concerns nouns and verbs; reduplication is used for deriving ideophones and adjectives.

3.1 Derivational morphology

Derivation is the process by which new words are formed from already existing ones by morphological processes such as affixation, compounding, reduplication etc., in most cases yielding a transcategorial lexical change. In the following section, I examine the formation of nominals from bare verbs and ideophonic words using the low tone nominalizing prefix ò-, reduplication and tone.

3.1.1 Unproductive derivation (deverbal nouns)

Before proceeding to the discussion of nominals derived from the verb category using the derivational affix, it should be noted that there exists in Etulo a set of deverbal nouns which, from a diachronic point of view, must have been derived by means of the prefixation of a vowel or syllabic nasal. As far as one can see, this process is irregular and no longer active (unproductive). No uniformity is observed in the prefixation pattern. The choice of a vowel prefix is unpredictable. Consider the following examples:

(1)		Noun		Base verb		
	a.	ìbɔ́	'prayer'	bɔ́	'pray'
	b.	áʃí	'song'	ʃí	'sing'
	c.	íʃá	'laugh/laughter'	ʃá	'laugh'
	d.	ùnâ	'sleep'	ná	'sleep'
	e.	òkíè	'load'	kíé	'carry'
	f.	úkíà	'trap'	kíá	'set (trap)'
	g.	ìmíò	'fear'	míó	'fear (be afraid)'
	h.	ólɛ́	'play'	lɛ́	'play'
	i.	ǹfìà	'sweetness'	fìà	'be sweet'
	j.	ǹfíú	'fatness'	fíú	'be fat'
	k.	ímíɛ́	'breath'	míɛ́	'breathe'

3.2 The nominalizing ò- vowel prefix

In contrast to the above described fossilized derivational process, Etulo presents a synchronically active one, to which this section is devoted.

The *ò-* vowel prefix is a hybrid affix that has both inflectional and derivational values. It forms paradigmatic relations with other verbs in the formation of infinitives and gerundives, changes verbs to (agentive) nouns and ideophones to attributive adjectives, and has a transcategorial feature, attaching to more than one lexical class. It bears an inherent low tone which is not subject to change or tonal modification in its occurrence. This prefix does not harmonize with the vowels of the verb root: it co-occurs with the two vowel sets.

3.2.1 The infinitive verb

In Etulo, the infinitive is a non-finite verb form. It is derived by means of the affixation of the low tone prefix to the bare verb. All identifiable verbs, copulas and the auxiliary in our data take this prefix in their infinitive form. As observed in the following examples, this prefix retains its tone in combination with verb roots of different tone types.

(2) **Verb root**   **Infinitive form**

	a.	gíé	'eat'	ògíé	'to eat'
	b.	lúū	'go'	òlúū	'to go'
	c.	ná	'sleep'	òná	'to sleep'
	d.	míɛ	'breathe'	òmíɛ	'to breathe'
	e.	kɩ̀ɔ̀	'do'	òkɩ̀ɔ̀	'to do'
	f.	sá	'wash'	òsá	'to wash'
	g.	lì	'be'	òlì	'to be'
	h.	dzɛ̀	'be (existential/locative)'	òdzɛ̀	'to have/be'
	i.	lè	'be'	òlè	'to be'

Infinitives exhibit verbal properties, such as allowing adverbial modification and taking nominal complements, as shown in the following examples:

(3) a. ò-kɛ̀   plé   tátásê
        PREF-go   early   be.better
        'To go early is better.'

     b. ò-gíé   ùnwógīē   dúmɔ́dúmɔ́   tíʃí   bā
        PREF-eat   food   slowly   be.good   NEG
        'To eat food slowly is not good.'

3.2.2 Gerundive nominals

In Etulo, gerundive nominals are derived from both eventive and stative verbs. Three processes are involved in their derivation: the affixation of the nominalizing prefix *o-*, the reduplication of the verb root and tonal modification. A fairly regular pattern emerges where the lexical tone of verb roots changes to either a falling or rising tone. In (4a), a falling tone is realized on the second part of the reduplicated verb form while in (4b), a rising tone is realized on the first or both parts of the reduplicated verb form. There are, however, instances where the inherent level tone of the verb root does not turn into a gliding tone, as in (4c). In terms of function, the derived form and its noun complement constitute the gerundive nominal.[1]

(4) a.

Verb root		Reduplicated form	Derived form	
ʃí	'dance'	ʃi-ʃi	(ífūē) ò-ʃíʃí	'dancing'
gbɔ̀	'read'	gbɔ-gbɔ	ò-gbɔ̀gbɔ̂	'reading'
mà	'cry'	ma-ma	(àkwɔ̀) ò-màmâ	'crying'
lɔ̀	'write'	lɔ-lɔ	ò-lɔ̀lɔ̂	'writing'

b.

Verb root		Reduplicated form	Derived form	
ʃí	'sing'	ʃi-ʃi	(áʃī) ò- ʃíʃí	'singing'
ʃá	'laugh'	ʃa-ʃa	(íʃá) ò-ʃǎʃǎ	'laughing'
wā	'sweep'	wa-wa	(ímbē) ò-wǎwǎ	'sweeping'
fá	'shout'	fa-fa	(èlâ) ò-fǎfǎ	'shouting'
wá	'drink'	wa-wa	(eni) òwǎwā	'drinking'

c.

Verb root		Reduplicated form	Derived form	
ná	'sleep'	na-na	(ùná) ò-nánā	'sleeping'
sá	'wash'	sa-sa	ò-sásā	'washing'
bā	'come'	ba-ba	ò-bábā	'coming'
nwɔ́	'kill'	nwɔ-nwɔ	ò-nwɔ́nwɔ̄	'killing'
nwá	'harvest'	nwa-nwa	ò-nwánwā	'harvesting'
fúá	'butcher'	fua-fua	ò-fúáfúā	'butchering'
fùà	'refuse'	fua-fua	ò-fùàfúà	'refusal'
gíé	'eat'	gie-gie	ò-gíégíē	'eating'
dzìlí	'destroy'	dzili-dzili	ò-dzìlízílī	'destruction'

The morphological processes of prefixation and reduplication employed in the derivation of gerundives are quite productive. They apply to many Etulo verbs. Further research is needed in order to ascertain whether this productive process is subject to semantic restrictions; for instance, whether it applies to permanent stative verbs.

At the syntactic level, gerundive nominals pattern like nouns by taking definiteness markers. In (5a), the gerundive takes the determiner *mà* 'the' while in (5b), it takes the possessive *ḿgbí ámá* 'their'.

---

1   In (4), the noun complements are optional and are therefore shown within brackets. However, gerundive nominals derived from verbs that obligatorily require noun complements mostly retain them in grammatical constructions. This is illustrated in the following example:

(i) mà àkwɔ̀ 'cry cry' → àkwɔ̀ ò-mà-mâ ḿgbī èmgbé tímbī
    cry PREF-cry-RED of children be.bad
    'The crying of the children is bad.'

(5) a. àʃí   ò-ʃí-ʃí   mà   kɨ̀ɔ̀ ání   ìtíngā
        song PREF-sing-RED   the do   1SG   anger
        'The singing angered me.'

   b. àʃí   ò-ʃí-ʃí   ḿgbí ámá   kɨ̀ɔ̀ ání   ìtíngā
        song PREF-sing-RED   POSS 3PL   do   1SG   anger
        'Their singing angered me.'

3.2.3 Derived agentive nominals

Agentive nominals are formed by a combination of the gerundive form and the generic noun *ǹgísè* 'person/someone'. There are however, few agentive nominals for which the use of the generic noun is not required such as *òtsètsê* 'teacher' derived from the verb *tsé* 'teach'. The following examples are illustrative:

(6) **Verb root**   **Derived agentives**

   a. fɔ́   'wipe/clean' → ǹgísè òfɔ́fɔ̄   'cleaner/cleaning person'
   b. kpájī 'learn'   → ǹgísè òkpájīkpájī 'learner/learning person'
   c. gíá   'buy'   → ǹgísè ògíágíá   'buyer/buying person'
   d. gíé   'eat'   → ǹgísè ògíégīē   'eater/eating person'
   e. wá   'drink'   → ǹgísè òwǎwā   'drinker/drinking person'
   f. lɔ̀   'write'   → ǹgísè òlɔ̀lô   'writer/writing person'

3.2.4 Adjectives derived from ideophones

Many ideophones may take the low tone nominalizing prefix when they function as adjectives or nominal modifiers. Below are some examples:

(7) **Ideophone**   **Nominal modifier**

   a. tétété   'sound of dripping water' ènì òtététɛ   'dripping water'
   b. fèlèfèlè 'silky'   ànwúntò òfèlèfèlè 'silky cloth'
   c. trɔ̀trɔ̀   'smooth'   èwô òtrɔ̀trɔ̀   'smooth body'

3.3 The -*lu* suffix

The *lu* morpheme is a verbal suffix that may be attached to a subset of Etulo. It is a grammaticalized form which may have been derived from the motion verb *lúū* 'go'. Based on the available data, the specific meaning or grammatical function of this suffix is still unclear. The vagueness of its meaning emerges in its optionality (see 9–11). For instance, the verb *kíé* 'take' allows the suffixation of -*lu* which results in the verb form *kíélū* 'take'. In grammatical constructions, these forms may substitute each other without a major change in meaning. Native speakers use both forms alternatively and see no semantic distinction between them. However, a closer look at the subset of verbs that take the *lu* suffix reveals a semantic interpretation suggestive of removing or moving something/an object from an extraction point. For instance, the verb forms *fíá-lú* 'peel' and *ʃé-lū* 'pluck' imply extracting an object such as dirt away from the floor or a fruit from a tree. It is suggested here that the -*lu* morpheme serves as a verbal extension suffix that connotes the removal of an object as in *fíálū* 'peel off', *sálū* 'wash away', *kíélū* 'take away'. Examples:

(8) **Verb root**			**Verb form**	
a.	fíá	'peel'	fíá-lú	'peel off'
b.	fɔ́	'clean'	fɔ́-lū	'clean out'
c.	sá	'wash'	sá-lū	'wash away'
d.	kíé	'take'	kíé-lū	'take away'
e.	ʃɛ́	'pluck'	ʃɛ́-lū	'pluck out'

Illustration of the suffix as used in grammatical constructions:

(9) a. ìɲànì fíá ángwɔ́
    PN peel yam
    'Inyani peeled yam.'

  b. ìɲànì fíá-lú ángwɔ́
    PN peel-SUFF yam
    'Inyani peeled yam.'

(10) a. éjî lè sá úgâ
    2PL:SUBJ PROG wash plate
    'We are washing plates.'

  b. éjî lè sá-lū úgâ
    2PL:SUBJ PROG wash-SUFF plate
    'We are washing plates.'

(11) a. á   kà   fɔ́   òdzû
         3PL:SUBJ   FUT   clean   house
         'They will clean the house.'
     b. á   kà   fɔ́-lū   òdzû
         3PL:SUBJ   FUT   clean-SUFF   house
         'They will clean the house.'

3.4 Reduplication

Reduplication is a morphological process that basically involves the repetition of a word or part of it. This motivates the distinction made in languages between partial and full reduplication. Depending on the language, reduplication may be inflectional or derivational in function. Reduplication in Etulo is mostly full and is associated with categories such as verb, ideophone and noun. As noted in the previous sections (Section 3.2.2 and Section 3.2.3), Etulo utilizes full reduplication in the derivation of gerundive/agentive nominals from the verb.

3.4.1 Reduplication of ideophones and nouns

Etulo ideophones have a repetitive structure. They are characterized by full repetition of the nuclear element (mono- or disyllabic). For most ideophones, this element has no lexical meaning and its reduplication has no identifiable grammatical function, except being a lexical marker of ideophonicity. Examples:

(12) **Base**   **Reduplicated form**
  a. *fele   fèlèfèlè   'silky'
  b. *trɔ   trɔ̀trɔ̀   'smooth'
  c. *tɛ   tɛ́tɛ́tɛ́   'depiction of dripping water'
  d. *gi   gìgìgì   'depiction of shivering'

From a diachronic perspective, a few adjectives (mostly colour terms) seem to have been derived from the noun by partial reduplication. This process is however unproductive. In the following examples, the word initial vowel of the base is replaced by a high tone vowel /o/. Examples:

(13) **Base (noun)**   **Reduplicated form (adjective)**
  a. úmbí   'dirt'   ómbímbí   'black/dark'
  b. úndzé   'whiteness'   óndzúndzé   'white'
  c. úmá   'fairness'   ómúmá   'red'

3.5 Compounding

Compounding involves the combination of two or more lexemes to create a new word (cf. Bauer 2003, Scalise and Forza 2011). From a cross-linguistic perspective, Lieber and Stekauer (2009) propose three major criteria for establishing compounds in languages, possibly in addition to other language internal criteria. These yardsticks include:

1. stress and other phonological means such as tonal pattern
2. syntactic impenetrability, inseparability, and unalterability
3. the behaviour of the complex item with respect to inflection

The third criterion has little or no relevance to Etulo nominal compounds since the noun category hardly undergoes any form of inflection. Compounds in Etulo are of two types: nominal and verb compounds. Both compound types are further classified as being endocentric or exocentric. The nominal compounds are distinguished from other N+N (noun phrases) constructions such as the associative, genitive or possessive structures. The meaning of a compound may be inferred from its components. The V+V compounds comprise two verb roots. In some cases, one root is analyzed as the main verb and the other root as its modifier (minor verb). The meaning of the verb compound is largely derived from the main verb; the minor verb may be semantically bleached or grammaticalized in its role as component of a verb compound. This type of V+V compound may be diachronically described as a type of serial verb. From a synchronic point of view, however, I analyze them as verb compounds.

3.5.1 Nominal compound

The Etulo nominal compounds are discussed under three major groupings: genitive, amalgamated and synthetic compounds.

3.5.1.1 Genitive compound

In Etulo, genitive compounds are formed by a combination or juxtaposition of at least two free-standing nouns. Their literal meaning corresponds to that of a genitive construction. For instance, the compound *m̀búɛ́ énî* 'fish' has the literal meaning, 'meat of water'. Such compounds denote a single conceptual unit and may be left-headed. The meaning expressed by Etulo genitive compounds could be partially derived from the literal meaning of their components. The lexical tone of individual nouns may change when they are realized as constituents of a compound noun. Note that in spoken or fast speech, the final vowel of N_1 and its tone is often assimilated and deleted. A compound noun such as *ònɔ́-ékìò* 'sea' would be realized as *ònékìò*.

(14)

	Noun	Noun		Compound noun
a.	ònwè	èjîèjî	→	ònwè-èjéjî
	child	blood		'infant'
b.	ìfîê	ìkíé	→	ìfìè-íkīē
	fat	head		'brain'
c.	m̀búé	ènì	→	m̀búé-énî
	meat	water		'fish'
d.	ìkíé	ìdúù	→	ìkíé-ídūù
	head	market/ week		'weekend'
e.	ònwè	òngìâ	→	ònwè-óngìâ
	child	woman		'girl'
f.	ónô	èkìô	→	ònɔ́-ékìò
	mother	river		'sea'

3.5.1.2 Amalgamated compound

Amalgamated compounds include forms with structures such as N+N, N+V, V+N, whose meanings may not always be transparent. In some cases, one of the constituents lacks independent semantic content outside the compound. These compounds are characterized by tonal change and vowel/tone deletion, which gives rise to highly lexicalized forms. Native Etulo speakers consider such compounds to be unified words. The deleted vowel is usually the last vowel of N_1 or the first vowel of N_2. Amalgamated compounds may be derived from two nouns, as shown in (15) below:

(15)

	Noun	Noun		Compound noun
a.	àkwô	àdé	→	àkwádê
	nut/seed	oil palm		'palmnut/ palmkernel'
b.	òkpâ	àfɔ̀	→	òkpáfɔ̀
	skin	leg		'shoe'
c.	ábô	àdé	→	àbàdê
	branch	oil palm		'palm frond'
d.	òndû	ùdzɛ́	→	òndúdzē
	mouth	tribe		'language'
e.	ìfô	òdzû	→	ìfòdzû
	hole	house		'room'

Another set of amalgamated compounds comprises a noun and an infinitive verb form. The noun may precede or follow the infinitive verb form.

(16)

	Noun	Infinitive		Compound noun
a.	ùnwɔ̂	ògíé	→	ùnwógīē
	thing	to eat		'food'
b.	ònú	òfɛ̀	→	ònùfɛ̂
	to give	way		'door'

A further set of compounds comprises two nouns. They are characterized by the possible loss of the semantic and phonological makeup of the first or second constituent. This is in contrast to examples (14 and 15).

(17)

	Noun	Noun		Compound noun
a.	*ìkp	òndû	→	ìkpóndû
		mouth		'lips'
b.	*ìkp	èsɛ́	→	ìkpésē̄
		ground/ down		'land'
c.	*and	èbìɔ̀	→	àndébíɔ̀
		chin		'beard'
d.	*ìmgb	èʃò	→	ìmgbàʃò
		heaven		'God'
e.	*ab	ògbé	→	àbógbē
		stream		'a small stream'
f.	*if	ògbé	→	ìfógbē
		stream		'a big stream'
g.	ángwɔ́	*umɔ	→	ángwúmɔ̂
		yam		'a specie of yam'
h.	*àbú	gíé	→	àbúgíē
		eat		right hand (eating hand)
i.	*àbú	*bē̄	→	àbúbē̄
				'left hand'

3.5.1.3 Synthetic compound

Synthetic compounds are derived from the combination of a noun and a gerundive nominal (nominalized verb). The noun that accompanies the gerundive is often syntactically associated with it either as an object or as an indirect complement. The gerundive serves as the modifier of the noun. The compound as a whole follows a head-modifier structure.

(18)		Noun	Gerundive	Nominal compound
	a.	èkwɔ́	ò-ònwɔ̌nwɔ̌	èkwɔ́ ònwɔ̌nwɔ̌
		tree	drying	'firewood'
	b.	ɔ̀nɔ̀	ò-tsétsē	ɔ̀nɔ̀ òtsétsē
		sun	shinning	'sunshine'
	c.	élélá	ò-dǐdǐ	élélá òdǐdǐ
		grace	seeing	'act of showing mercy'

3.5.2 Nominal compounds vs associative constructions

Compound nouns are structurally similar to associative constructions NPs. Both involve a concatenation of nouns and tonal change. One of the cross-linguistic criteria that defines compounds is syntactic atomicity, which entails that constituents of a compound word cannot be operated upon by syntactic rules. In other words, no lexical word may be inserted, moved or deleted from such complex words. In contrast with some associative constructions (particularly those with a possessive meaning), Etulo compounds do not allow the insertion of the possessive marker *mgbi*. Its insertion yields ungrammatical constructions as in (19) or gives a possessive reading as in (20).

(19)	a.	m̀búé	énî	
		meat	water	
		'fish'		
	b.	*m̀búé	ḿgbī	énî
		meat	of	water
		'fish'		
(20)	a.	ònwὲ	óngìâ	
		child	woman	
		'girl'		
	b.	?ònwὲ	ḿgbī	óngìâ
		child	of	woman
		'a woman's child'		

With nominal compounds, it is impossible to join one of the constituents with another noun. As shown in (21a), joining the N_2 with other nouns results in ungrammaticality. For coordination to occur, the whole compound must be included in the coordinating process. In contrast, associative constructions allow joint coordination with other nouns using the coordinating morpheme *jì* as illustrated in (22a and 22b).

(21) a. *m̀búɛ́ énî jì òʃɛ́
       meat water and forest
       'fish and bush meat'

   b. m̀búɛ́ énî jì m̀búɛ́ óʃɛ̃
      meat water and meat forest
      'fish and bush meat'

(22) a. újá ítùmátû jì òlòmû
       basket tomato and orange
       'a tomato and orange basket'

   b. újá ítùmátû jì újá òlòmû
      basket tomato and basket orange
      'a tomato basket and an orange basket'

The features of genitive nominal compounds and associative constructions are summarized in Table 3.

Table 3.1 Features of associative constructions and nominal compounds

Characterization	Associative constructions (N+N)	Compounds (N+N)
Partial co-ordination	Yes	No
Use of the possessive marker	Yes (possible in some cases)	No
Tonal change of N2	Yes	Yes
Headedness	Left headed	Left headed or non-headed

3.5.3 Verbal Compound

Three groups of Etulo verb compounds are identified. The first group comprises at least two verbs (V_1-V_2) which may also occur as independent verbs. Verb compounds classified under group I are more or less lexicalized serial verbs. They are typically non-headed and have a non-compositional meaning (exocentric) except for a few, such as *gbónwɔ́* 'kill' with a cause-effect meaning.

(23) **Verb**   **Verb**   **Verb compound**

a. mùà + dzɛ́   mùàdzɛ́
   reduce   cut   'cut into pieces'

b. gbó + nwɔ́   gbónwɔ́
   beat   kill   'kill by beating/beat to death'

c. kwú + dzɛ̀   kwúdzê
   catch   stay   'stand'

d. lúū + bā   lúbā
   go   come   'come back/go inside'

e. bí + lúū   bílúū
   hold   go   'lose (something)'

One of the ways by which lexicalized serial verbs (verb compounds) differ from serial verbs is on the basis of inseparability. Components of verb compounds are inseparable while those of a serial verb construction may be separated by other constituents. In (24a–b), one observes that the separation of the components of the lexicalized serial verb *gbónwɔ́* 'beat to death/kill' by the object results in ungrammaticality. In contrast, the separability of the components of a serial verb construction does not yield ungrammaticality as shown in (25a–b).

(24) a. àdì   gbó-nwɔ́   ìsɛ̀sɛ́
        PN   beat-kill   PN
        'Adi killed Isɛsɛ.'

    b. *àdì   gbó   ìsɛ̀sɛ́   nwɔ́
        PN   beat   PN   kill
        'Adi killed Isɛsɛ.'

(25) a. àdì   kwó-wō   ótsé
        PN   inject-put   medicine
        'Adi sprayed fertilizer.'

    b. àdì   kwó   ótsé   wō
        PN   inject   medicine   put
        'Adi sprayed fertilizer.'

The second group of Etulo verb compounds comprises the verb and a particle or two verbs. They are endocentric compounds with a compositional meaning. The structure of the constituents is that of head-modifier. The particle *nto* is semantically linked to the notion of length. In verb compounds however, the particle and the grammaticalized verb *kɛ* 'go' denote prepositional ideas involving motion/direction and location (see 26 and 27). Further investigation may reveal other particles and grammaticalized verbs that are used in the formation of Etulo verb compounds.

(26)	a.	kìέ	+	ǹtó	→	kìàtóō
		rise		length		'rise up'
	b.	dzè	+	ǹtó		dzùntó
		COP		length		'stand/stay up'
(27)	a.	sɔ́	+	ké	→	sɔ́kéè
		sit		go		'sit on'
	c.	dɔ́	+	ké	→	dɔ́kè
		keep		go		'keep on'
	d.	tɔ́	+	kè	→	tɔ́kè
		climb		go		'climb on'

The third group of verb compounds comprises inseparable forms. From a diachronic view, some of these compounds may have been derived from a verb+noun construction. In modern usage, however, the components are semantically opaque. The verb component is hardly recoverable most likely as a result of vowel elision or contraction. In (28), for instance, the verb compounds comprise a *V (now semantically and phonologically non-recoverable) and the noun *umbi* 'dirt/blackness'. This is most likely a case of verb+noun complement that has become lexicalized into a mono-morphemic form in meaning and structure.

(28)	a.	*ti	+	umbi	→	tímbí	'be bad'
	b.	*ʃi	+	umbi	→	ʃímbí	'be dirty'
	c.	*lu	+	umbi	→	lúmbī	'be dark'

3.6 Conclusion

The Etulo language is predominantly an isolating/analytic language with agglutinative features. Only one productive hybrid affix is attested, the nominalizing *o-* prefix, which forms the infinitive and contributes to the formation of gerundive nominals. There is also an unclassified verbal suffix *-lu*. Affixation of the nominalizing prefix is restricted to Etulo verbs and ideophones. Etulo makes productive use of reduplication and compounding. Reduplication is involved in the formation of gerundive nominals, together with tonal changes and affixation. It is also involved in the formation of ideophones. Noun compounds and verb compounds are prominently present in Etulo. Genitive nominal compounds are distinguished from associative constructions by the absence of the morpheme used in associative constructions. Some compound verbs are described as lexicalized serial verbs and distinguished from SVCs.

4. Word Classes

4.0 Introduction

This chapter characterizes the lexical categories attested in Etulo using both semantic and morpho-syntactic criteria. The categories discussed include pronoun, noun, verb, adverb, qualificative and preposition. It also examines the status of the Etulo ideophone and how it cuts across different word classes. In addition, it describes the Etulo numeral system.

4.1 The pronominal system

'Pronominal' is used here as a cover term for subtypes of pronouns including personal pronouns, possessives, reflexives, and relative pronouns. These categories are examined with the aim of identifying their morphological and syntactic characterization, as well as their interaction with other categories like number, gender and case. Though case as a grammatical category is not overtly marked in Etulo, some pronominals show case distinctions to a limited extent. This is especially observed in the distinction between subject and object pronoun forms. Other related categories such as demonstratives and possessive determiners are also discussed.

4.1.1 Personal pronouns

According to Dixon (2010), personal pronouns are a small closed class of grammatical words that vary for person. The three-way distinction made for the personal pronoun in Etulo includes 1st, 2nd and 3rd person. The 1st and 2nd person pronouns refer to participants in a speech act and function as shifters, while the 3rd person denotes a referent (animate or inanimate) which is neither the speaker nor addressee. In relation to number, only the singular and plural forms are distinguished for the three persons. No specific plural morpheme can be isolated for the plural forms. No gender distinction is observed for the 3rd person or any other member of the paradigm. Bhat (2003) proposes a typological classification that basically groups pronouns into two categories, free vs bound pronouns. Free pronouns generally function as the head of an NP while bound pronouns attach to the predicate. The Etulo pronominal system comprises both free and bound pronouns. However, some of the seemingly bound forms are still in an evolving process.[1] In other words, some of the pronouns categorized as bound forms are possibly phonologically reduced pronouns that are still in the process of turning into bound forms (see Table 4.1). Dixon (2010) identifies such a phonological reduction as one of the pathways leading from a free form to a bound form. It is observed that bound forms have a restricted distribution in grammatical constructions in comparison with their free counterparts (see Section 4.1.3). When functioning as NP heads, plural personal pronouns (to the exclusion of singular ones) have combinatorial possibilities with modifiers like numerals. The nominative-accusative case split is morphologically expressed for some pronoun forms as the subject vs object pronouns, while others bear the same form in both nominative and accusative function. Below, I present a table and concrete examples showing the subject and object forms of personal pronouns, as well as the free and bound forms.

Table 4.1 Etulo personal pronouns

Person (subject)	Full/Free forms	Reduced/Bound forms
1SG	ánî	ń
1PL	éjî	í
2SG	ábû	o
2PL	émâ	í
3SG		o/í
3PL		á
Person (object)		
1SG	ánî	ń
1PL	éjî	
2SG	ábû	
2PL	émâ	
3SG	ónwú[2]	nasalization+n[3]
3PL	ámá[4]	má

---

1 In this work, only the bound forms for the 1st and 3rd person singular object pronouns are consistently represented as being cliticized to a host.
2 The 3SG pronoun *onwu* also serves as a logophoric pronoun (see Section 4.1.4).
3 The 3SG OBJ pronoun is realized as *n* and triggers the nasalization of the preceding vowel.
4 Note that the full pronoun forms *ónwú* (3SG) and *ámá* (3PL), although listed as object pronouns in Table 4.1, are not exclusively restricted to the function of object pronouns. They occasionally occupy subject argument slots in constructions such as relative and focus constructions (see Section 4.1.1.3).

4.1.1.1 Subject pronouns

In Etulo, subject pronouns generally precede the verb. Their inherent tones are often retained in grammatical constructions except in fast speech where, for instance, the high-falling tone of the 1SG, 2SG, 1PL and 2PL pronouns changes to high-high or high-mid tones. The full and reduced forms of the 1SG pronoun *ánî* and *ń* are used interchangeably in the subject argument slot. The 1st person plural is realized as *éjî* and *í*. These two forms are interchangeable. Note that the form *i* realizes three different pronouns as shown in Table 4.1. One therefore relies on the context of usage to ascertain its interpretation in a construction. No distinction is made between the possible values of 'We' (inclusive and exclusive). Below are some examples:

(1) a. ánî   ká   mà   àkwɔ̀
       1SG:SUBJ FUT   cry   cry(N)
       'I will cry.'
    b. ń   ká   mà   àkwɔ̀
       1SG:SUBJ FUT   cry   cry(N)
       'I will cry.'

(2) a. éjî   lé   kìɔ̀   ùnwógīē
       1PL:SUBJ PROG   cook   food
       'We are cooking food.'
    b. í   lè   dɔ́   ótsē
       1PL:SUBJ PROG   SYMV   sickness
       'We are sick.'

The 2nd person subject pronoun has two forms in the singular, *ábû* and *o*. These two forms are in a paradigmatic relationship i.e., one can be substituted by the other. It seems that the form *ábû* is predominantly used. In most cases, there is an arbitrary rather than a motivated choice by the speakers. The 2nd person plural form is realized as *émâ* or *í*. Note that the 2PL pronoun shares the same form and tone with the 3SG pronoun. However, these forms rarely imply any ambiguity because they occur in different contexts. In particular, the 2PL pronoun is assigned the feature [+ human] while the 3SG pronoun is assigned a [- human] feature.

(3) a. ábû   lí   ná   úná   mì   ègbégbè
       2SG:SUBJ HAB   sleep   sleep (N)   in   morning
       'You sleep in the morning.'
    b. ó   lè   ná   ùnâ
       2SG:SUBJ PROG   sleep   sleep (N)
       'You are sleeping.'

(4) a. émâ lè lé ólē
       2PL:SUBJ PROG play play(N)
       'You are playing.'
    b. í lè lé ólē
       2PL:SUBJ PROG play play(N)
       'You are playing.'

The 3SG subject pronoun can be overt or covert. In the overt form, it is expressed by *o* for [+animate] referents or marginally as *ónwú*, and by *í* for [-animate] referents. The 3SG pronoun *o* mostly bears a low tone, but may be marked by a high tone in constructions with past temporal reference (compare 5a and 5b). The covert feature of the 3SG is evident in copula constructions. Examples (5d and 5f) illustrate the covertness of the 3SG person in contexts that require the inanimate pronoun *í*. Insertion of the pronoun in such contexts results in ungrammaticality or a different semantic interpretation (see 5e and 5g). As noted earlier, the *í* form of the inanimate 3SG subject pronoun overlaps with a variant of the 1PL and 2PL subject pronoun, except that it contrasts with them with respect to the animacy feature. The 3rd person subject plural pronoun is usually realized as a high tone vowel *á*, derived from the full form *ámá*. The latter is not considered a full variant of the 3PL subject, partly because of its restricted occurrence in the subject slot. In other words, a sentence like **ámá lé gìè ùnwógīē* 'They are eating' would be considered ill-formed. There are, however, a few contexts where it may occur in the subject position as a substitute of the reduced form or when it cannot be substituted by the reduced form, as in (6b). One of the motivating factors for the obligatory occurrence of the 3PL pronoun *ámá* in the subject position in (6b) is its occurrence with numerals. One may assert that the 3PL pronoun ámá occupies the subject slot whenever it co-occurs with some sort of modifier. In the absence of a modifier (numeral or relative marker), the full form *ámá* is replaced by the reduced form *á*.

(5) a. ò lé kìɔ ùnwógīē
       3SG:SUBJ PROG cook food
       'He/she is cooking food.'
    b. ó dí ánî
       3SG:SUBJ see 1SG:OBJ
       'He saw me.'
    c. ónwú nwú lè dɔ́ ótsē ké àdúà
       3SG:SUBJ REL PROG SYMV sickness go church
       'He that is sick went to church.'
    d. lì ìnwíndà
       COP beautiful
       'It is beautiful.'

	e.	ʔí	lì	ìnwíndà	
		3SG	COP	beautiful	
		'It is beautiful.'			
	f.	dzè	mmènénǐ		
		COP	here		
		'It is here.'			
	g.	ʔí	dzè	mmènénǐ	
		3SG	COP	here	
		'It is here.'			

(6) a. á lē kɔ̀ ùnwógīē
    3PL:SUBJ PROG cook food
    'They are cooking food.'

b. ámá èfà lé mà àkwɔ̀
   3PL:SUBJ two PROG cry cry(N)
   'They two are crying (two of them are crying).'

4.1.1.2 Object pronouns

As shown in Table 4.1, Etulo relies mostly on constituent order for a distinction between pronouns in subject and object function, except for the 3SG/PL pronoun. Object pronouns are generally preceded by the verb. The 1SG object pronoun is realized as *ánî*. The reduced *n* form also occurs in the object slot as cliticized to a host which could be a verb or a preposition. In such cases, the final vowel of the host is phonologically conditioned. See for instance (7b), where the vowel *i* changes to *ɛ*. One also observes that the bound 1SG pronoun is not assigned any tone in the object function. This is in contrast with its subject function, where it is assigned a high tone (see Section 4.1.1.1). There is no difference observed in the form and tone of the 1PL pronoun *ejî* in both subject and object functions. Its counterpart *í* does not function as object.

(7) a. ábû lé gbɔ̀ jì ánî
       2SG:SUBJ PROG speak to 1SG:OBJ
       'You are speaking to me.'

   b. ábû gbɔ̀ jèn
      2SG:SUBJ speak to.1SG:OBJ
      'You spoke to me.'

(8) a. àdì kwú éjî èlâ
       PN call 1PL:OBJ voice
       'Adi called us.'

   b. *àdì kwú í èlâ
      PN call 1PL:OBJ voice
      'Adi called us.'

For the 2nd person object pronoun, the singular and plural forms are realized as *ábû* and *émâ* just as their subject counterparts excluding the *o* and *i* forms which rarely occur as objects (see 9 and 10).

(9) ání   ʃá   ábû   íʃá
     1SG:SUBJ   laugh   2SG:OBJ   laugh(N)
     'I laughed at you.'

(10) àdì   kwú   émâ   èlâ
     PN   call   2PL:OBJ   voice
     'Adi called you.'

Three variants of the 3SG object are identified; nasalization, zero realization and the *onwu* form. The final vowel of a verb or preposition is nasalized as exemplified in (11a) to express the 3SG. There is a zero realization of the 3SG object in (11c) and an overt realization in (11b). These variants have different animacy features. The overt form is [+animate,], covert form [-animate], and the nasalized form [+/- animate]. The 3PL is realized as *má* and occasionally as *ámá*. It seems that the only formal subject-object pronoun distinction obtained in Etulo is with the 3rd person pronoun.

(11) a.   àdì   kwṹn   èlâ
          PN   call.3SG:OBJ   voice
          'Adi called him/her.'

     b.   kĩ̀ɔ̃n   dàfí   ónwú   mànì
          do.3SG:OBJ   like   her   PTCL
          'Do it like her.'

     c.   àdì   kíé-lū
          PN   take-SUFF
          'Adi took it.'

(12) a.   àdì   lè   kwú   má   èlâ
          PN   PROG   call   3PL:OBJ   voice
          'Adi is calling them.'

     b.   éjî   lè   gbɔ́   jì   ámá
          1PL:SUBJ   PROG   speak   to   3PL:OBJ
          'We are speaking to them.'

4.1.1.3 A note on free and bound forms

The term free pronoun is used here for pronominal forms that are not phonologically reduced, serve as NP heads without a restricted distribution, and do not require a host, while the term bound pronoun subsumes pronominal forms that may have been phonologically reduced, have a restricted distribution, and may require a host. Although it is still difficult to make a clear-cut distinction between both forms of pronoun, the context of usage comes in handy. In focus and relative constructions, for instance, only the free pronouns may function as NP heads. The replacement of the free pronouns with the bound ones results in ungrammaticality. Some examples are given below of focus constructions:

(13) a. lì ání nwɔ́ ùndɔ̀ mà
        COP 1SG kill goat the
        'It is I that killed the goat.'

   b. *lì ń nwɔ́ ùndɔ̀ mà
        COP 1SG kill goat the
        'It is I that killed the goat.'

   c. lì éjî nwɔ́ ùndɔ̀ mà
        COP 1PL kill goat the
        'It is we that killed the goat.'

   d. *lì í nwɔ́ ùndɔ̀ mà
        COP 1PL kill goat the
        'It is we that killed the goat.'

(14) a. lì ábû nwɔ́ ùndɔ̀ mà
        COP 2SG kill goat the
        'It is you that killed the goat.'

   b. *lì ó nwɔ́ ùndɔ̀ mà
        COP 2SG kill goat the
        'It is you that killed the goat.'

   c. lì émâ nwɔ́ ùndɔ̀ mà
        COP 2PL kill goat the
        'It is you that killed the goat.'

   d. *lì í nwɔ́ ùndɔ̀ mà
        COP 2PL kill goat the
        'It is you that killed the goat.'

(15) a. lì ónwú nwɔ́ ùndɔ̀ mà
        COP 3SG kill goat the
        'It is her/him that killed the goat.'

   b. *lì ó nwɔ́ ùndɔ̀ mà
        COP 3SG kill goat the
        'It is her/him that killed the goat.'

   c. lì ámá nwɔ́ ùndɔ̀ mà
        COP 3PL kill goat the
        'It is them that killed the goat.'

	d.	*lì	á	nwɔ́	ùndɔ̀	mà
		COP	3PL	kill	goat	the
		'It is them that killed the goat.'				

This pattern is replicated in relative constructions where only the free forms are applicable. The occurrence of bound forms in 16b and 17b is considered ungrammatical. I illustrate this using the 1SG and the 3SG pronouns. Examples:

(16)	a.	ánî	nwú	lè	dɔ́	ótsē	ké	àdúà
		1SG	REL	PROG	SYMV	sickness	go	church
		'I that is sick went to church.'						
	b.	*n	nwú	lè	dɔ́	ótsē	ké	àdúà
		1SG	REL	PROG	SYMV	sickness	go	church
		'I that is sick went to church.'						
(17)	a.	ónwú	nwú	lè	dɔ́	ótsē	ké	àdúà
		3SG	REL	PROG	SYMV	sickness	go	church
		'He that is sick went to church.'						
	b.	*ó	nwú	lè	dɔ́	ótsē	ké	àdúà
		3SG	REL	PROG	SYMV	sickness	go	church
		'He that is sick went to church.'						

Also, the plural pronouns that co-occur with modifying numerals only allow a combination of free pronouns and numerals but not of a bound form and a numeral. In (18a, 19a and 20a) for instance, the plural pronouns *éjî* 'we', *émâ* 'you' and *ámá* 'they/them' are modified by the numerals *èfà* 'two' and *ètà* 'three'. In contrast, the co-occurrence of their bound counterparts *í* 'you/we', *á/má* 'they/them' with these numerals in (18b, 19b and 20b) yields ungrammatical constructions.

(18)	a.	éjî	ètà	lú	údē	
		1PL	three	go	home	
		'We three went home.'				
	b.	*í	ètà	lú	údē	
		1PL	three	go	home	
		'We three went home.'				
(19)	a.	émâ	èfà	bá	náà	
		2PL	two	come	PL	
		'You two should come.'				
	b.	*í	èfà	bá	náà	
		2PL	two	come	PL	
		'You two should come.'				
(20)	a.	ámá	èfà	lé	mà	àkwɔ̀
		3PL	two	PROG	cry	cry(N)
		'Two of them are crying.'					

	b.	*á/má	èfà	lé	mà	àkwɔ̀
		3PL	two	PROG	cry	cry(N)
		'Two of them are crying.'				

4.1.2 Possessives

Possessive constructions may be predicative (see the verbs *have* and *belong* in English) or (ad) nominal when they involve a direct relationship between the possessor and possessed. [5] In this section, emphasis is on nominal possessives (N+N combination, possessive determiner + noun) and possessive pronouns. Etulo lacks a distinct paradigm of possessive pronouns. Rather, it uses personal pronouns in combination with the possessive morpheme *mgbi* or the apposition of the possessor and the possessed. The choice of these strategies depends on the item being possessed, but in certain contexts both can be used. No formal distinction is made between possessive pronouns and possessive determiners. The alienable and inalienable dichotomy is also not formally marked. Examples (21–26) illustrate the use of possessive pronouns and possessive determiners in NPs and copula constructions. No morphological distinction is observed in the realization of both forms of possessives, except perhaps in structural terms. When a personal pronoun combines with the possessive morpheme, the possessed noun is always adjacent to the possessive morpheme (i.e. directly precedes it). This is illustrated in (21a, 22a, 23a, 24a, 25a and 26a). The possessive pronoun, on the other hand, involves just the possessive morpheme and the personal pronoun. Thus, one can say *ḿgbí ánî lì m̀mènénǐ* 'mine is here'. Note that the occurrence of the possessive morpheme is obligatory in these constructions. This obligatoriness particularly applies to constructions denoting several possessive relationships, excluding kinship relationships which involve a pronoun as the possessor and a noun as the possessed. Consider the following examples:

(21)	a.	ùdé	ḿgbí	ánì	dzè	m̀mànání
		house	POSS	1SG	COP	there
		'My house/compound is there.'				
	b.	ùdé	nâ	lì	ḿgbí	ánì
		house	that	COP	POSS	1SG
		'That house is mine.'				

---

[5] Etulo expresses predicative possession using the copula *dzè* as in *àdì dzè jì ájàtù* 'Adi has a car'. The English predicative construction indicating possession which is formed with the verb belong as in 'The book belongs to me' is equivalent to the non-predicative possessive in Etulo. Example:

(i)		àfè	lì	ḿgbí	ánî
		book	COP	POSS	1SG
		'The book is mine./The book belongs to me.'			

(22) a. ùdé m̀gbí éjì dzè m̀mànání
house POSS 1PL COP there
'Our house/compound is there.'

b. ùdé nâ lì m̀gbí éjî
house that COP POSS 1PL
'That house/compound is ours.'

(23) a. àfè m̀gbí ábû lì òfùfê
book POSS 2SG COP new
'Your book is new.'

b. àfè nâ lì m̀gbí ábû
book that COP POSS 2SG
'The book is yours/belongs to you.'

(24) a. àjàtù m̀gbí émâ lì | ófúfê
car POSS 2PL COP new
'Your cars are new.'

b. àjàtù ńtónâ lì m̀gbí émâ
car those COP POSS 2PL
'Those cars are yours.'

(25) a. ùdé m̀gbǎn dzè m̀mànǎnǐ
house POSS.2SG COP there
'His house is there.'

b. ùdé nâ lì m̀gbǎn
house that COP POSS.3SG
'That house is his.'

(26) a. àjàtù m̀gbí ámá ʃē
car POSS 3PL be.big
'Their car is big.'

b. àjàtù nê lì m̀gbí ámá
car this COP POSS 3PL
'This car is theirs.'

Possessive constructions that express kinship relationships are exclusively coded by apposition, i.e. the juxtaposition of the possessed and the possessor. The possessed generally precedes the possessor. The usage of some bound pronouns is possible, alternating with their full variants. Thus, it is grammatical to say ónên as an alternative to ónó ánî 'my mother' or ótsóò as an alternative to ótsó ábû 'your father'. The possessive morpheme 'mgbi' is barred in such constructions. Examples (27a–f) illustrate the juxtaposition of pronouns and nouns in possessive constructions.

(27) a. ónɔ́ ánî
mother 1SG
'my mother'
b. ónɔ́ éjî
mother 1PL
'our mother'
c. ótsó ábû
father 2SG
'your father'
d. ónɔ́ émâ
father 2PL
'your father'
e. ótsɔ́n
father.3SG
'his/her father'
f. ótsó mā
father 3PL
'their father'

Possessive constructions that involve two NPs may adopt either of the two strategies, i.e. apposition (as with kinship relationships) or use of the possessive morpheme in combination with personal pronouns. This is exemplified in (28a and 28b).

(28) a. ìkíé (ḿgbī) úndɔ̂
head POSS goat
'goat's head/ head of a goat'
b. ònwè (ḿgbī) ímgbàʃò
child POSS God
'God's child/' child of God'

In Etulo, the possessed generally precedes the possessor and both may be further separated by the possessive morpheme, as with non kinship terms (possessive determiners and N+N constructions).

4.1.3 Reflexive pronouns

Reflexives are pronouns co-referential with their antecedent, which is often the subject. In the generative syntax approach, they are considered to belong to the set of anaphors. According to König et al. (2013), reflexive pronouns are expressions that are prototypically used to indicate that a non-subject argument of a transitive predicate is bound by the subject. They typically occupy the object slot in most languages and are expressed by different means. In English, for instance, reflexive pronouns are derived by a combination of personal/possessive pronouns and the reflexive morpheme *self*. In many languages, an etymological link has been attested to exist between reflexive morphemes and terms denoting body parts. Thus, in place of the English *self*, some languages such as Igbo, Japanese, Evenki and Ngiti derive reflexive morphemes from terms like body, head, skin and soul (König et al. 2013). There are, however, languages that possess a separate paradigm of reflexives.

Reflexives in Etulo are expressed by a combination of personal pronouns and the reflexive morpheme. This reflexive morpheme is derived from the morpheme *èwô*, an Etulo word for body. It always precedes the personal pronouns and is phonologically conditioned when followed by the reduced form of the 1SG pronoun *n* and the 3SG object pronoun. Example (29b) illustrates the change of the final vowel of the reflexive morpheme from *o* to *e* following the cliticization of *n*. The tone of the 2SG pronoun *o* changes from a high to a low tone when it functions as a reflexive clitic as illustrated in (30b). This tonal change is also applicable in intensifier constructions (see 36b). In (31), the word final vowel of *èwô* undergoes nasalization indicating the marking of the 3SG object pronoun. Other personal pronouns used in reflexive constructions retain their inherent tones. As shown in Table 4.1, some personal pronouns are excluded from the reflexive function. The object or accusative pronouns are typically employed in the formation of reflexives. There are, however, some object pronouns that are incompatible with the reflexive morpheme, such as the full pronominal forms *ámá* 3PL, *ónwú* 3SG.[6] Consider the following examples:

(29) a.
ánî	nwɔ́	èwó	ánî	wá
1SG:SUBJ	kill	body	1SG	PERF

'I have killed myself.'

b.
ń	ʃá	èwén	íʃá
1SG:SUBJ	laugh	body:1SG	laugh(N)

'I laughed at myself.'

(30) a.
ábû	nwɔ́	èwó	ábû
2SG:SUBJ	kill	body	2SG

'You killed yourself.'

b.
ō	nwɔ́	èwóò
2SG:SUBJ	kill	body:2SG

'You killed yourself.'

c.
ō	lè	nwɔ́	èwóò	ábû
2SG:SUBJ	PROG	kill	body	2SG

'You killed yourself.'

---

6   The following constructions are perceived as ungrammatical by native speakers: *onwu ka nwɔ ewo onwu 'He will kill himself', *a ka nwɔ ewo ama 'They will kill themselves'.

(31) ò kà nwɔ́ èwɔ́n
3SG:SUBJ FUT kill body:3SG
'He will kill himself.'

(32) éjî lè nwɔ́ èwó éjî
1PL:SUBJ PROG kill body 1PL
'We are killing ourselves.'

(33) émâ nwɔ́ èwó émâ
2PL:SUBJ kill body 2PL
'You killed yourselves.'

(34) á nwɔ́ èwó má wà
3PL:SUBJ kill body 3PL PERF
'They have killed themselves.'

The function of reflexive pronouns may be extended to include the marking of emphasis on the antecedent. This is usually the case in languages that make no grammaticalized distinction between reflexive pronouns and intensifiers. The term 'intensifiers' as used here refers to expressions like the German *selbst* or English *self*, which can be adjoined to NPs and are invariably focused, as in 'The director himself opened the letter' or 'The director opened the letter himself' (cf. König et al. 2013). The extended use of reflexives in languages like English, German and Igbo does not apply in Etulo. Reflexives and intensifiers are clearly differentiated in form and function though they are both derived in a similar way. Just like reflexives, the intensifier is formed by a combination of personal pronouns and the morpheme *àbúwò* meaning 'self' which always precedes the pronoun.[7] An 'intensifier' construction serves to emphasize or reinforce the preceding NP or subject. It occupies the post object position in a sentence (35–40).

(35) ánî gíá àjàtù àbúwò ánî
1SG:SUBJ buy car self 1SG
'I bought the car myself.'

(36) a. ábû gíá àjàtù nâ àbúwò ábû
2SG:SUBJ buy car that self 2SG
'You bought that car yourself.'

b. ō gíá àjàtù nâ àbúwōò
2SG:SUBJ buy car that self.2SG
'You bought that car yourself.'

---

7   It is possible that the reflexive morpheme *àbúwò* is derived from the words *àbɔ* 'hand' and *èwô* 'body'. As is common in Etulo, a phonological process may account for the loss of the word final vowel in *abɔ* and the word initial vowel in *èwô* (see Section 2.6.4). A similar instance is observed with verb *fùwó* which is a combination of the monosyllabic verb *fò* 'bath' and the noun *èwô* 'body'. Both the vowel of the monosyllabic verb and the word initial vowel of the noun ewo are elided and replaced by the vowel /u/.

(37)	ò	gíá	àjàtù	ná	àbúwṍn		
	3SG:SUBJ	buy	car	that	self-3SG		
	'He bought the car himself.'						
(38)	éjî	gíá	àjàtù	àbúwò	éjî		
	1PL:SUBJ	buy	car	self	1PL		
	'We bought the car ourselves.'						
(39)	émâ	kà	gíá	àjàtù	nâ	àbúwò	émâ
	2PL:SUBJ	FUT	buy	car	that	self	2PL
	'You will buy that car yourselves.'						
(40)	á	gīā	àjàtù	nâ	àbúwò	má	
	3PL:SUBJ	buy	car	that	self	3PL	
	'They bought that car themselves.'						

Table 4.2 Reflexive pronouns

	Reflexive pronoun	Intensifier
1SG	èwó ánî	àbúwò ánî
	èwén	
2SG	èwó ábû	àbúwò ábû
	èwóò	àbúwōò
3SG	èwṍn	àbúwṍn
1PL	èwó éjî	àbúwò éjî
2PL	èwó émâ	àbúwò émâ
3PL	èwó má	àbúwò má

4.1.4 Anaphoric and logophoric reference

Anaphors subsume all pronominals that refer back to their antecedents such as reflexives, reciprocals, the 3rd person pronoun and some demonstratives[8]. Reflexives however differ from the 3rd person pronoun in that they are obligatorily bound to their antecedents. In this section, emphasis is laid on the syntactic characterization of the anaphoric 3rd person pronoun and its logophoric realization. According to Huddleston and Pullum (2002: 1453), 'Anaphora is the relation between an anaphor and an antecedent where the interpretation of the anaphor is determined via that of the antecedent'. In other words, anaphoric

---

8   Here, the term 'anaphor' is used in a more generic sense. I do not adopt the generative syntax position concerning the contrast between anaphors and pronouns.

reference broadly describes the relationship that exists between a pronoun and its antecedent in a text (sentence) or discourse. In contrast with anaphora which makes a 'backward' reference to something stated earlier, the term cataphora is used to refer to forms stated later in the text (cf. Dixon 2010). In some anaphoric contexts, the 3rd person pronoun can be ambiguous in its reference. For instance, the 3rd person pronoun in the English sentence 'John said that he saw me' has two likely interpretations. It can possibly refer back to the antecedent *John* or to some other referent outside the sentence. While English depends solely on discourse context for meaning disambiguation, some West African languages like Ewe, Gokana and Lele (cf. Hyman and Comrie 1981, Ameka 1995) adopt the use of logophoric marking, as in Gokana, or a distinct logophoric pronoun. Logophoric pronouns function primarily to remove the ambiguity associated with pronouns in reported speech which is often biclausal. Logophoric pronouns are mostly used with complement verbs such as *say, know, hear* and *see*.

In Etulo, the 3rd person pronoun bears an anaphoric relation with its antecedent in a construction or with an unspecified referent. This is observed in (41a) where the 3rd person pronoun *o* (subject) obligatorily refers back to its antecedent *adi* which is the subject of the main clause. In contrast, in (41b), its reference is ambiguous between its antecedent and some other unspecified referent. Such ambiguity can however be resolved in specific predicate constructions with the use of some sort of logophor. Etulo has no logophoric marking in the form of affixation or as an entirely distinct 3rd person logophoric pronoun, but it can employ the 3rd person free pronominal form in logophoric contexts. In other words, *ónwú* gets the logophoric interpretation in addition to other uses. The use of the logophoric pronoun in disambiguating contexts in Etulo is triggered by verbs of communication and psychological state. In (42a and 43a) the logophoric pronoun *ónwú* is coreferential with its antecedents indicating that the source of information (*Àdì* and *Ìnyànì* 'proper names') is the same as the subject of the embedded clause. On the other hand, the 3rd person pronoun *o* as used in (42b and 43b) makes disjoint reference to some other referent not included in the sentence. Observe, by contrast, the diverging function of the 3rd person pronoun *o* in (42b and 43b) as opposed to (41a and 41b). In logophoric contexts, its reference is strictly exophoric but may be either exophoric or endophoric in non-logophoric contexts. Examples:

(41) a. àdí$_i$ gbō òmbàdí èwô ìkékíé ó$_i$ gbó àfè bá
        PN fail test body because 3SG:SUBJ read book NEG
        'Adi failed his exam because he did not read/study.'

    b. àdì$_i$ dí ánî ònò nwí ó$_{i/j}$ bā mànì
        PN see 1SG:OBJ time REL 3SG:SUBJ come DET
        'Adi saw me when he came.'

(42) a. àdì$_i$ gbɛ̌ɛ̄ ónwú$_i$ kà bá
    PN say 3SG FUT come
    'Adi said that he will come.'

  b. àdì gbɛ̌ɛ̄ ò$_j$ kà bá
    PN say 3SG:SUBJ FUT come
    'Adi said that he will come.'

(43) a. ìŋànì$_i$ jé gbɛ̌ɛ̄ ónwú$_i$ kà bá
    PN know COMP 3SG:SUBJ FUT come
    'Inyani knows that she will come.'

  b. ìŋànì$_i$ jé gbɛ̌ɛ̄ ò$_j$ kà bá
    PN know COMP 3SG:SUBJ FUT come
    'Inyani knows that she will come.'

4.1.5 Interrogative pronouns

Interrogative pronouns in Etulo comprise interrogative words which may replace or be replaced by nominals. They occur in object argument position and retain their inherent tones in grammatical constructions. Interrogative words in Etulo are further discussed in Chapter 5. The four interrogative pronouns are èmé 'who', èkíé 'what', òlé 'where/which' and èngá 'when'. These are used in constructions such as the following:

(44) ábû lì èmé?
    2SG COP who
    'Who are you/You are who?'

(45) á kwúlú èngá?
    3PL:SUBJ die when
    'When did they die?'

(46) ábû kè òlé?
    2SG:SUBJ go where
    'Where did you go?'

(47) ábû mìná òlé?
    2SG:SUBJ want which
    'Which (one) do you want?'

(48) nénê lì èkíé ?
    this COP what
    'What is this?

4.1.6 Relative pronouns

Etulo has two relative pronouns: *ònwú* which is characterized by the [+human] feature and *ònwí* which is assigned a [-human] feature. Both relative pronouns are derived from the two relative markers *nwú* and *nwí* with which they share the same semantic features. In a relative clause, both relative pronouns perform the dual function of a nominal and a relative marker. The relative pronouns may modify the head noun and introduce a relative clause as in (49a and 49b). They may also function as both the head noun and the relative marker in a relative clause. In (50a and 50b) for instance, the relative pronouns perform a dual function: the direct English translation of the constructions would be 'We saw the one who ate our food' and 'I bought the one that I want'. Just like the head noun of a relative clause, both relative pronouns are modified by the definite article *mànì* 'the' which usually occurs in the clause-final position of a relative clause. The use of the relative pronouns in Etulo is further discussed in Chapter 5.

(49) a. ánî dí óngìâ ònwú tá òngìùlɔ̀ àfè
       1SG:SUBJ see woman REL.P hit man slap
       'I saw a woman who slapped a man.'

   b. ánî dí m̀dà ònwí àdì ʃé ŋà
       1SG:SUBJ see cow REL.P PN be.big surpass
       'I saw a cow that Adi is bigger than.'

(50) a. éjî dí ònwú gíé éjî ùnwógīē mànì
       1PL:SUBJ see REL.P eat 1PL food DET
       'We saw who ate our food.'

   b. ánî gíá ònwí ánî mìná mànì
       1SG:SUBJ buy REL.P 1SG want DET
       'I bought what I want.'

4.1.7 Demonstratives

Languages typically have demonstratives, though their characterization in terms of syntactic function, morphological realization and meaning tend to vary. Dixon (2010) observes that the majority of languages have at least two demonstratives relating to 'near the speaker' and 'not near the speaker'. The terms 'proximal' and 'distal' demonstratives are often used to convey this difference (see Diessel 1999). Demonstratives are primarily used as deictic expressions that indicate a contrast in relation to the location of their referents; whether they are near or far, visible or not visible, of a higher or lower level. They also perform pragmatic and anaphoric functions. The most common distinction made for demonstratives is between nominal demonstratives which point to entities (animate and inanimate) and adverbial demonstratives which may point to a location/place. Demonstratives may be realized as affixes, clitics or independent words. Syntactically, they may function as full NP heads or nominal modifiers. In a typological study of demonstratives, Diessel (1999) claims that the most frequent inflectional features of this category include number, gender and case.

In this section, emphasis is laid on the morphological and syntactic characterization of demonstratives in Etulo (excluding their pragmatic or discourse function). Etulo has just two distance-oriented degrees within the distance-oriented system (near vs far from the deitic centre), i.e. proximal vs distal demonstratives (nominal/adverbial). Nominal demonstratives are morphologically realized as independent words and are marked for number. They basically occur as determiners and in some contexts as pronouns. Examples (51–54) illustrate the use of these demonstratives as determiners, indicating their various morphological forms in different syntactic positions. The proximal demonstrative *nê* and the distal demonstrative *nâ* are both marked with a falling tone. They are always preceded by the noun which they modify. Their morphemic shape can, however, exhibit partial change in tone and form in certain syntactic environments. In (51a, 51b, 52a and 52b) both demonstratives retain their monosyllabic forms in the subject and object sentential slots. In contrast, they are realized as *nénǐ* and *nánǐ* respectively when they appear in sentence final positions (see 51c, 52c, 53c, and 54b). Thus one cannot have the phrase *àfè nénǐ* 'this book' in the subject slot. Number is expressed on demonstratives by a combination of the morpheme *nto* and the singular proximal and distal forms *né(nǐ), ná(nǐ)*, resulting in *ńtóné(nǐ)* 'these', *ńtóná(nǐ)* 'those'. The disyllabic and trisyllabic demonstratives are morphologically decomposable, though the exact meaning of the morphemes *nto* and *ni* is not quite clear. Below are some examples of demonstratives as determiners:

(51) a. àfè nê lì ḿgbí ánî
book this cop poss 1SG
'This book is mine.'

b. àdì wā òdzú nê nònwúnĕ
PN sweep house this today
'Adi swept this house today.'

c. á lè sá íʃídɔ̀ nénǐ
3PL:SUBJ PROG wash pot this
'They are washing this pot.'

(52) a. ùndɔ̀ òfiúńfíú nâ lì ḿgbí ánî
goat fat that cop poss 1SG
'That fat goat is mine.'

b. ánî tù àfè nâ èdĕdĕ
1SG:SUBJ find book that yesterday
'I found that book yesterday.'

	c.	á	gbɔ̀	àfɛ̀	nánǐ	
		3PL:SUBJ	read	book	that	
		'They read that book.'				
(53)	a.	èmgbɛ́	ńtónê	lé	ʃì	ífúé
		children	these	PROG	dance	dance(N)
		'These children are dancing.'				
	b.	àdì	gíá	àjàtù	ńtónê	èdědě
		PN	buy	car	these	yesterday
		'Adi bought these cars yesterday.'				
	c.	á	lè	sá	íʃídɔ̀	ńtónénǐ
		3PL:SUBJ	PROG	wash	pot	these
		'They are washing these pots.'				
(54)	a.	àfɛ̀	ńtónâ	lì	ḿgbí	ábû
		book	those	COP	POSS	2SG
		'Those books are yours.'				
	b.	ánî	mìná	m̀tsà	ńtónánǐ	
		1SG:SUBJ	want	mango	those	
		'I want those mangoes.'				

When singular demonstratives are realized as pronominals, they are restricted to the subject function. In object function, they obligatorily co-occur with words like *ùnwɔ́* 'thing' and they function as nominal modifiers rather than pronominals (see 55–58). One observes a change in the morphological forms of singular demonstratives in pronominal function in contrast to their forms as determiners. In pronominal function, the singular demonstratives are realized via the reduplication of proximal and distal demonstrative stems *nê* and *nâ*, resulting in the disyllabic forms *nénê* and *nánâ* with high and falling tones. The occurrence of these reduplicated forms is restricted to the subject slot (sentence initial position). Plural demonstratives require no morphological modification in their pronominal and adjectival functions. The forms *ńtónê* 'these' and *ńtónâ* 'those' are used both as determiners and as pronouns. Unlike their singular counterparts, they occur in both subject and object slots as pronominals. Their forms are, however, modified in sentence-final positions (mostly in the object slot), in analogy with singular determiner demonstratives in object function (see 55b, 56b, 57b and 59b).[9] Examples:

---

9   In isolation, the forms *nâ* and *nánǐ*, *nê* and *nénǐ* may be alternated as determiners. It is possible to have *àjàtù ná(nǐ)* 'that car', *àjàtù né(nǐ)* 'this car', *àjàtù ńtóná(nǐ)* 'those cars', *àjàtù ńtóné(nǐ)* 'these cars'.

(55) a. nénê   lì   àfè   ḿgbī   íngíú
        this   COP   book   POSS   PN
        'This is Ingiu's book.'

   b. ánî   mìná   ò-kíé   ùnwɔ́   nénǐ
        1SG:SUBJ   want   INF-take thing   this
        'I want to take this (thing).'

(56) a. nánǐ   lì   ḿgbí   ánî
        that   COP   POSS   1SG
        'That is mine.'

   b. ánî   mìná   ùnwɔ́   nánǐ
        1SG:SUBJ   want   thing   that
        'I want that.'

(57) a. ńtónê   tíʃí   bā
        these   be.good NEG
        'These (ones) are not good.'

   b. ánî   mìná   ńtónénǐ
        1SG:SUBJ   want   these
        'I want these.'

(58) a. ńtónâ   tíʃí   bā
        those   be.good NEG
        'Those (ones) are not good.'

   b. àdì   mìná   ńtónánǐ
        PN   want   those
        'Adi wants those.'

In interrogative copula constructions, the subject nominal demonstratives *nɛnɛ* and *nana* alternate with the morphemes *dɛ̀n* 'this' and *dâ* 'that'; the obvious similarity being the corresponding vowels *ɛ* and *a*, as observed in both proximal and distal demonstratives. The latter forms are however restricted to interrogative constructions where they constitute a NP.

(59) a. lì   èkíé   dɛ̀n?
        COP   what   this
        'What is this?'

   b. nénê   lì   èkíé?
        this   COP   what
        'What is this?'

(60) a. lì   èkíé   dâ?
        COP   what   that
        'What is that?'

   b. nánâ   lì   èkíé?
        that   COP   what
        'What is that?'

For adverbial demonstratives, two types are identified in Etulo: the proximal *m̀méné(nǐ)* 'here' and the distal *m̀máná(nǐ)* 'there'. For further discussion on adverbial demonstratives, see Section 4.5.

Table 4.3 Demonstratives

	Demonstrative pronouns	Demonstrative determiners	Demonstrative adverbials
proximal (SG)	nénê	nê/nénǐ	m̀ménénǐ/m̀ménê 'here'
distal (SG)	nánâ	nâ/nánǐ	m̀mánánǐ/m̀mánâ 'there'
proximal (PL)	ńtónê	ńtónê/ńtónénǐ	
distal (PL)	ńtónâ	ńtónâ/ńtónánǐ	

4.1.8 A note on the indefinite pronoun quantifiers

Etulo does not have a large class of indefinite pronouns and quantifiers. Only two such elements have been identified: *ámgbéká* 'some' and *dúú* 'all'. Both occur in the subject and object positions (61–62). They also function as determiners (see Section 4.2.4). Indefinite pronouns in English such as *nobody*, *somebody* and *nothing* are expressed in Etulo with the words *ǹgísè* 'person' and *ńká* 'thing' in negative constructions (see 63a–63b). The English quantifier pronoun *many* is realized as *kpákpá* (animate) and *kwùbà* (inanimate), but it strictly functions as a determiner rather than a pronoun (see Section 4.2.4 for a discussion on determiners).

(61) a. ámgbéká giè ùnwógīē bá
       some   eat food   NEG
       'Some did not eat.'

   b. ánǐ kíé   ámgbéká
      1SG take some
      'I took some.'

(62) a. dúú kà   kwúlúū
       all FUT die
       'All will die.'

   b. ánǐ gíá dūū
      1SG buy all
      'I bought all (of them).'

(63) a. ńká   kā   kìɔ̀ bá
       thing FUT do   NEG
       'Nothing will happen.'

	b.	ǹgísè		bá		bá
		person		come		NEG
		'Nobody came.'				

4.1.9 Conclusion

This section has outlined the features of the Etulo pronominal system: personal pronoun, reflexive pronoun, interrogative pronoun, relative pronoun, anaphoric and logophoric reference. Also discussed are possessives and demonstratives. Personal pronouns comprise free and bound forms with no semantic gender distinction. The 3rd person singular can only be dropped in copula constructions. Etulo has no separate paradigm of possesive pronouns. Possessives are mostly expressed using the possessive morpheme *ḿgbī* in combination with personal pronouns. Reflexives are formed with the word *ewo* 'body' plus personal pronouns while intensifiers are formed with the word *àbúwò* 'self' plus personal pronouns. Etulo is characterized by partial logophoricity. The use of the logophoric pronoun is triggered by verbs of communication and psychological state. Animacy distinction is relevant for the relative pronouns. Four interrogative pronouns are identified. One of them, *ole* 'which/where', functions as an interrogative determiner (see Section 4.2.4). Etulo has a two-way deictic system (proximal and distal) with number distinction singular/plural.

4.2. The noun category and noun phrase

This section addresses the noun category and its properties. It also discusses the category of determiners and the associative construction, focusing on definiteness, quantifiers and interrogative words that function as determiners. It then examines how some of these constituents combine to form the noun phrase. More specifically, Section 4.2.1 outlines the structural criteria for establishing the noun category as a distinct word class in Etulo; Section 4.2.2 and Section 4.2.3 describe the phonological and morphosyntactic characterization of the noun category; Section 4.2.4 discusses a class of Etulo determiners. This is followed by a discussion of the Etulo noun phrase in Section 4.2.5 and a discussion of a subtype of the NP known as the associative construction in Section 4.2.6. In Section 4.2.7, nouns that denote property concepts are distinguished from adjectives. A semantic classification of Etulo nouns is given in Section 4.2.8, while Section 4.2.9 provides a summary.

The universality of the major lexical categories (noun and verb) has been questioned in recent literature (Everet 2005). In a typological study of word classes, Hengeveld (1992) makes a distinction between languages with flexible word classes and those with rigid word classes. He identifies languages in which no clear cut distinction is made between the noun and verb categories. The view adopted here is that of the universality of the major lexical categories (see Schachter 1985, Baker 2003, Croft 2005, Dixon 2010). Evidently, the semantic characterization of nouns on the basis of their reference to entities, objects etc. does not serve as a sufficient criterion for establishing a distinct lexical class in human languages. A given concept may be realized as a verb in language A but as a noun in language B. Similarly, the morpho-syntactic features of a noun vary from one language to the next. One thus needs to rely on a combination of semantic, morpho-syntactic and distributional properties in order to establish a distinct noun category in a language.

4.2.1 Theoretical backdrop

For some languages, the distinction between the noun and other categories (verb and adjective) is clear cut, while in others such distinction is rather fuzzy. One of the most common yet problematic means of establishing the noun category in individual languages is by notional characterization. In the traditional view, the noun category typically includes words which refer to entities (both concrete objects and abstract concepts). As noted earlier, this notional approach falls short in the light of cross-linguistic variation. From the morpho-syntactic perspective, Hengeveld (2004) defines a nominal as a predicate which, without further measures, can be used as the head of a term (NP). This implies that a prototypical noun does not require any morpho-syntactic operation to function as an NP or the head of an NP. Different languages adopt several language internal criteria in characterizing their class of noun. In English, for instance, a distinguishing feature of nouns is their capacity to be marked for definiteness or non-definiteness using prenominal articles. In general, English nouns may be preceded by an article but need not be followed by another word. Grammatical categories often associated with the noun include gender or noun class, case, number and definiteness. In Etulo, only two of these categories (number and definiteness) seem, to an extent, applicable to the noun class. The noun category is established using the following prototypical and language-internal phonological criteria (as detailed in Section 4.2.2):

- Semantic criteria (reference to entities; animate vs inanimate, concrete vs abstract concepts, mass vs count; though Etulo lacks a morphological distinction between mass and count nouns, their compatibility with the plural morpheme tends to vary)
- Morphological criteria (characteristic inflectional and derivational possibilities)

- Syntactic criteria (distributional properties, such as compatibility with definite and non-definite morphemes as well as markers of number)

4.2.2 Phonological structure of Etulo nouns

Etulo nouns begin with a vowel or syllabic nasal but rarely with a consonant. Borrowed nouns are adapted to this phonological pattern.[10] The lexical or inherent tones of a noun may be influenced in grammatical constructions. This is often the case in associative constructions. Moreover, a noun comprises at least two syllables, in contrast to verbs which can be monosyllabic or disyllabic. In the table below, Etulo nouns are classified according to their syllabic structure into dysillabic, trisyllabic and polysyllabic nouns.

Table 4.4 Syllabic structure of the Etulo noun

Disyllabic	Trisyllabic	Polysyllabic
ùtɔ̀ 'king'	àbúbē 'left'	íkínábō 'tortoise'
àtsé 'age grade'	àjíwī 'shame'	òkpákpágìdì 'butterfly'
àdzè 'poverty'	ùnwógīē 'food'	m̀màlídzɔ̀dzɔ̀ 'a type of fly'
ùnwɔ̂ 'thing'	ímgbífōò 'toad'	òbùkúsè 'a type of leaf'
ùkà 'friend'	íʃákwú 'chameleon'	òkpɔ́lɔ́ŋgɔ́ɔ̀ 'crab'
àŋgá 'drum'	m̀màfà 'youth'	

4.2.3 Morpho-syntactic characterizations of nouns

Nouns in Etulo lack any form of morphological inflection, at least from a synchronic perspective. There are, however, a subset of disyllabic nouns that are cognate with some verb roots and thus suggest that a derivational process must have been exploited. For instance, the noun *ibɔ* 'prayer' is cognate with the verb *bɔ* 'pray'. The phonological structure of such nouns is **v+cv (v)**. The first syllable is realized as a vowel or syllabic nasal (see also Section 3.1.1). Examples:

(64) a. íbɔ́ 'prayer' → bɔ́ 'pray'
b. ùnâ 'sleep' → ná 'sleep'
c. àʃí 'song' → ʃí 'sing'
d. m̀fìà 'fatness' → fìà 'be fat'
e. íʃá 'laughter' → ʃá 'laugh'

---

10 Borrowed English nouns like *tomato* and *bucket* are pronounced as *itumato, ibokoti*. This also applies to borrowed words from neighbouring languages such as Tiv and Hausa (see Section 2.6.5).

Grammatical categories or features such as number, case, definiteness etc. (which are cross-linguistically associated with the noun category) are marginally realized as morphological markings on nouns. Number/plurality is expressed via different means: vowel substitution, numerals, plural morpheme (*èmí*) and irregular forms. Number marking may be optional or obligatory depending on the noun. Most animate [-human] and inanimate nouns may but need not be marked for number while animate [+human] (i.e. mostly kinship terms) nouns are obligatorily marked for number. The table below illustrates the use of vowel substitution and of the plural morpheme as number marking strategies. Many nouns with animate reference (human/kinship terms) express plurality by vowel substitution. In the first two columns, one observes that the word-initial vowel /o/ in singular nouns is substituted by /e/ and /i/ in their plural forms. For the non-human animate and inanimate nouns, the prenominal plural morpheme *emi* is used.

Table 4.5 Number marking

Kinship terms (+human)		Inanimate/non-human	
Singular	Plural	Singular	Plural
óbâ 'husband'	ébâ 'husbands'	ìfà 'snake'	èmí ìfà 'snakes'
ònwè 'child'	ènwè 'children'	àfè 'book'	èmí àfè 'books'
óngìâ 'woman'	éngìâ 'women'	ǹgísè 'person'	èmí ǹgísè 'persons'
òngìùlɔ̂ 'man'	èngìùlɔ̂ 'men'	èkwɔ́ 'tree'	èmí èkwɔ́ 'trees'
òwàkwádē 'widow'	èwàkwádē 'widows'	ákpúkpû 'bone'	èmí ákpúkpû 'bones'
ònwé óngìùlɔ̂ 'boy'	ènwé éngìùlɔ̂ 'boys'	àbɔ̂ 'hand'	èmí àbɔ̂ 'hands'
ònwé óngìâ 'girl'	ènwé éngìâ 'girls'	òdzû 'house'	èmí òdzû 'houses'

4.2.4 A class of determiners

Determiners are a class of words that co-occurs with a noun to qualify its referential value. They typically include possessives, demonstratives, quantifiers, interrogative words and definite/indefinite articles. Some members of this class are known to share an affinity with other categories such as adjectives with respect to their syntactic behavior.

The Etulo determiners include demonstratives, possessives, quantifiers, interrogative words and the definite article. The determiner function of possessives and demonstratives have already been discussed in Section 4.1.5

and Section 4.1.10. In this section, I focus on the modifying functions of the definite article, interrogative words and quantifiers.

4.2.4.1 The category of definiteness

Definiteness is a category typically associated with the noun phrase. A definite NP refers to an entity which is identifiable to the speaker and the hearer in a given context. Languages vary in regards to the expression of definiteness: some have a grammaticalized way to express it and others lack it altogether.

In Etulo, definiteness is marked by the low tone definite article *mà* 'the' (65a), which may also be realized as *mànì* depending on its position of occurrence. The latter form is realized in the sentence-final position (65b). This variation in form is not peculiar to the definite article. It is also applicable to the demonstrative morphemes (see Section 4.1.7). The position of the definite marker is postnominal. Examples:

(65) a. ònwè òngìùlɔ̂ mà gíá m̀tsà
       child man the buy mango
       'The boy bought mangoes.'
    b. àdì dí ònwè òngìùlɔ̂ mànì
       PN see child man the
       'Adi saw the boy.'

4.2.4.2 Interrogative determiners

There are two interrogative items which can function as determiners in Etulo: *òlé* 'which' and *àlí* 'what/which'. Their position in relation to the modified noun varies. The determiner *òlé* is postnominal while *àlí* is prenominal. In (66a) for instance, the interrogative determiner *òlé* follows the noun *àjàtù* whereas in (66b), the noun follows the determiner *àlí*.

(66) a. lì àjàtù òlé nwí ábû dí
       COP car which REL 2SG see
       'Which car did you see?'
    b. lì àlí àjàtù nwí ábû dí
       COP what car REL 2SG see
       'What/which car did you see?'

4.2.4.3 Quantificational determiners

A quantifier is a type of determiner that specifies the numerosity of the noun phrase. They include numerals and other quantifiers such as *kpákpá* 'many', *kwùbà* 'many', *ámgbéká* 'some' *dúú* 'all'. As determiners, their position is postnominal.

(67) ǹgísè kpákpá lú údē
     person many go home
     'Many people went home.'

(68) ánî gíá ájàtù kwùbà
     1SG buy car many
     'I bought many cars.'

(69) ǹgísè ámgbéká gìè ùnwógīē
     people some eat food
     'Some did not eat.'

(70) ánî gíá ájàtù (mà) dúú
     1SG buy car the all
     'I bought all the cars.'

4.2.5 The noun phrase

The term noun phrase (NP) is used here to refer to the noun and its dependents. It serves as a sentential argument: the grammatical subject, direct or indirect object. The Etulo NP comprises a noun/pronoun or a head noun in combination with one or more dependents. Noun modifiers in Etulo include numerals, quantifiers, adjectives, demonstratives, the definite article, genitives (pronouns and nouns), plural morpheme, interrogative determiner and the relative clause. Several of the noun dependents are subsumed under the determiner category. In the absence of these dependents, all noun types (proper, common, etc.) function independently as individual NPs in main and peripheral argument positions. This draws from the fact that Etulo lacks an indefinite article. Even the use of the definite article *mà* is restricted to referential contexts in discourse (to a large extent). Within an NP, the head noun may be preceded or followed by a dependent. In examples (71–78), the noun dependents follow the head noun in an NP with the exception of the plural morpheme, the interrogative determiner (see 66b), and a few adjectives which occur prenominally. Consider the following examples:

(71) àfè ètá
     book three
     'three books'

(72) àjàtù   ófúfê
      car   new
      'new car'

(73) a. àfè   nâ
        book   that
        'that book'
     b. àfè   nê
        book   this
        'this book'

(74) m̀tsà   mà
      mango   the
      'the mango'

(75) a. àjàtù   kwùbà
        car   many
        'many cars'
     b. ǹgísè   kpákpá
        person   many
        'many people'

(76) èmí   àjàtù
      PL   car
      'cars'

(77) ìnwíndà   óngìâ
      beauty   woman
      'beautiful woman'

(78) àjàtù   dúú
      car   all
      'all cars'

Etulo requires a regular pattern in the ordering of noun dependents (adjectives, demonstratives, numerals) in relation to each other and to the head noun. In a head initial NP that consists of these dependents, the adjective directly precedes the numeral which is, in turn, followed by the demonstrative, resulting in the order N > Adj > Num > Dem (see 79a). When the adjective is prenominal, the order becomes Adj > N > Num > Dem as in (79b). Further discussion on the constituent order within the NP is in Section 5.7.

(79) a. òbúé   ómbímbí   ìjúó   ńtónénǐ
        dog   black   ten   these
        'these ten black dogs'
     b. ìnwíndà éngìâ   ètá   ńtónénǐ
        beautiful women   three   these
        'these three beautiful women'

4.2.6 Associative constructions

The associative construction is observed in some of the world's languages. According to Welmers (1973: 275), 'Associative constructions constitute an important aspect of noun modification in a variety of Niger Kordofonian languages'. In Igbo, for instance, associative constructions are strictly characterized by the juxtaposition of two nouns as in *oche osisi* 'wooden chair (a chair made of wood)', *nkata ose* 'basket of pepper', *isi ewu* 'goat head', *akwa Ifeoma* 'Ifeoma's cloth'. In Swahili and some other languages, the nouns are linked or joined by an associative morpheme (see Williamson 1986, Welmers 1973: 276) as shown by the following example from Swahili:

(80) a. chupa ya maji
'a bottle of water'
b. saa ya mkono
'wrist watch (clock for the arm)'
c. miti ya kujengea
'sticks for building'

(Welmers 1973: 276; no glosses in original)

Typical semantic relations expressed by associative constructions include possession, content, origin, material etc. From a broad perspective, an associative construction is used as a cover term for NP configurations which may express the above semantic notions. It is a type of NP which involves a N+N combination where N_1 may be modified by N_2 or vice versa. There are, however, instances where the two nouns jointly attain the status of an exocentric compound with none of them modifying the other. In this subsection, I focus on associative construction as a type of NP in Etulo. A noun may be modified by another noun in a possessive relation. The example *ònwè (m̀gbī) ímgbàfò* 'child of God/God's child' indicates possession or ownership. While it is relatively simple to assign a possessive interpretation to the above example, it seems quite problematic for other constructions. The following examples illustrate various semantic readings expressed by associative constructions:

(81) a. ugà   ùnwógīē   content/purpose
plate   food
'plate of food/plate for food'
b. òbá   ángíà   content
bag   millet
'bag of millet'

	c.	ìtsè	ɛ́kwɔ́	material/source
		chair	wood/tree	
		'wooden chair'		
	d.	ìkíé	úndɔ̀	possession/type
		head	goat	
		'head of a goat/goat head'		

Associative constructions are left-headed. In other words, the N$_1$ functions as the head and is modified by N$_2$. The use of the possesive morpheme ḿgbī may be optional or obligatory in contexts where a possessive meaning is at stake. With other semantic readings such as content, purpose, and type, its use is unacceptable. A tonal change is often observed with N$_2$ in associative constructions. In (81c) for instance, the inherent tone of the N$_2$ ɛ̀kwɔ́ changes from LH to HM, while in (81d), the tone of the N$_2$ ùndɔ̀ changes from LL to HF. It is still unclear if such tonal changes follow a regular pattern. The constituents of an associative construction may be jointly modified by demonstratives, quantifiers, possessive determiner, and adjectives. No structural difference is observed in instances where the N$_2$ is modified or where both N$_1$ and N$_2$ are jointly modified. Consider example (82a) in contrast to (82b).

(82)	a.	újá	ìtùmátù	ómúmá	
		basket	tomato	ripe	
		'a basket of ripe tomatoes'			
	b.	újá	ìtùmátù	òkwúkwó	
		basket	tomato	big	
		'a big basket of tomatoes'			
(83)	a.	ìkíé	úndɔ̀	òkwúkwó	
		head	goat	big	
		'head of a big goat'			
	b.	ìkíé	úndɔ̀	òkwúkwó	
		head	goat	big	
		'a big goat head'			

Associative constructions allow joint coordination with other nouns using the coordinating morpheme *jì*, as illustrated in (83a and 83b):

(83)	a.	újá	ìtùmátò	jì	òlòmû	
		basket	tomato	and	orange	
		'a basket of tomato and orange'				
	b.	újá	ìtùmátò	jì	újá	òlòmû
		basket	tomato	and	basket	orange
		'a basket of tomato and orange'				

Associative constructions also share similarities with nominal compounds. A comparison of both N+N construction types is discussed in Section 3.5.2.

4.2.7 Distinguishing nouns from adjectives

Some Etulo nouns denote property concepts. At the syntactic level, a subset of nouns that express property concepts may function as predicative expressions in copula constructions, just like adjectives. Example (84a) shows the noun *ìnwíndà* 'beauty' in this function. In (84b), the same noun functions as a noun modifier, while in (84c) it is the head noun modified by the possessive form *ḿgbí ábû*. Examples:

(84) a. ìɲànì   lì   ìnwíndà
        PN   COP   beauty
        'Inyani is beautiful.'

     b. àdì   dí   òngìà   ìnwíndà
        PN   see   woman   beauty
        'Adi saw a beautiful woman.'

     c. ìnwíndà   ḿgbí   ábû   tíʃí
        beauty   POSS   2SG   be.good
        'Your beauty is good.'

Other nouns such as *ìtíngā* 'anger', *èmbúà* 'hunger', *ótsē* 'sickness', which denote property concepts (see 85 and 86), also function as nominal modifiers in noun phrases such as *ǹgísè ìtíngā* 'angry man/person', *ǹgísè émbúà* 'hungry man'. In such N+N constructions, N₂ expresses a qualitative meaning. Unlike adjectives, these nouns may serve as arguments in a clause and may take modifiers such demonstratives and possessives.

(85) a. ánî   dɔ́   èmbùà
        1SG:SUBJ SYMV   hunger
        'I am hungry.'

     b. èmbúà   kà   nwɔ́   éjî
        hunger   FUT   kill   1PL:OBJ
        'Hunger will kill us.'

(86) a. àdì   lé   kìɔ̀   ìtíngā
        PN   PROG   do   anger
        'Adi is feeling angry.'

     b. ìtíngā   tíʃí   bā
        anger   be.good NEG
        'Anger is not good.'

4.2.8 Semantic classification of nouns

Nouns are typically categorized into different semantic classes based on the characterization of what they denote. Common semantic classes include concrete vs abstract nouns, count vs mass nouns, animate vs inanimate nouns, common vs proper nouns etc. Noun categories thus often overlap, for one noun may belong to more than one semantic class. In the table below, only four semantic classes of Etulo nouns (concrete, abstract, count, mass) are illustrated. Other subclasses are subsumed in these four classes.

Many abstract nouns that denote property concepts perform an adjectival function in Etulo, while some concrete nouns may also function as modifiers in N+N constructions. Count nouns which have [+human +kinship] features are more likely to express number (pluralization) via vowel substitution, while others express pluralization with the plural morpheme èmí.

Table 4.6 Semantic classification of nouns

Semantic class	Examples
Concrete noun	ìkíé 'head'
	ítsēē 'chair'
	ìsèsé 'name of person'
Abstract noun	ìtíngā 'anger'
	émbúà 'hunger'
	ìmíò 'fear'
Count noun	àfè 'book'
	òngìâ 'woman'
	m̀dà 'cow'
Mass noun	ènì 'water'
	àngìà 'millet'
	èkìè 'sand'

4.2.9 Conclusion

Etulo nouns have some predictable phonological features common in Niger Congo languages; the noun begins with a vowel or syllabic nasal. Nouns with non-human or inanimate referents are optionally marked for number, while nouns with human referents are obligatorily marked for number. Number is marked either with initial vowel alternation or with prenominal free plural morpheme. Etulo has a class of determiners that may combine with the noun within the NP. The determiner class comprises quantifiers, demonstratives, the definite article, indefinite pronouns and the interrogative determiner. Etulo has no indefinite article. Associative constructions are characterized by functions such as content, purpose and possession.

4.3 The verb category

This section discusses the Etulo verb as a lexical category. Section 4.3.1 examines the phonological structure of the Etulo verb root. A classification of the verb class is given in Section 4.3.2; a distinction is made between complement and non-complement types in Section 4.3.2.1; the verbs are further classified into simple and complex predicates in Section 4.3.3; the selectional restriction that characterizes semantically related verbs is briefly discussed in Section 4.3.4. This is followed by a conclusion in Section 4.3.5. At the morphological level, the Etulo verb has no inflection in relation to TAM (tense-aspect-mood) categories. The morphological characterization of the verb is discussed in Chapter 3.

4.3.1 Phonological structure of verb roots

Armstrong (1983) notes that many Idomoid languages have the common 'Eastern Kwa' trait that allows verbs to begin with a consonant and nouns to begin with a vowel. This observation holds in Etulo. The verb root typically begins with a consonant or syllabic nasal and the last syllable is open-ended. Verb roots in Etulo consist of not more than three syllables. Monosyllabic verb roots seem more common than disyllabic and trisyllabic verb roots. Trisyllabic verb roots are in fact rarely attested. Besides, it is possible that some of the verb roots analysed as disyllabic and trisyllabic are a combination of different verbal elements. The prosodic structure of verbs is represented as follows:

[CV(V)]	(monosyllabic)
[CV(V): CV(V)]	(disyllabic)
[NCV]	(disyllabic)
[CV:CV:CV]	(trisyllabic)

Table 4.7 Phonological structure of the Etulo verb

CV(V)		NCV(V)		CV:CV		CV:CV:CV	
mà	'cry'	ǹdéē	'be tired'	bùlù	'fly'	kwúlésĕ	'stop'
kpà	'pay'	m̀bùò	'be full'	kwùlú	'open'	gbìlímɔ̆	'forget'
kìà	'plant'	ǹdzì	'bury'	wítá	'start'		
dzè̩	'be'			kàkà	'enter'		
kìɔ̀	'cook'			mìná	'want/ desire'		

CV(V)		NCV(V)		CV:CV		CV:CV:CV	
fìà	'try'			gbíkīē	'break'		
ná	'sleep'			fàwá	'tear'		
gbá	'peel'			tsàmú	'push'		
kíé	'take'			míní	'roll'		
wé	'remember'			gbèlá	'scrub'		
lúū	'go'			ɲìné	'change/swap'		
kíá	'set (trap)'						
gbō	'fall/fail'						
kpā	'grind'						
fīā	'sweep'						

The vowels and syllabic nasals of verb roots are assigned specific tones. The monosyllabic verb roots could be classified into different classes on the basis of their inherent tone. There are high tone, mid tone and low tone verb roots. This tonal classification has an implication for some preverbal tense-aspect morphemes that are tonologically conditioned, such as the future marker *ka* and the progressive marker *le*. The tone of these preverbal markers is in polarity relation with the inherent tone of the following verb (especially the monosyllabic verb). Both markers bear a high tone when followed by inherently low and mid tone verbs and a low tone when followed by a high tone verb. Examples (87 and 88) illustrate the occurrence of the progressive and future markers followed by low and mid tone verbs while (89a and 89b) illustrate the high tone verb being preceded by both markers:

(87) a. ò ká kìà ìsíkápá
       3SG:SUBJ FUT plant rice
       'He will plant rice.'

   b. àdì lé kìà ìsíkápá
      PN PROG plant rice
      'Adi is planting rice.'

(88) a. ìɲànì ká kpā àtsúbō
       PN FUT grind pepper
       'Inyani will grind pepper.'

   b. àdì lé kpā àtsúbō
      PN PROG grind pepper
      'Adi is grinding pepper.'

(89) a. àdì   kà   gbá   ángwɔ́
         PN   FUT   peel   yam
         'Adi will peel yam.'
    b.   àdì   lè   gbá   ángwɔ́
         PN   PROG   peel   yam
         'Adi is peeling yam.'

4.3.2 Verb classification

Besides the typical classification of verbs on the basis of their transitivity value, semantics (for instance motion, experiential verbs etc.) or the dynamic-stative divide, many African languages distinguish between simple and complex predicates. Depending on the language, a complex predicate may correspond to a serial verb construction (SVC) or a verb compound. Additionally, Benue Congo languages like Igbo, Idoma, Ewe and Esan also classify verbs into groups based on their capacity to take complements. In the following section, I attempt to classify Etulo verbs in two ways, based on the distinction between complement and non-complement verbs and between simple and complex predicates. Both classifications are basic to the Etulo verb system.

The phenomenon of complement verbs in West African languages has been widely studied and has been a subject of controversy. In the study of the Igbo verb, Nwachukwu (1976) distinguishes between inherent complement and non-inherent complement verbs. He describes inherent complement verbs as a subset of verbs whose roots require a noun in their citation form for the full specification of their meaning. He argues that the functional semantic load of such verbs rests on their noun complements. Emenanjo (2015) also classifies Igbo verbs into five classes based on the nature of their noun complements. Similar to Nwachukwu, he defines a subset of the Igbo complement verbs as dummy units that rely on their noun complements for the full realization of their meaning.

In the study of Ewe, Essegbey (1999) adopts a different approach to the study of verb complementation. He identifies a set of verbs in Ewe that obligatorily requires noun complements. He distinguishes between obligatory complement verbs (OCVs) and non-obligatory complement verbs. He argues against analysing OCVs as light verbs and rather adopts a compositional approach. Compositionality entails that the meaning of an expression is a function of its parts and their manner of combination. From a semantic viewpoint, Essegbey argues that OCVs and their complements form two clines with one relating to verb specificity and the other to complement specificity. The less specific verbs occur with more specific complements and the more specific verbs occur with less specific complements.

I use the term 'obligatory complement verbs' to refer to a class of Etulo verbs in that requires a noun complement. In some cases, the meaning of the verb is underdetermined and the noun complements perform the function of further specifying their meaning.

4.3.2.1 Obligatory complement verbs (OCVs)

Verbs that obligatorily co-occur with a noun as meaning specifier are prevalent in Etulo, hence the need to group verbs into two classes. OCVs co-exist at the underlying structure with a nominal complement for the full specification of their meaning, while non-obligatory complement verbs (NCVs) require no such complement. The verb root and nominal complement could be interwoven in meaning to the extent that native speakers intuitively think of some of them (verb + complement) as one word. Another motivation for such assumption by native speakers could emanate from the phonological process of vowel elision and contraction which is quite common in spoken or fast speech. The final vowel of the verb root is often elided. A verb such as *ʃí áʃí* 'sing' would be realized as *ʃáʃí*. A list of some Etulo complement verbs is given in Table 4.8 showing their full forms and the resulting forms after the application of phonological processes in spoken speech. The choice of writing the verb and its complement in their full form or otherwise is a matter of convention. Subsequently, the conventions |V| (verb) and |OC| (obligatory noun complement), shall be used to represent the two components of the OCV.

Table 4.8 Contracted Verb+Noun forms

Full forms of verb and complement	Deleted/ contracted vowels	Realized form in speech	Retained/resulting vowel
tsé ɔ̀ɲà 'run race'	/ɛ/, /o/	tsíɲà 'run (race)'	/ɪ/
ná úná 'sleep sleep'	/a/	núná 'sleep (sleep)'	/u/
bɔ́ íbɔ́ 'pray prayer'	/ɔ/	bíbɔ́ 'pray (prayer)'	/i/
mà àkwɔ̀ 'cry cry'	/a/	màkwɔ̀ 'cry (cry)'	/a/
jí úmí 'steal theft'	/u/	jímí 'steal (theft)'	/i/
lé ólē̄ 'play play'	/o/	lélē̄ 'play (play)'	/ɛ/
ʃá íʃá 'laugh laugh (N)'	/a/	ʃíʃá 'laugh (laugh)'	/i/
ʃí áʃí 'sing song'	/i/	ʃáʃí 'sing (song)'	/a/
ʃí ìfúé 'dance dance (N)'	/i/	ʃífúé 'dance (dance)'	/i/

Full forms of verb and complement	Deleted/ contracted vowels	Realized form in speech	Retained/resulting vowel
ʃò èwô 'bath body'	/o/, /e/	ʃùwó 'bath (body)'	/u/
tá ámgbá 'greet greeting'	/a/	támgbā 'greet (greeting)'	/a/
gbó ábɔ̂ 'clap hand'	/o/	gbábɔ̂ 'clap (hand)'	/a/
dí ìnê 'look' see eye	/i/	dínê 'look'	/i/
gbò èsɛ́ 'fall ground'	/o/, /e/	gbèsɛ́ 'fall (down)'	/ɛ/
lá èsɛ́ 'lie ground'	/e/	lásɛ́ 'lie (down)'	/a/
sɔ̄ èsɛ́ 'sit ground'	/ɔ/, /e/	sìsɛ́ 'sit (down)'	/i/
dó ésɔ́ 'send message'	/o/, /ɛ/	désɔ́ 'send (message)'	/ɛ/

An OCV may receive different semantic interpretations depending on the noun that is assigned as its complement. The basic characterization of the Etulo OCV stems from the nature of the noun that it selects as a complement and the semantic content of the verb in isolation (without its complement). There are OCVs that have a fixed collocation with the noun that they select such as *ʃá íʃá* 'laugh', *ná únâ* 'sleep', *bɔ́ íbɔ́* 'pray'. These verbs (with their semantic interpretation) can only co-occur with specific nouns. Their inherent meaning is usually underdetermined. In contrast, other OCVs have no fixed collocation with their noun and may select their complement from a plethora of nouns. Verbs such as *gie unwogie* 'eat food', *gba angwɔ* 'peel yam' select nouns which may be replaced by other nouns in the realization of the same meaning. The generic noun *unwogie* 'food' can be replaced by another type of food like *gie inatse* 'eat beans'.

On the semantic content of OCVs, two possibilities are observed. There are OCVs whose numerous semantic interpretations are not related in meaning. The verb is more or less semantically underdetermined in the absence of a complement. Take for instance the V *fí* in (90) and *kpà* in (96) which realize unrelated meanings. Such verbs (identical verb roots) are here analysed as different verbs (homonyms) that draw their full meaning from the OC that co-occur with them. Other OCVs tend to have an identifiable meaning which could sometimes be vague. In (92), the V *gbò* expresses the event of striking a person or an object. In all of its pairing with different OCs, the derived interpretations (beat, drum, clap) are loosely linked to the overall meaning. The *kìɔ̀* cluster in (95) expresses the core meaning 'do' which implies performing or undergoing an event. The OC that it selects determines the exact type of the event involved. One could argue that this is a case of different but semantically related realizations of an individual verb. The more specific the verb meaning, the less specific it's complement. It follows from the foregoing that some Etulo OCVs could assume an ambiguous reading in the absence of their noun complement. Some of these Vs are cognate with their OCs (see 96–99).

(90) a. ʃí-áʃí   'sing'   **ʃí cluster**
        sing-song.oc

     b. ʃí-òdzɛ́   'quarrel'
        quarell-talk.oc

     c. ʃí-òkwɔ̀   'farm'
        farm-farm.oc

(91) a. tá-àfè   'slap'   **ta cluster**
        hit-slap.oc

     b. tá-àsá   'punch'
        hit-blow.oc

     c. tá-òdákâ   'shoot'
        shoot-gun.oc

     d. tá-ámgbá   'greet'
        greet-greeting.oc

(92) a. gbó-àbɔ̂   'clap/beg'   **gbó cluster**
        beat-hand.oc

     b. gbó-íbé   'beat'
        beat-fight.oc

     c. gbó-àngá   'drum'
        beat-drum.oc

(93) a. tsé-ènì   'swim'   **tsé cluster**
        hit-water.oc

     b. tsé-òɲà   'run'
        hit-race.oc

     c. tsé-àfɔ̀   'kick'
        hit-leg.oc

(94) a. wó-édē   'be mad'   **wó cluster**
        wear.madness.oc

     b. wó-èwô   'prepare'
        wear-body.oc

     c. wó-élélá   'dream'
        dream-dream.oc

     d. wó-ànwúntò   'wear'
        wear cloth.oc

(95)	a.	kìɔ̀-ìdɔ́	'work'	**kìɔ̀ cluster**
		do-work.OC		
	b.	kìɔ̀-ùnwógīē	'cook'	
		do-food.OC		
	c.	kìɔ̀-m̀náóʃī	'pound'	
		do-yam.OC		
	d.	kìɔ̀-ìtíngā.OC	'be angry'	
		do anger		
(96)	a.	kpà-àkpà	'vomit'	**kpà cluster**
		vomit-vomit.OC		
	b.	kpà-m̀kpâ	'pay debt'	
		pay-debt.OC		
(97)		lɛ́-ólɛ́	'play'	
		play-play.OC		
(98)		ʃá-íʃá	'laugh'	
		laugh-laugh.OC		
(99)		bɔ́-íbɔ́	'pray'	
		pray-prayer.OC		
(100)		gbò-èsɛ́	'fall'	
		fall-ground.OC		
(101)		gbá-ángwɔ́	'peel'	
		peel-yam.OC		
(102)		gbɔ́-àfɛ̀	'read'	
		read-book.OC		
(103)		gíé-ùnwógīē	'eat'	
		eat-food.OC		

A verb and its complement are not always bound together but can be split by another constituent. This is often the case in grammatical constructions where the complement co-occurs with the object of the verb (see 104a and 104b).

(104)	a.	àdì	tá	òkà	ánî	àfè
		PN	hit	friend	1SG:POSS	slap.OC
		'Adi slapped my friend.'				
	b.	àdì	tá	ábû	ámgbá	
		PN	greet	2SG:OBJ	greeting.OC	
		'Adi greeted you.'				

A further discussion is provided in chapter 6 about the transitive/intransitive status of Etulo verbs.

4.3.2.2 Non-obligatory complement verbs (NCVs)

As noted earlier, non-obligatory complement verbs (NCVs) do not require an obligatory noun as complement for the full realization of meaning. Many disyllabic verbs fall in this group.[11] Below are some examples:

(105) a. bùlù   'fly'
       b. m̀bùò   'be full'
       c. ǹdéɛ̄   'be tired'
       d. jágbá   'be able'
       e. jé   'know'
       f. ʃímbí   'be dirty'
       g. mìná   'want'
       h. ǹdzî   'bury'
       i. gbíkīē   'break'

4.3.3 Simple vs complex predicates

The alternative method of Etulo verb classification is based on the distinction between simple and complex predicates. Simple predicate constructions involve a single verb which functions as the sole predicate of a clause. On the other hand, the term 'complex predicate' serves as a cover term for language specific constructions such as serial verb constructions, particle+verb constructions and verb+verb constructions. According to Butt (2010: 13), 'complex predicate is used to designate a construction that involves two or more predicational elements (such as nouns, verbs and adjectives) which predicate as a single unit, i.e. their arguments map onto a monoclausal syntactic structure.' Adopting this definition, V+V constructs that make up a monoclausal structure could be analysed as complex predicates. In traditional linguistic literature of languages like Chinese and Igbo, V+V sequences are alternatively termed compound verbs, especially when they are analysable as one word (cf. Thompson 1973, Lord 1975).

Both OCVs and NCVs may be classified as simple predicates when they function independently as sole predicate of a clause. The Etulo complex predicate subsumes two groups of verbs, namely: verb compounds and serial verbs. Verb compounds such as *gbónwɔ́* 'kill', *tsénwɔ́* 'kill', *mùàdzé* 'cut into pieces', *lúbā* 'go back/go inside', etc. are complex predicates that function as a single unit in a clause. The first two examples denote cause-effect events: the action of beating and hitting is expressed by V_1 *gbó* 'beat' and *tsé* 'hit' and the final effect which is

---

[11] From a diachronic perspective, some of the verbs analysed as disyllabic could involve a historical process of fusion; possibly of V+V or even V+N.

of killing is expressed by V₂ *nwɔ́* 'kill'. They are immune from the ambiguity that characterizes most simple predicates and therefore hardly require any nominal complement for the full specification of their meaning. A discussion of serial verbs as a type of complex predicate is given in Chapter 6.

4.3.4. Selectional restriction

The term 'selectional restriction' is used here to describe the semantic distinction made with regards to the specific type of argument (object) a verb co-occurs with. There seems to exist, for some events, a subset of verbs with similar or same meaning. The usage of a member of each subset is partly determined by the semantic specification of the object, which is in most cases a noun. To describe the event of grinding, a choice is made among the three verbs that express the concept of grinding based on the item that is being ground (see the first column). Thus, it is ungrammatical to use the verb *já* with *àtsúbō* or vice versa.

Table 4.9 Selectional restriction

'grind'	'pound'	'break'	'peel'	'wash'
kpáā àtsúbō	só ólógó	gbíkīē	gbá angwɔ	nwú ìnê
'grind pepper'	'pound cassava'	'break (stick)'	'peel yam (raw)'	'wash face'
já ìnátsè	kìɔ̀ ùnáóshī	gbóbū	fíá angwɔ	sá àjàtù
'grind beans (wet)'	'pound yam'	'break (head/pot)'	'peel yam (cooked)'	'wash car'

4.3.5 Conclusion

A phonological description is given of Etulo verb roots as being predominantly monosyllabic. The verbs begin either with a consonant or a syllabic nasal and can be classified according to their tonal characteristics. The tone class of a verb has consequences for some TAM particles which show tone polarity with the verb. Two types of distinctions are proposed for the Etulo verb: simple vs complex predicates. In addition, OCVs are distinguished from NCVs. OCVs are described as verbs that co-occur with OCs which may or may not be a cognate of the V. The nominal complement could be semantically fixed or not. With respect to meaning, the less specific OCVs occur with more specific or fixed noun complements and vice versa. A discussion of the transitive/intransitive dichotomy is found in Chapter 6.

4.4 Qualificatives

The adjective is cited as one of the major lexical categories in the world's languages, next to nouns and verbs. There are, however, languages for which claims are made about the absence of a distinct adjectival class, such as Korean (Martin 1992, Yu 1998), and Lao (Enfield 2004). Some of these claims remain controversial (see Dixon 2004). For languages in which there is an indisputable adjective class, a variation in the size of the class is observed. Some languages have a relatively large and open class, while others have a small and closed one. One feature of many Niger Congo languages is their limited number of pure (underived) adjectives. Welmers (1973: 250) states that 'In almost all Niger Congo languages which have a class of adjectives, the class is rather small, and many concepts expressed by adjectives in European languages are expressed by other kinds of constructions using noun, verb or both.' Igbo, for instance, has about eight antonymic pairs of adjectives. In Ewe, only five simple adjectives are attested (Ameka 2002). Other Niger Congo languages like Jukun and Edo lack a separate adjectival class (cf. Welmers 1973, Omoruyi 1986). In Jukun, qualificatives are derived from verbs by reduplication, while Edo employs adjectival verbs. The existence of verb-like and/or noun-like adjectives is, of course, not peculiar to Niger Congo languages. Genetti and Hildebrandt (2004) distinguish between pure adjectives and verb-like adjectives in Manange (a Tibeto-Burman language). Fiona (2004) identifies a set of adjectival verbs as distinguished from non-adjectival verbs in Wolof (an Atlantic language spoken in Senegal).

The term 'qualificatives', as used here, covers a wide range of categories that denote property concepts. These categories include a small class of adjectives, a subset of stative verbs, ideophones and a small class of nouns. Since Etulo has few adjectives, it relies largely on other categories to express typical qualification functions. In the following sections, I discuss the adjective class using language internal criteria in conjunction with the typological criteria proposed by Dixon (2004) for identifying an adjectival class. The use of other categories as qualificatives is also discussed. In addition, the use of intensifiers and the expression of comparison will be described.

4.4.1 Typological criteria

From a purely semantic point of view, adjectives prototypically denote property concepts relating to nouns. The semantic view, however, falls short as a sufficient yardstick for establishing a separate class of adjectives, since property concepts are notably expressed by other categories such as nouns, verbs or both in some languages. To avoid the common pitfall of passively analysing the semantic equivalents of, for example, English adjectives as adjectives in other languages, one needs to adopt language specific criteria (semantic, phonological, or morphosyntactic). In Hausa (a Chadic language), for instance, adjectives are syntactically defined by their use as nominal modifiers or predicators, in addition to the semantic criterion (cf. Newman 2000). In Manange, simple adjectives are morphologically distinguished from some other categories by their lack of inflectional or derivational morphology, and syntactically by their attributive function and ability to occur in a complement clause (cf. Genetti and Hildebrandt 2004).

Dixon (2004) proposes a typological framework for establishing adjectives as a distinct category. He proposes different sets of semantic categories, distinguished as core and peripheral. The core semantic type includes four semantic primitives (dimension, age, value and colour) and is likely to be the only type found in languages with a small adjective class. The peripheral semantic type includes semantic primitives such as physical property, human propensity, speed, difficulty, similarity, qualification, quantification, position and number. This peripheral type is associated with medium and large adjective classes. I present below a summary of Dixon's typological criteria (semantic and syntactic). A lexical class is considered an adjective class if it:

- denotes some or all of the semantic types (which are viewed as property concepts)
- is grammatically distinct from the noun and verb class
- functions either as a copula complement or intransitive predicate
- performs attributive function as a nominal modifier

In addition to underlying language internal criteria, in the following sections, I examine how the above characterization applies to the Etulo adjectival category.

4.4.2 The adjective class

A total of ten adjectives have been identified in Etulo. They are trisyllabic and have the phonological structure V-CV-CV. They tend to have a systematic tone pattern with the exception of *ìtsítsî* 'short'. Their inherent tones may, however, change in grammatical constructions. Etulo adjectives are characterized by partial reduplication of the consonant and sometimes vowel segments. In some cases, the reduplication is part of the morphological process which derives an adjective from a noun or verb. In other cases, the reduplication is not linked to a synchronically interpretable derivational process. Four Etulo adjectives are derived in this way. They include the three adjectives of color *ómúmá* 'red', *óndzúndzé* 'white', *ómbímbí* 'black' and *ómgbūmgbē* 'young'. In Table 4.10, I list the ten adjectives, their reduplicated segments, and the words from which they are derived.

Table 4.10 Etulo adjectives

Adjectives		Reduplicated segments	Derived from	
ómúmá	'red'	/m/	má	'be ripe (be fair)'
ómbímbí	'black'	/mbi/	úmbí	'dirt'
óndzúndzé	'white'	/ndz/	úndzé	'white'
ómgbūmgbē	'young/small'	/mgb/	òmgbé	'small'
òfùfè	'new'	/f/		
òsùsè	'good'	/s/		
òbúbé	'bad'	/b/		
ókwúkwó	'big'	/kw/		
ìtsítsî	'short'	/tsi/		
ògbùgbè	'old'	/gb/		

In the attributive function, Etulo adjectives may precede or follow the modified noun. Below are some examples:

(106) a. ǹgísè ògbùgbè
person old
'old person'
b. ògbùgbè ǹgísè
old person
'old person'
(107) a. àjàtù ókwúkwó
car big
'big car'
b. ókwúkwó ájàtù
big car
'big car'
(108) a. àbù ìtsìtsî
gown short
'short gown'
b. ìtsítsí àbù
short gown
'short gown'

(109) a. ùnwɔ̂   òsùsè
         thing   good
         'good thing'
     b. òsùsè   ùnwɔ̂
         good   thing
         'good thing'
(110) a. àjàtù   òfùfè
         car   new
         'new car'
     b. òfùfè   àjàtù
         new   car
         'new car'
(111) a. ùndɔ̀   ómbímbí
         goat   black
         'black goat'
     b. ómbímbí   úndɔ̂
         black   goat
         'black goat'
(112) a. ùndɔ̀   óndzúndzé
         goat   white
         'white goat'
     b. óndzúndzé úndɔ̂
         white   goat
         'white goat'

These adjectives are characterized by their ability to function as complements in a copula construction (to use Dixon's terminology), i.e. as adjectival predicates (in Hengeveld's (1992) conception). The structure can be represented as (CS) COP CC where the copula subject CS may be omitted. In Etulo, this applies to contexts where the subject is the 3SG pronoun with [-animate] feature. The following examples are illustrative:

(113) òdzú   nâ   lì   ókwúkwó
      house   that   COP   big
      'That house is big.'
(114) lì   ómbímbí
      COP   black
      'It is black.'
(115) àjàtù   ḿgbí   ánî   lì   òfùfè
      car   POSS   1SG   COP   new
      'My car is new.'

Most adjectives may function as the predicate in a relative clause. In such constructions, they are preceded by the relative marker and the copula as shown in (116 and 117).

(116) a. àbù nwí lì ìtsítsî
gown REL COP short
'a gown that is short'
b. òngìâ nwú lì òbùbè
woman REL COP bad
'a woman that is bad'

All the identified adjectives can also function as nominals. They co-occur with the demonstratives *nâ* 'that', *nê* 'this', *ńtónâ* 'those', *ńtónê* 'these and the definite article *mà* 'the'. Consider the following examples:

(117) a. ókwúkwó nê
big this
'this big one'
b. ìtsítsí mà
short the
'the short one'

4.4.3 Verbs as qualificatives (adjectival verbs)

Adjectival verbs are a subtype of semantically intransitive predicate denoting property concepts. Most property concepts are expressed by this group of stative verbs in Etulo. As any other verb, adjectival verb roots begin with a consonant or syllabic nasal but never with a vowel. They also take the nominalizing vowel prefix in the infinitive form. Below is a list of adjectival verbs in Etulo.

Table 4.11 Adjectival verbs

CV (V)		NCV(V)		CV(N)CV	
nwɔ́ɔ̄	'be dry'	ǹdéē	'be tired'	mámā	'be sour'
má	'be ripe'	m̀bùò	'be full'	gígìè	'be sharp'
fìù ǹfìà	'be sweet'	ǹdù	'be dirty'	sùndô	'be heavy'
fíú ńfíú	'be fat'			dútsà	'be heavy'
fìù ǹfíé	'be strong'			túntó	'be long/far'
jí ùjù	'be cold'			tímbī	'be bad/ugly'
ʃé	'be big'			tíʃî	'be good'

CV (V)		NCV(V)		CV(N)CV	
ʃé ìgbô	'be tall'			lúmā	'be fair'
gìè ǹgìè	'be small'			lúmbī	'be dark'
kíɛ̄	'be old'			sùmsè	'be beautiful'
				kpɔ́kɔ́	'be hard'
				ʃímbí	'be dirty'
				tsídzâ	'be dirty'

These verbs function as the sole predicate in an intransitive construction. At the syntactic level, two main argument slots are filled by nouns namely: subject and object (provided the verb belongs to the OCV set, as many of those in the above table). As detailed in Section 4.3.2, the object position is occupied by the nominal complement that specifies the full meaning of the verb. The syntactic frame of adjectival verbs is represented as NP+V (+ nominal complement). Thus, even in intransitive predicate constructions, Etulo may (in many cases) superficially retain the SVO basic word order. Many adjectival verbs are compatible with tense-aspect morphemes (the future marker *ka*, progressive marker *le*, habitual marker *li* and the perfect marker *wa*), but to varying degrees.[12] Below are examples of adjectival verbs used in grammatical constructions:

(118) òn ɔ́   éjî   fíú   ńfíú
      mother   1PL   be.fat   fatness
      'Our mother is fat'

(119) òngìà   nê   kíɛ̄
      Woman   this   be.old
      'This woman is old.'

(120) ùnwógīē   nâ   jí   ùjù
      food   that   be.cold   cold
      'That food is cold.'

(121) ànwúntò   ḿgbí   ánî   ʃímbí
      cloth   POSS   1SG   be.dirty
      'My clothes are dirty.'

---

12 The compatibility of tense-aspect morphemes with adjectival verbs requires further investigation. In comparison with activity verbs, it seems that some TAM morphemes receive a different semantic interpretation in occurrence with different groups of verbs. For instance, the progressive morpheme *le* gives rise to an inceptive meaning with at least some adjectival verbs (see Chapter 7 for further discussion).

4.4.3.1 Verbs in attributive function

Adjectival verbs may modify the noun in attributive contexts. To function as modifiers, they occur in relative clause constructions or alternatively take the low tone nominalizing prefix *o-* (see 122–124). In both cases, they are preceded by the modified noun. In a relative clause, the relative markers *nwí* and *nwú* are preceded by the modified noun and followed by the adjectival verb. Note that adjectival verbs do not take a prefix when they function as a predicate in a relative clause. Some of the nominalized verbs additionally require a full reduplication of the verb root in attributive function. As illustrated in (122a), the verb *kíē* 'be old' which modifies *ǹgísè* 'person' obligatorily takes the low tone prefix and has its root reduplicated. Among the verbs that require prefixation and reduplication in attributive function, one finds *tímbī* 'be ugly', *ʃímbí* 'be dirty' and *ǹdù* 'be dirty'.

(122) a. ǹgísè ò-kíé-kíē
person/man PREF-be.old-red
'an old person'

b. ǹgísè nwú kíē
person REL be.old
'a person that is old'

(123) a. ánî kíé ígbé ò-sùndô
1SG:SUBJ carry bag PREF-be.heavy
'I am carrying a heavy bag.'

b. ánî kíé ígbé nwí sùndô
1SG:SUBJ carry bag REL be.heavy
'I am carrying a bag that is heavy.'

(124) a. ɔ̀dɔ̀ ò-mámā
soup PREF-be.sour
'a sour soup'

b. ɔ̀dɔ̀ nwí mámā
soup REL be.sour
'soup that is sour'

4.4.4 Other means of expressing property concepts

Besides the use of adjectives and verbs, other categories such as a subset of abstract nouns and ideophones may equally denote property concepts. Such nouns include *m̀màfà* 'youth', *òtsé* 'sickness', *ìtíngā* 'anger', *èmbúà* 'hunger', àdzè 'poverty', ìnwíndà/m̀nwàzá 'beauty'. Some of them function as copula complements just like adjectives (125a–b) or as nominal modifiers (125c). Like typical nouns, this subset of nouns can be accompanied by determiners such as demonstratives and possessives.

(125) a. ò   lì   m̀màfà
          3SG   COP   youth
          'She is young.'
      b. à   dzέ   àdzὲ   sáān
          3PL   COP   poverty   INT
          'They are very poor.'
      c. ábû   lé   kìɔ̀   ìtíngā
          2SG:SUBJ   PROG   do   anger
          'You are feeling angry.'

They also function as nominal modifiers. Consider the following examples:

(126) a. òngìâ   ìnwíndà
          woman   beauty
          'beautiful woman'
      b. ṅgísὲ   ìtíngā
          person   anger
          'angry person'

Etulo has a class of ideophones which perform a variety of functions (see Section 4.7). One of these is to describe the properties of a noun. Such ideophones include fèlèfèlè 'silky', trɔ̀trɔ̀ 'smooth', léngéléngé 'slim', tétété 'sound of dripping water', plédédédé 'white', bìùùù 'black' etc. In examples (127a–b), the ideophones give a vivid description of the attributes of the NP subjects. When ideophones serve as nominal modifiers, they take the nominalizing prefix o- (128a and 128b). Examples:

(127) a. ìkíé   m̀gbí   ánî   lè   trὲtrὲ
          head   POSS   1SG   is   IDEO
          'My head is bald.'
      b. ànwúntò   nê   lè   fèlèfèlè
          cloth   this   is   IDEO
          'This cloth is silky.'
(128) a. ànwúntò   ò-fèlèfèlè
          cloth   PREF-IDEO
          'silky cloth'
      b. òngìâ   ò-léngéléngé
          woman   PREF-IDEO
          'slim woman'

4.4.5 Semantic characterization of qualificatives

Some property concepts are expressed by a subset of qualificatives with the same or a similar meaning. The semantic feature of the modified noun informs the use of one form or the other. As an example, the English adjective *heavy* is expressed by two adjectival verbs namely *sùndó* and *dúùtsà*. Inanimate nouns are qualified by *sùndó* while animate nouns are qualified by *duutsa*.[13] A similar example occurs with the English adjective *beautiful*, which is denoted by the nouns *ìnwíndà* [+female], *m̀nwàzá* [+male] and the adjectival verb *sumse* [+inanimate]. Additionally, some adjectives tend to have a corresponding adjectival verb. They are listed in the table below.

Table 4.12 Corresponding adjectives and adjectival/stative verbs

Adjectives		Adjectival verbs	
òsùsè	'good'	tíʃī	'be good'
òbúbé	'bad'	tímbī	'be bad'
ókwúkwó	'big'	ʃé	'be big'
ómbímbí	'black'	lúmbī	'be dark'
ómúmá	'red'	lúmā	'be fair/red'
ògbùgbè	'old'	kíē	'be old'
ómgbúmgbé	'small'	gìè ǹgìè	'be small'

4.4.6 Differentiating between adjectives and adjectival verbs

As stated earlier, both categories share in common their ability to denote property concepts. They, however, differ in their phonological, morphological and syntactic characterization. Just like most nouns, adjectives commence with a vowel while adjectival verbs begin with a consonant, although both may begin with a syllabic nasal (/m/ or /n/). Only adjectival verbs and ideophones may take the low tone *ò-* prefix. Adjectives and adjectival verbs are characterized by reduplication. With the former, this reduplication is partial and lacks an identifiable semantic denotation. With the latter, reduplication is full and only occurs when the relevant (indeed few) adjectival verbs are in attributive function. Most adjectives are classified as core semantic types while adjectival verbs may be grouped in both core and peripheral semantic categories (see Section 4.4.1). In their predicative function, both adjectives and adjectival verbs are intransitive predicates; however, the former must be accompanied by the

---

13 The verb *sùndó* 'be heavy' may modify the Etulo noun for a human corpse (but then, a human corpse is [-animate]).

copula, while the latter may take an obligatory nominal complement. Their differences and similarities are further summarized in the table below:

Table 4.13 Summarized features of adjectives and adjectival verbs

Features	Adjective	Adjectival verb
Occurs in attributive function	Yes	Yes (but only in relative clause/ taking a nominalizing prefix)
With the copula	Yes	No
As intransitive predicate	Yes	Yes
Is morphologically marked	No	Yes
Undergoes reduplication	Yes (partial)	Yes (full)
Is prenominal in attributive function	Yes (optional)	No
Begins with a vowel	Yes	No
Occurs in a relative clause	Yes (not all)	Yes

4.4.7 Expression of degree

Degree is expressed via verb serialization based on the verb ŋà 'surpass'. This applies to both adjectives and adjectival verbs. In the comparative constructions exemplified below, the verb ŋà co-occurs with the copula lì and the adjective òfùfè 'new' in (129a) and with the adjectival verb gígíè 'be sharp' in (130a). For the superlative construction, ŋà is used in combination with dúú 'all' (see 129b and 130b). The verb ŋà always follows the adjectival verb as well as the copula construction (copula + adjective). There are, however, few instances of superlative constructions where ŋà may precede both the copula and the adjective. In (129c) for instance, the superlative marker is preverbal.[14]

(129) a. àjàtù ḿgbí àdì lì òfùfé ŋà ḿgbí ánî
car POSS PN COP new surpass POSS 1SG
'Adi's car is newer than mine.'

b. àjàtù ḿgbī ánî lì òfùfé ŋà dúū
car POSS 1SG COP new surpass all
'My car is the newest.'

---

14 The superlative marker ŋa is realized as ŋao in (129c) where it precedes the copula and adjective. This construction may be realized alternatively as àjàtù ḿgbī ádî lì òfùfè ŋà mì ìgbókò dúū 'Adi's car is the newest in Gboko'. The reason for this alteration of the phonetic shape is still unclear.

c. àjàtù ḿgbī ádî ŋàô lì òfùfê mì ìgbókò dúū
car POSS PN surpass COP new in PN all
'Adi's car is the newest in Gboko.'

(130) a. èbà ḿgbī ìsèsé gígíè ŋà ḿgbí ánî
knife POSS PN be.sharp surpass POSS 1SG
'Isɛsɛ's knife is sharper than mine'

b. èbà ḿgbī ìsèsé gígíè ŋà dúū
knife POSS PN be.sharp surpass all
'Isɛsɛ's knife is the sharpest.'

For the expression of the equivalence comparison, Etulo uses the morpheme *dàfí* 'as/like' as in (131). Negative comparison is marked by *dàfí* in combination with the negative marker *ba* as shown in (132).

(131) àdì fíú ńfíú dàfí òlá
PN be.fat fatness as PN
'Adi is as fat as Ola.'

(132) àdì fíú ńfíú dàfí òlá bá
PN be.fat fatness as PN NEG
'Adi is not as fat as Ola.'

4.4.8. Use of the intensifier *sáān* with qualificatives

Across languages, many adjectival concepts are gradable. In Etulo, degree modification involves adjectives and adjectival verbs. It is expressed periphrastically with the intensifier *sáān*. This morpheme bears a high-mid tone contour. It modifies the adjective and adjectival verb in both attributive and predicative function. Examples (133a and 134b) illustrate its use with the adjective *ìtsítsî* 'short' in attributive and predicative function. In (134a and 134b), it modifies the adjectival verbs *má* 'be ripe' and *ʃé* 'be big'. The intensifier occurs in the sentence final position in the examples below.

(133) a. ìsèsé lì ìtsítsí sáān
PN COP short INT
'Isɛsɛ is very short.'

b. ìɲànì lì ònwè óngìâ òsùsè sáān
PN COP child woman good INT
'Inyani is a very good girl.'

(134) a. m̀tsà nâ mà sáān
mango that be.ripe INT
'That mango is very ripe.'

b. àdì gíá ájàtù nwí ʃé sáān
PN buy car REL be.big INT
'Adi bought a very big car.'

4.4.9 Conclusion

From the above analyses, it is evident that property concepts in Etulo are expressed by a distinct small adjective class, and a larger set of stative verbs called adjectival verbs. These two categories are alike in terms of semantic content but differ in their phonological, morphological and syntactic characterization. In addition, there are other categories (nouns and ideophones) that may denote property concepts.

From a typological perspective, the expression of property concepts in Etulo is typical of many Niger Congo languages of West Africa such as Etulo, Igbo, Yoruba and Ewe. These languages are characterized by a small class of adjectives, and therefore adopt other means of encoding property concepts.

4.5 The adverb category

The adverb class is often regarded as comprising heterogeneous linguistic elements. Givon (1993: 71) observes that, among all lexical categories, adverbs are the least homogeneous and the hardest to define. In traditional grammar, the adverb is viewed as a category which may function as the modifier of a verb, an adjective or another adverb. It is seen as an open class in many languages where it is attested (cf. Schachter & Shopen 2007). Adverbs may be classified into subtypes (e.g. temporal adverbs, place adverbs, manner adverbs) based on the semantic notions they denote. This is captured in Trask's (1993: 3) definition of adverbs as 'a lexical category whose members are grammatical adjuncts of a verb and most typically express semantic notions such as time, manner, place, instrument or circumstance.'

This section discusses words which belong to the adverb class (adverbs) or perform adverbial functions (adverbials) in Etulo. It establishes the different semantic types, pointing out their phonological, morphological and syntactic properties. It proposes two major classifications for the adverb: morphological and functional classification.

4.5.1 The classification of adverbs

In Etulo, an adverb is a word, or closely knit group of words, that serves to modify the verb or qualificative. They express a variety of meanings such as manner, time, frequency, location and magnitude/intensity. As noted earlier, two classifications are made for the Etulo adverb. The morphological classification makes a distinction between simple and derived adverbs, while the functional classification distinguishes different adverb types on the basis of their semantic function. In the discussion of the adverb category, adverbial clauses are excluded; their study is taken up in a separate chapter.

4.5.1.1 The morphological classification of adverbs

Morphologically, adverbs are grouped into two types: simple and complex. Simple adverbs comprise individual words that are not derived from any other category and are not a combination of different words. By contrast, complex adverbs are often words from other word classes, such as nouns (noun phrases), and ideophones which perform adverbial functions.

4.5.1.1.1 Simple adverbs

Few adverbs belong to this group. They include:

- Adverbs of time: *téjî* 'already/before'; *dzíkân* 'earlier/before'; *nósē* 'before'; *plɛ́* 'early'
- Adverb of degree: *sáān* 'a lot, very'

4.5.1.1.2 Complex adverbs

Many adverbs belong to the complex class. Two forms are observed. The first group comprises noun phrases in adverbial function. They are formed by a combination of nouns and determiners which jointly express an adverbial meaning. I call this group 'phrasal adverbials'. The second type is formed from other group of words such as ideophones, and is characterized by reduplication.

4.5.1.1.2.1 Phrasal adverbials

Phrasal adverbials include temporal NPs such as *àlí ɔ̀nɔ̀* (*dúú*) 'every time/all the time', *ɔ̀nɔ̀ òká* 'sometimes'. The use of the morpheme *dúú* 'all' in the above mentioned phrasal adverb is optional. The phrasal adverb, *àlí ɔ̀nɔ̀*, which literally means 'every time', translates into English as *often, always* and *frequently*.[15] In the spoken form, the word final vowel of the first morpheme is elided (*àlí ɔ̀nɔ̀* → *àlɔ́nɔ̀*), while for the adverb *ɔ̀nɔ̀ òká* it is the word initial vowel of the second word that is elided giving rise to *ɔ̀nɔ̀ká*. The above phrasal adverbials belong to the semantic class of time adverbials. Examples:

---

15 The phrase *àlí ɔ̀nɔ̀* has an ambiguous reading. Besides its adverbial meaning, it is used in interrogatives to imply which time?

(135) a. ánî   lí   ná   úná   àlí   ɔ̀nɔ̀   dúū
         1SG:SUBJ HAB   sleep sleep every time   all
         'I sleep always.'
     b. ònɔ̄   ánî   lí   kɪ̀ɔ̀   ùnwógīē ɔ̀nɔ̀   òká
        mother 1SG   HAB   do   food   time   another
        'My mother cooks sometimes.'

4.5.1.1.2.2 Adverbs formed by reduplication

Adverbs characterized by reduplication are mostly derived from ideophones. They are otherwise referred to as ideophonic adverbs. Many of them express the semantic notion of manner.

(136) a. dúmɔ́ dúmɔ́   'slowly'
     b. pléplé   'quickly'
     c. tétété   'depiction of dripping water'
     d. gígígí   'depiction of shivering'
     e. pìàpìàpìà   'description of a sweet taste'

Some locative adverbs are derived from the noun category. For instance, the Etulo adverbs èsɛ́ 'down' and èfò 'up' derive from the nouns 'ground' and 'heaven'.

4.5.1.2 The functional classification of adverbs

Adverbs can be classified according to their function in a construction. Etulo adverbs are grouped into five basic classes: manner, place, time, frequency and degree. They are discussed in the following sections.

4.5.1.2.1 Manner adverbs

Manner adverbs describe the way in which an activity or event takes place. Manner adverbs as discussed here subsume a subset of adverbs referred to in the literature as pace adverbs. Pace adverbs denote manner but are restricted to describing speed or pace of movement involved in an activity. Manner adverbs modify the verb. Regarding their syntactic distribution, they follow the verb or verb phrase they modify. As shown in examples (137b, 138b and 139b),

Etulo manner adverbs cannot be fronted in the sentence; their occurrence is restricted to sentence final positions. Etulo manner adverbs include *pléplé* 'quickly', *ʃílídìdì* 'slowly', *dúmɔ́ dúmɔ́* 'slowly'. Their usage in constructions is illustrated in examples (137a–139a).

(137) a. ó lúū ʃílídìdì
         3SG:SUBJ go quietly
         'He went away quietly.'
    b. *ʃílídìdì ó lúū
         quietly 3SG:SUBJ go
         'He went away quietly.'

(138) a. ìsèsè nwɔ́ ùndɔ̀ pléplé
         PN kill goat quickly
         'Isɛsɛ killed the goat quickly.'
    b. *pléplé ìsèsé nwɔ́ ùndɔ̀
         quickly PN kill goat
         'Isɛsɛ killed the goat quickly.'

(139) a. ìɲànì lí gbɔ̄ ódzé dúmɔdúmɔ́
         PN HAB talk talk slowly
         'Inyani talks slowly'
    b. *dúmɔ́dúmɔ́ ìɲànì lí gbɔ̄ ódzé
         slowly PN HAB talk talk
         'Inyani talks slowly.'

A subset of ideophonic adverbs denote manner by depiction or imitation of an activity, event or state expressed by the verb. Just like typical manner adverbs, ideophonic adverbs answer the question 'How is the activity of X' or 'How is the state of X'? This is illustrated in (140a and 140b).

(140) a. ènì lè fú kwútùkwùtù
         water PROG boil IDEO
         'The water is boiling.'
    b. àdì lí kìkíé ɲáɲáɲá
         PN HAB walk IDEO
         'Adi walks gracefully.'

4.5.1.2.2 Temporal adverbs

Temporal adverbs indicate the time at which an event or activity takes place. Etulo temporal adverbs have scope over an entire proposition and are particularly relevant in resolving the ambiguity associated with the bare verb in non-future constructions (see Chapter 7). They may consist of single words such as èdědě̂ 'yesterday', ékéká 'tomorrow', íně̌ 'today', plé 'early/on time', téjî 'already/before', dzíkân 'previously/earlier', nósē 'before', or phrasal adverbials such as ɔ̀nɔ́ néní̌ 'now (this time)', ègbètáně̌ 'next tomorrow/day before yesterday'. Temporal phrasal adverbials are NPs consisting of a noun and a determiner. For instance, the adverb meaning 'now' is realized by a combination of the noun ɔnɔ and the demonstrative nɛnɪ 'this' which translates literally as 'this time'. The phrasal adverb ègbètáně̌ inglobates via the fusion of three words: egbe 'day', eta 'three' and mɛ 'today'. It can be both future and past-referring (three days before or after the speech time). This is shown in examples (141a and 141b). Some of these time adverbs (ékéká 'tomorrow' èdědě̂ 'yesterday' mɛ 'today') are in fact nouns that function as adverbs. They may occur in sentence final or sentence initial position as in (142a and 142b). In sentence final position, they are directly preceded by a verb or verb phrase, while in sentence initial position they precede the verb or verb phrase. No change in meaning is observed when they occur in either position.

(141) a. àdì bā ègbètáně̌
         PN come day.three.today
         'Adi came the day before yesterday.'
      b. ìɲànǐ kà bā ègbètáně̌
         PN FUT come day.three.today
         'Inyani will come a day after tomorrow.'
(142) a. ánî̀ gìè ùnwógīē èdédě̌
         1SG:SUBJ eat food yesterday
         'I ate food yesterday.'
      b. èdédě̌ ánî̀ gìè ùnwógīē
         yesterday 1SG:SUBJ eat food
         'Yesterday I ate food.'

Two kinds of past temporal reference are denoted by the time adverbials téjî 'already/before' and dzíkân 'previously/earlier': remote and recent past. The recent past reference is expressed by dzíkân 'earlier'. Etulo speakers only use dzíkân for events that have just occurred or occurred earlier in the day, but never for events that occurred a day before the speech time. The adverb dzíkân occurs in either preverbal or postverbal positions (cf. 143a–b). On the other hand, the adverb téjî expresses a variety of meanings, such as remote past reference, completive and experiential meaning. Depending on the context of occurrence, it may be translated into English as 'before, already, first'.[16] Unlike *dzíkân*, the adverb *teji* does not occur in sentence initial or final position. It is strictly preverbal. Constructions such as **teji adi na una* or **adi na una teji* are considered ungrammatical. In (144a), where *téjî* directly precedes the habitual morpheme and verb, it denotes remote past reference. It may also be replaced by another time adverbial, namely *nose* 'before', which occurs in sentence initial positions (see 144b). The adverb *téjî* expresses a perfectal or completive meaning when it co-occurs with the perfect morpheme *wà* (see 145). Note that this time adverb may equally occur in constructions with past reference reading without any accompanying tense-aspect particle.

(143) a. ìsèsɛ̀   dzíkân   lè   dí   ání   inê
         PN   before   PROG   see   1SG   eye
         'Isɛsɛ was looking at me.'

     b. ìsèsɛ́   lè   dí   ání   inê   dzíkân
         PN   PROG   see   1SG   eye   before
         'Isɛsɛ was looking at me.'

(144) a. èkwɔ́   nê   téjí   lī   nwɔ́ɔ́
         tree   this   before   HAB   be.dry
         'This tree used to be dry'

     b. nósē   èkwɔ́   nê   lí   nwɔ́ɔ́
         before   tree   this   HAB   dry
         'This tree used to be dry.'

(145) ò   téjí   kwúlú   wà
       3SG:SUBJ   already   die   PERF
       'He has already died.'

4.5.1.2.3 Place adverbs

Place adverbs are used to indicate the location of an event and the animate or inanimate entities involved. They typically answer the question: *where?* Two contrastive place adverbs have been identified in Etulo: *m̀mènê/m̀mènénǐ* 'here' and *m̀mánâ/m̀mánánǐ* 'there'. The adverbs *m̀ménê* and *m̀mánâ* respectively

---

16 The use of *téjî* in constructions such as *àdì téjí gìè ùnwógīē* is ambiguous between two readings: Adi first ate and Adi had eaten. In the first meaning, it translates into 'first' in English to indicate the order of an event rather than the time of its occurrence, while in its second reading, it denotes past reference.

denote a location near vs away from the speaker.[17] The forms m̀méné̂ and m̀máná̂ are used in clause initial and medial positions while m̀ménénǐ and m̀mánánǐ only occur in clause final positions. The occurrence of the latter forms (m̀ménénǐ and m̀mánánǐ) in sentence initial positions results is ungrammatical (146c and 147c):

(146) a. àdì bā m̀mèńénǐ
        PN come here
        'Adi came here.'

 b. àdì bā m̀méné bá
        PN come here NEG
        'Adi did not come here.'

 c. *m̀ménénǐ àdì bā
        here PN come
        'Adi came here.'

 d. m̀méné̂ àdì bā bá
        here PN come NEG
        'Adi did not come here.'

(147) a. éjî sɔ̄ m̀mánánǐ
        1PL:SUBJ sit there
        'We sat there.'

 b. éjî sɔ̄ m̀máná bá
        1PL:SUBJ sit there NEG
        'We did not sit there.'

 c. *m̀mánánǐ éjî sɔ̄
        there 1PL:SUBJ sit
        'We sat there.'

 d. m̀máná̂ éjî sɔ́ bá
        there 1PL:SUBJ sit NEG
        'We did not sit there.'

---

17 Both adverbial forms also have nominal functions. In such case function, they are realized as adverbial demonstratives and may occur in sentence initial positions, as in the following examples:

i) m̀méné̂ lì ímbé ánî dí isèsé
   here COP place 1SG:SUBJ see PN
   'Here is the place I saw Isɛsɛ'

ii) m̀máná̂ lì ímbé ánî dí isèsé
    there COP place 1SG:SUBJ see PN
    'There is where I saw Isɛsɛ'

Other place adverbs indicating position or location include *kwékwé* 'nearby/ near', *èsɛ́* 'down (ground)', *èʃò* 'up (heaven)'. Some of them are derived from nouns. The last two adverbs, for instance, are clearly nouns that perform adverbial functions. These derived adverbs only occur in postverbal position and sentence final position. However, the adverb *kwékwé* which also occurs postverbally may be placed in sentence medial and sentence final positions. Consider the following examples:

(148) àdì   tsɛ́   ònà   lú   èʃò
      PN   run   race   go   up
      'Adi ran upstairs.'

(149) ìnwúnɔ́   nê   bùlù   lú-bā   èsɛ́
      bird   this   fly   go-come down
      'This bird flew down.'

(150) òkwɔ̀   ḿgbī   ónɔ́   ánî   dzὲ   kwékwé
      farm   POSS   mother 1SG   COP   nearby
      'My mother's farm is nearby.'

4.5.1.2.4 Frequency adverbs

Frequency adverbs are verb modifiers that denote how often an event expressed by the verb takes place. Etulo frequency adverbs are derived from noun phrases such as *àlí égbè (dúú)* 'everyday', *àlí ɔ̀nɔ̀* 'every time/always/often', *ɔ̀nɔ̀ òká* 'sometimes', *àkpí óɲíī* 'once', *àkpó étā* 'three times'. These adverbs may occur in sentence final position where they are directly prīeceded by the verb that they modify (see 151a, 152a 153a and 154a). They may also occur in sentence initial position (see 151b, 152b, 153b and 154b).

(151) a. ánî   lí   ná   úná   àlí   égbē   (dúú)
          1SG:SUBJ HAB   sleep   sleep   every   day   all
          'I sleep every day.'

      b. àlí   égbē   dúú   ánî   lí   ná   únâ
          every   day   all   1SG:SUBJ HAB   sleep   sleep
          'Every day I sleep.'

(152) a. éjî   ná   únâ   àkpó   étá
          1PL:SUBJ sleep   sleep   times   three
          'We slept three times.'

      b. àkpó   étá   éjî   ná   únâ
          times   three   1PL:SUBJ sleep   sleep
          'We slept three times.'

(153) a. òká ánî lí ʃá íʃá àlí ɔ̀nɔ̀
friend 1SG HAB laugh laugh every time
'My friend laughs every time/always.'

b. àlí ɔ̀nɔ̀ òká ánî lí ʃá íʃá
every time friend 1SG HAB laugh laugh
'Everytime, my friend laughs.'

(154) a. ónɔ́ ánî lí kɪ̀ɔ̀ ùnwógīē ɔ̀nɔ̀-òká
mother 1SG HAB do food time-another
'My mother cooks food sometimes'

b. ɔ̀nɔ̀-òká ónɔ́ ánî lí kɪ̀ɔ̀ ùnwógīē
time-another mother 1SG HAB do food
'My mother cooks food sometimes.'

4.5.1.2.5 Adverbs of magnitude

This group of adverbs encompasses degree words and intensifiers. They are used to indicate the intensity or degree of an event or activity. The adverbs of magnitude attested in Etulo include *sáān* 'very/a lot/ really', *gwéé* 'a little' and *kpákpá* 'a lot'. These adverbs may modify verbs, adjectives, adverbs, and even nouns. It is worthy of note that words that function as adverbs of magnitude (as mentioned above) may belong to other word categories. For instance, the adverbs *gwéé* and *kpákpá* function not just as adverbs but also as nominal modifiers, as in *ngisɛ kpakpa* 'many people (a lot of people)', *ǹgísɛ̀ gwéé* 'few people'. The word *sáān* is also realized as a qualificative where it denotes the meaning 'clear/clean', as in the constructions *eni le saan* 'the water is clean', *eni osaan* 'clean water'. The two adverbs *sáān* and *kpákpá* express a similar meaning in some contexts and are loosely translated into English as *very/alot/really*. In grammatical constructions, the occurrence of these adverbs is restricted to sentence final position. They are usually preceded by the word they modify, be it a verb phrase, adverb or adjective. In examples (155–157), one finds the adverbs *sáān, kpákpá* and *gwéé* in sentence final position, where they modify the verb *má àkwɔ̀* 'cry'. In (158a and 158b), *sáān* 'very' modifies two other adverbs *plɛ́* 'early' and *dúmɔ́ dúmɔ́* 'slowly'.

(155) à má àkwɔ̀ sáān
3PL:SUBJ cry cry INT
'They really cried/They cried a lot.'

(156) à má àkwɔ̀ kpákpá
3PL:SUBJ cry cry INT
'They really cried.'

(157) á   mà   àkwɔ̀   gwéé
      3PL:SUBJ cry   cry   little
      'They cried a little.'

(158) a. ó   bā   ùmákárántá plé   sáān
         3SG:SUBJ come   school   early INT
         'He came to school very early.'
      b. ìɲànì lí   gbɔ̄   ódzé   dúmɔ́dúmɔ́ sáān
         PN   HAB   talk   talk   slowly   INT
         'Inyani talks very slowly.'

The adverbs *sáān* modifies the adjective *òfùfè* 'new' in (159).

(159) àjàtù nê   lì   òfùfè sáān
      car   this   COP   new   very
      'This car is very new.'

4.5.2 The relative order of adverbs

In Etulo, two or more adverbs which belong to different semantic groups may co-occur in a construction. For instance, a manner and a temporal adverb may co-occur, just as manner, degree, and frequency adverbs. The emphasis is however, on the ordering of these adverbials when they occur together. In (160a–b), the manner adverbial *pléplé* 'fast/quickly' may either precede or follow the temporal adverb *èdědě* 'yesterday'. In (161), three adverbs co-occur (manner, degree and frequency adverbs). The degree adverb *sáān* 'very' is obligatorily preceded by the manner adverbial *dúmɔ́ dúmɔ́*, while both are followed by the frequency adverb *àlí ɔ̀nɔ̀* 'every time/always'. It is observed that when a manner adverb co-occurs with a degree adverb (magnitude), the manner adverb always precedes. A reversal of this order yields ungrammatical constructions (161b). If both adverbs co-occur with a frequency adverb as in (161a and 161b), both are directly followed by the frequency adverb except in cases where the frequency adverb is moved from sentence final position to sentence initial position. Examples:

(160) a. àdí   kìkíé   pléplé   èdědě
         PN   walk   fast   yesterday
         'Adi walked fast yesterday.'
      b. àdí   kìkíé   èdědě   pléplé
         PN   walk   yesterday fast
         'Adi walked fast yesterday.'

(161) a. àdì lí gìè ùnwógīē dúmɔ́dúmɔ́ sáān àlí ɔ̀nɔ̀
      PN HAB eat food   slowly   INT every time
      'Adi always goes to school very early.'
   b. *àdì lí ké ùmákárántá sáān plé àlí ɔ̀nɔ̀
      PN HAB go school   INT early every time
      'Adi always goes to school very early.'

4.5.3 Conclusion

In summary, the adverb class in Etulo is made up of simple adverbs, phrasal adverbials and ideophonic adverbs. Simple adverbs are non-derived while the adverbials are derived. The adverbials comprise words that belong to other lexical classes but perform adverbial functions. From a functional perspective, Etulo adverbs are grouped into four classes: temporal, place, frequency adverbs and adverbs of magnitude.

4.6 The preposition category

Across languages, thematic roles such as location, comitative and instrumental etc. are expressed in a myriad of ways. In many languages, these roles are expressed by a distinct class of words which may be small or large, known as 'adposition'. Adpositions are realized as postpositions or prepositions depending on their position relative to the noun. In languages with very few prepositions, many prepositional ideas are additionally expressed by other word classes, such as verbs or nouns. Migeod et al. (2013) observe that some African languages, like Hausa, correspond to European languages as regards the nature and use of prepositions, while in others, like Kanuri, true prepositions are very few. In many serial verb languages of West Africa which have few prepositions, indirect object meanings (most notably: recipient/benefactive semantic roles) are expressed by verbs. The paucity of prepositions in such languages has probably led to previous claims that prepositions are not expected to occur in serial verb languages or that serial verbs grammaticalize into prepositions.

This section focuses on establishing a distinct category of prepositions in Etulo as well as other means by which recipient/benefactive meanings may be expressed. It explores the syntactic characterization of Etulo prepositions and the etymology of some of these prepositions.

4.6.1 Etulo prepositions

The Etulo preposition category comprises words that are obligatorily followed by the nominals they govern. They typically express locative, benefactive and instrumental meaning. Like many African languages, Etulo has few prepositions. About four true prepositions are attested in Etulo: *mì* 'at, on, in, from', *jì* 'with', *m̀bí/m̀bó* 'to (direction towards)' and *ŋátāā* 'until'. These four prepositions are distinguished from other prepositions such as *ìkíé* 'for' and *ìdzídzê* 'between' which are derived from nouns. Other indirect object meanings are expressed by verbs or the existential copula.

4.6.1.1 The preposition mì

This preposition is a low tone morpheme that expresses a variety of meanings which includes purpose, location in time, location or position of an object and the provenance of an object or person. It is translated into English as *at, in, on, from* and *by*. The preposition final vowel /i/ is phonologically conditioned via assimilation by the initial vowel of the following word. For instance, the prepositional phrase (PP) *mì òtú* 'at night' is realized in fast speech as *mò òtú*. In examples (162a and 162b), *mì* forms a PP with the following nouns *ègbégbè* 'morning' and *ɔ̀nɔ̀* 'time', in both instances, denoting time. The PP may also be transposed to the sentence initial position as in *mì ègbégbè á kà dí ánî* 'in the morning they will see me'. Examples:

(162) a. á   kà   dí   ánî   mì   ègbégbè
         3PL:SUBJ FUT   see   1SG:OBJ   LOC   morning
         'They will see me in the morning.'

     b. àdì   dɔ́   ótsé   mì   ɔ̀nɔ̀   nâa
         PN   be   sick   LOC   time that.Q
         'Was Adi sick at that time?'

In examples (163a and 163b), the preposition *mì* expresses the location or position of an object. It seems that Etulo employs *mì* in the location of both inanimate and animate entities. There are however instances where the location or position of an object or person is expressed by an existential copula or a complex predicate. This is discussed in Section 4.6.5.

(163) a. ánî   dzàtà   ùnwógīē   m̀gbí   ábû   mì   òtélá
         1SG:SUBJ leave   food   POSS   2SG   LOC   table
         'I left your food on the table.'

     b. ánî   kíé   àwújá   m̀gbí   ánî   dá   mì   ígbé   nánî
         1SG:SUBJ take   money   POSS   1SG   hide LOC   bag   that
         'I hid my money in that bag.'

In examples (164a–c), *mì* expresses the provenance especially when it refers to a place or location. If, on the other hand, the source is an animate entity, an alternative preposition is used. In the construction *ánî gíá ájàtù nê m̀bí ìsèsé* 'I bought this car from Isɛsɛ', the preposition '*m̀bí*' is used. It should be noted that there are also verbs which may also express provenance (see Section 4.6.5.2).

(164) a. ó jē̠ mì ìlégósò
       3SG:SUBJ return LOC PN
       'He returned from Lagos.'
   b. ánî tsé ònà mì àdì ké kàtsínà-álá
       1SG:SUBJ run race LOC PN go PN
       'I ran from Adi to Katsina-ala.'
   c. àdì jí úmí áwūjā mì ígbé nánǐ
       PN steal theft money LOC bag that
       'Adi stole money from that bag.'

4.6.1.2 The preposition *jì*

The preposition *jì* is a low tone morpheme which expresses two meanings: comitative (165a) and instrumental (165b). It translates into English as *with* and obligatorily precedes pronoun, noun or noun phrase. Note that the comitative or instrumental meanings may alternatively be expressed by a verb (see Chapter 6 on SVCs). The low tone morpheme *jì* also functions as a co-ordinating marker (see Section 5.3).

(165) a. ánî ké ìdû jì újá
       1SG:SUBJ go market with basket
       'I went to market with a basket.'
   b. èmgbé lè lé ólē̠ jì ùbô
       children PROG play play with ball
       'The children are playing with a ball.'

The preposition *jì* serves as a host to the 3rd person singular object pronominal clitic *n*. Its vowel /i/ is conditioned in the environment of this clitic, changing into /a/ and becomes nasalized. This is illustrated in examples (166a and 166b).

(166) a. àdì ké ùmákárántá jàn
       PN go school with.3SG:OBJ
       'Adi went to school with her.'
   b. ìsèsé lé ólē̠ jàn
       PN play play with.3SG:OBJ
       'Isɛsɛ played with him'

4.6.1.3 The preposition m̀bí

The preposition m̀bí expresses two basic notions: provenance and direction (motion towards a person). It is sometimes realized as m̀bó especially when followed by a plural pronoun (see example 167c). In constructions where m̀bí denotes source, it co-occurs with specific motion verbs which include kìè 'come' or bā 'come', while in constructions where it expresses a directional meaning, it co-occurs with motion verbs such as ké 'go' or lúū 'go' bā 'come'. It seems that the m̀bí preposition only derives its meaning in conjunction with the appropriate motion verb. There are hardly instances where it independently expresses provenance or directional meaning. Examples (167a)-(167c) illustrate the use of m̀bí in expressing 'directional meaning' while example (168) illustrates the use of m̀bí in expressing 'provenance'.

(167) a. òtsètsé nâ tsò àbó kê m̀bí ìsèsé
teacher that point hand go to PN
'That teacher pointed at Isɛsɛ.'

b. ó nwì ìkwútê bá m̀bí ánî
3SG:SUBJ throw stone come to 1SG:OBJ
'He threw a stone at me.'

c. éjî tsé òɲà kè m̀bó má
1PL:SUBJ run race go to 3PL:OBJ
'We ran to them.'

(168) éjî kíé kìè m̀bí àdì
1PL:SUBJ take come from PN
'We took it from Adi.'

4.6.1.4 The preposition ŋátāā

The ŋátāā preposition indicates a specified point in time at which an event terminates. This preposition translates into English as *until* or *till*. It may co-occur with the motion verb bā 'come' followed by a noun. It is the only preposition in Etulo that is directly followed by a motion verb which also expresses a prepositional idea.

(169) a. àdì ná úná mì ègbégbè ŋátāā bā òtú
PN sleep sleep from morning until come night
'Adi slept from morning till night.'

b. ó fé ánî ŋátāā bá ònòdé
3SG:SUBJ wait 1SG:OBJ until come evening
'He waited for me until evening.'

4.6.2 Derived prepositions

Two most common derived prepositions are ìkíé 'for' and ìdzídzé 'between'. The preposition *ikie* derived from the noun *ikie* 'head', translates into English as *'for, about, because of'*. Among the notions expressed by ìkíé, one finds purpose and benefactivity (different interpretations of reason). Constructions in which this preposition denotes such meanings answer the questions *'For whom did you X?* (benefactive) and *Why did you X?* (purpose). Examples (170a and 170b) illustrate the benefactive meaning.[18] Note however that in Etulo, the benefactive meaning may alternatively be expressed by serial verbs or by a dative construction (see Chapter 6). In example (171), *ikie* denotes purpose. The use or occurrence of the possessive morpheme *mgbi* with *ikie* is optional. Consider the following examples:

(170) a. á   gíá   ájàtù   nê   ìkíé   ánî
         3PL:SUBJ buy   book   this   for   1SG:OBJ
         'They bought this car for me.'

     b. ìsèsé   nwɔ́   m̀dà   ìkíé   émī   òkàân
         PN   kill   cow   for   PL   friend.3SG:POSS
         'Isɛsɛ killed a cow for his friends.'

(171)   ánî   kìɔ̀   ùnwógīē ìkíé   (m̀gbī) àdì
         1SG:SUBJ cook   food   head   POSS   PN
         'I cooked food because of Adi.'

The morpheme ìkíé also functions as a preposition in constructions where it is translated as 'about'. This is illustrated in examples (172a and 172b):

(172) a. á   ɲá   ánî   òdzé   ìkíé   ábû
         3PL:SUBJ tell   1SG:OBJ talk   about   2SG:OBJ
         'They told me about you.'

     b. ánî   wá   élélá   ìkíé   ábû
         1SG:SUBJ dream   dream   about   2SG:OBJ
         'I dreamt about you.'

The word ìdzídzê is basically a noun meaning 'centre' or 'middle'. As a noun, it may be preceded or governed by the preposition *mì*. This morpheme also functions as a preposition indicating the position of a person or object. It translates as

---

18 Some Etulo speakers place the preposition mi before ikie as in *á gīā ájàtù nê (mì) ìkíé (m̀gbí) ánî* 'They bought this car for me'. In this sentence, the prepositional phrase 'mì ìkíé mgbi ánî' literally translates as 'in head of me/in my head'. The use of *ikie* as a preposition in (171a and 171b) may have been derived from such a construction.

between in English. In example (173a), *ìdzídzê* occurs as a preposition governing a noun phrase, while in (173b) it occurs as a noun governed by the preposition *mì*. Even though both constructions have the same meaning, the use of *ìdzídzé* as 'between' in (173a) without the preposition *mì* confirms its use as a derived preposition.

(173) a. àfɛ̀ nâ dzɛ̀ ìdzídzé ádî jì ìsésé
book that COP middle PN and PN
'That book is between Adi and Isɛsɛ.'

b. àfɛ̀ nâ dzɛ̀ mì ìdzídzé ḿgbí àdì jì ìsèsɛé
book that COP in middle POSS PN and PN
'That book is between Adi and Isɛsɛ.'

Concerning the two derived prepositions *ikie* and *ìdzídzé*, it is observed that despite their function as prepositions, they may also be optionally preceded by the preposition *mì* especially in the environment of a following possessive *ḿgbī*. It is likely that the function as prepositions may have evolved from such constructions.

4.6.3 Phonological features of prepositions

Etulo prepositions are typically monosyllabic, disyllabic or trisyllabic words whose inherent tones are mostly retained in grammatical constructions. In fast speech, the word final vowels of the prepositions *mì* and *jì* usually undergo assimilation by the initial vowel of the following word (see 174a and 174b). As noted earlier (see Section 4.6.1.2), phonological alteration is observed with the preposition *jì/béjī* when it hosts the 3rd person object pronoun. The /i/ vowel in *jì/beji* changes to /a/ and becomes nasalized as in (175a and 175b).

(174) a. mì + òtú → mò òtú 'at night'
b. jì + ánî → jà ánî 'with me'
(175) a. jì → jã̀ 'with her/him'
b. beji → bèjã̀ 'with her/him'

4.6.4 The syntactic distribution of prepositions

Etulo prepositions mostly precede a noun, a noun phrase or a pronoun with which they form a PP. The only exception is *ŋátāā* 'until', which is directly followed by the motion verb, in turn followed by a noun. A preposition cannot be separated or displaced from its position in a PP. There are therefore no instances of preposition stranding. Some PPs may be moved to the clause initial position.

This is particularly the case with the prepositions *mì*, and *ìkíé* (176 and 177). With others, like *m̀bí* and *ìkíé*, such transposition yield unacceptable sentences (178 and 179). The following examples show the occurrence of prepositional phrases in two different positions (clause initial and clause final).

(176) a.

ń	ká	bā	údé	mì	òngíégīē	ófíá	nénî
1SG:SUBJ	FUT	come	home	LOC	PREF. finish:RED	month	this

'I will come home by the end of this month.'

b.

mì	òngíéngīē	ófíá	nê	ń	ká	bā	údé
LOC	PREF. finish:RED	month	this	1SG:SUBJ	FUT	come	home

'By the end of this month I will come home.'

(177) a.

á	gīā	ájàtù	nê	ìkíé	ánî
3PL:SUBJ	buy	car	this	for	1SG:OBJ

'They bought this car for me.'

b.

ìkíé	ánî	á	gīā	ájàtù	nê
for	1SG:OBJ	3PL:SUBJ	buy	car	this

'For me they bought this car.'

(178) a.

èmgbé	lè	lé	ólē	jì	ùbô
children	PROG	play	play	with	ball

'The children are playing with a ball.'

b.

?jì	ùbô	èmgbé	lè	lé	ólē
with	ball	children	PROG	play	play

'With a ball the children are playing.'

(179) a.

ó	nwī	ìkwútsê	bá	m̀bí	ánî
3SG:SUBJ	throw	stone	come	to	1SG:OBJ

'He threw a stone at me.'

b.

*m̀bí	ánî	ó	nwī	ìkwútsê	bá
to	1SG:OBJ	3SG:SUBJ	throw	stone	come

'At me he threw a stone.'

4.6.5 Other means to express locative and related meanings

Besides the use of prepositions, locative meanings may also be expressed in Etulo by the use of the existential copula *dzè*, motion verbs such as *ké* 'go' (direction towards), *kìè* 'come from (source)', *bā* 'come', and other verbs such as *nū* 'give' (benefactivity). Both the existential copula and some of these verbs occur in complex predicates (serial verbs and compound verbs). For details on the use of some of these verbs in prepositional functions, see chapter 6 on verb serialization. In the current section, the focus is on the use of some of these verbs as prepositional markers in seemingly compound verbs.

In some cases, a locative meaning is simultaneously denoted by more than one device in the same construction. For instance, an existential copula may optionally co-occur with the locative preposition *mì* to denote location in a sentence while the preposition *m̀bí* 'to/from' obligatorily occurs with motion verbs to denote direction or provenance. These additional strategies used in denoting location, provenance and direction are discussed in the following sections.

4.6.5.1 The existential copula as a locative marker

The low tone existential copula *dzè* denotes the location or position of animate and inanimate entities. This copula has the plural variant *tó*. It agrees with the subject in number. Both forms are compatible with the locative preposition *mì*. However, the co-occurrence of the copula with the locative preposition *mì* is not obligatory. The preposition *mì* can be omitted with place names as shown in (180a and c). The locative copula takes a locative complement realized as NP, PP (180a–b) or a locative adverb as in (180e). The Etulo existential copula forms a complex predicate in combination with other verbs such as *sɔ́* 'sit', *wó* 'put', *dɔ́* 'climb'.

(180) a. àdì dzè ìlégósò
 PN COP PN
 'Adi is in Lagos.'
 b. àdì dzè mì ìlégósò
 PN COP in PN
 'Adi is in Lagos.'
 c. á tō ìlégósò
 3PL:SUBJ COP.PL PN
 'They are in Lagos.'
 d. á tō mì ìlègósò
 3PL:SUBJ COP.PL in PN
 'They are in Lagos.'
 e. òkwɔ̀ ḿgbī ónɔ́ ánî dzè kwɛ́kwɛ́
 farm POSS mother 1SG COP near
 'My mother's farm is nearby.'

4.6.5.2 The *kìè* verb as a preposition marker

The verb *kìè* 'come from' may be realized as the sole predicate in a clause where it denotes the source or origin of the subject as in (181a). It also indicates the starting point of an event of motion such as walking, dancing, running, journey etc. In examples (181b and 181c), the events of dancing and travelling commence from a point in space expressed by *kìè*, while the motion verbs *ké* 'go' and *bā* 'come' indicate the direction or terminating point of these events.

(181) a. ó kìè ílègōsò
       3SG:SUBJ come-from PN
       'He came from Lagos'
     b. ʃí ífúé kìè m̀ménê kè m̀bó
        dance dance come.from here go there
        'Dance from here to there.'
     c. ánî kìè ònìtshà bā àdì
        1SG:SUBJ come.from PN come PN
        'I came from Onitsha to Adi.'

4.6.5.3 Preposition markers in complex predicates: the verb kɛ, and the existential copula

It has been noted earlier that the existential copula may function as the sole predicate in a clause where it denotes location. On the other hand, the motion verb equally denotes direction especially in serial verb constructions. As shall be shown in the following examples, both predicates, i.e. the existential copula and the motion verb, may combine with other verbs to form a complex or compound predicate.[19] In such constructions, they denote location with or without the locative preposition *mì*. In examples (182 and 183), for instance, the verbs *sɔ̄* 'sit' and *wó* 'put' form a complex predicate with both prepositional markers. In these complex predicates, the verbal prepositional markers mainly express the position or location of an object. Observe that in all of these examples, the co-occurrence of the complex predicates with the locative preposition *mì* is optional. In (182a and 182b), the verb *kè* 'go' seems to be grammaticalized, having lost its inherent lexical meaning. A tonal change is equally observed with *kɛ*, whose tone changes from high (inherent) to a step or low in such constructions. Examples (183a–b) show that the *dzè/tó* copula retains its locative meaning and inherent tone.

(182) a àdì sɔ́-k̀ (mì) òndú ítsè
        PN sit-LOC LOC mouth chair
        'Adi sat at the edge of the chair.'

---

19 Most native speakers consider these V+V constructions as one grammatical word. This may be associated with the fact that the verb *ké* loses its original meaning as a motion verb in such contexts. The native speakers therefore find it difficult to assign a specific lexical meaning to it.

	b.	á	kíé	àfɛ̀	nâ	wó-kē	(mì)	ígbé
		3PL:SUBJ	take	book	that	put-LOC	LOC	bag
		'They put that book in a bag.'						
(183)	a.	àfɛ̀	wó-dzɛ́	(mì)	ígbé			
		book	put-COP	LOC	bag			
		'A book is in a bag/ There is a book in a bag.'						
	b.	àfɛ̀	wó-tō	(mì)	ígbé			
		book	put-COP.PL	LOC	bag			
		'There are books in a bag.'						
	c.	àdì	só-dzē	ìtsè				
		PN	sit-COP	chair				
		'Adi is sitting on a chair.'						
	d.	á	sò-tó	ìtsè				
		3PL:SUBJ	sit-COP.PL	chair				
		'They are sitting on a chair.'						

4.6.6 Conclusion

Like many West African languages, Etulo has a small class of prepositions. Four pure (non derived) prepositions are identified: *mì* 'locative', *jì* 'with', *m̀bí/m̀bó* 'to/from' and *ŋátāā* 'until'. Two classes of prepositions are distinguished: the non-derived and derived. The derived prepositions comprise grammaticalized nouns that function as prepositions. They include *ìkíé* 'head/for' and *ìdzídzé* 'centre/between'. In addition to this small class of prepositions, Etulo adopts other means of expressing propositional notions, such as verbal constructions.

4.7 The status of Etulo ideophones

The term 'ideophone' was first used by Doke (1935) to refer to a class of words that depict sensory or perceptual imagery. In earlier works, this group of words were labelled descriptive adverbs, picture words, onomatopoeic adverbs, interjections (cf. Welmers 1973). These labels are all related to the semantic or descriptive nature of ideophones. The study of ideophones is particularly advanced for African languages. They have been described in many languages including Yoruba (Courtenay 1969), Ewe (Ameka 1999), Igbo (Maduka 1983), Wolaitta (Amha 1999) and Emai (Egbokhare 1999). Many studies on ideophones focus on their phonological properties in relation to other lexical categories in the language. Such phonological features often include vowel lengthening, reduplication (partial or full), rigid tonal structure and deviant phonotactics. In addition to the phonological features, ideophones are also characterized by their morphological, syntactic and semantic features. One feature commonly associated with ideophones is that they have very little morphology (Childs 1999: 185). There are, however, languages where ideophones undergo derivation. In Dindinga, an Eastern Sudanic language, Jong (1999) observes that ideophones may undergo derivation to produce verbs, nouns or adjectives. In Wolaitta, some ideophones take the same inflection as the adjectives (Azeb 1999).

One of the controversies associated with the study of ideophones is centred on its categorial status. In many languages, it is quite difficult to assign ideophonic words to a particular word class. In Ewe for instance, Ameka (1999) observes that ideophones have no distinct grammatical or word class. They may fall into any syntactic class (nominal, adjectival, adverbial, intensifier, verbal) depending on their function. On the contrary, ideophones constitute a distinct grammatical category in languages like Siwu, a Ghananian language (Dingemanse 2011). There seem to be no valid cross-linguistic criteria for distinguishing ideophones from other word categories. Linguists therefore rely on language internal criteria.

In this section, I propose a working definition of ideophones in Etulo and establish their categorial status. I also examine their phonological, morphological, syntactic and semantic characterization.

4.7.1 Towards a definition

One of the most quoted definitions is found in the work of Doke (1935: 118), who defines an ideophone as a vivid representation of an idea in sound which describes a predicate, qualificative or adverbial in respect to manner, colour, smell, action, state or intensity. According to Dingemanse (2012: 655), 'Ideophones are marked words that depict sensory imagery.' Trask (1993: 131–132) views ideophones as 'a grammatically distinct class of words, which typically express either distinctive sounds, or visually distinctive types of action.' From a cross-linguistic perspective, all ideophones have one thing in common: they express different types of actions or states either by depiction or description.

4.7.2 The Etulo ideophone

Etulo ideophones are a group of words that vividly describe or depict the nature of an activity or state which can fulfill a range of syntactic functions (predicative, noun modifier and verb modifier). Very little research has been done on this. The only available but sketchy description is found in Okoye and Egenti (2015). They observe that Etulo ideophones are characterized by vowel lengthening and reduplication. They also describe the different semantic notions expressed by ideophones. Not much information is given as regards the categorial status of ideophones or their syntactic properties. In the following sections, I give a more detailed characterization.

4.7.2.1 The phonological characterization of Etulo ideophones

Etulo ideophones occur in single or reduplicated forms. They can have monosyllabic or disyllabic roots. Except for the common occurrence of the relatively rare CCV syllable structure, no peculiarity is observed with the ideophones as regards their syllable structure. In other words, they largely maintain the syllable structure of the language. Attested consonant clusters of ideophones involve a combination of a fricative/plosive and a trill/lateral ([fl] [tr] [dr]) as illustrated in (184a–b). Etulo ideophones are characterized by vowel lengthening, vowel copying and a uniform tone pattern. In single or non-reduplicated ideophones, the word final vowel is usually lengthened. In most cases, this lengthening offers no semantic modification to the meaning of the ideophone (see 185a–c). In some ideophones, the vowel of the first syllable is copied onto the following syllables as in (186a–b). As regards the tone pattern, ideophones are mostly realized as all high or all low. There are, however, a few instances showing contrasting tones especially in single ideophonic words (see 185a).

(184) a. trètrè 'bald (smooth surface)'
b. ǹdrèǹdrè 'silky'
c. flɔ̀flɔ̀flɔ̀ 'sound of shuffling feet'
(185) a. wúūū 'sound of a moving car'
b. tùùù 'horrible smell'
c. bìùùù 'extremely dark'
(186) a. pàpàpà 'sound of wing flapping'
b. kwɔ́kíɔ́kwɔ́kíɔ́ 'rough'
c. tétété 'sound of dripping water'
(187) a. kplédédédé 'white'
b. ʃílí-dìdìdì 'quiet'

4.7.2.2 The morphological characterization of Etulo ideophones

Many of the Etulo ideophones are characterized by reduplication or triplication. In most cases, reduplication is full rather than partial and does not always connote emphasis or intensity. Such ideophones are inherently repetitive. In other words, they are not derived (at least synchronically) from their monosyllabic or disyllabic forms (or what seems to be like the root) by reduplication. For instance, the ideophone *trètrè* is not derived from **trè*, neither is *flɔ̀flɔ̀flɔ̀* derived from **flɔ*. In a few ideophones however, reduplication serves as a morphological means of derivation from other lexical words. In other words, the reduplicated forms may be derived from an independent root. This is shown in examples (188a and 188b). On the contrary, examples (189a–c) show a set of ideophones for which derivation seems to play no derivational role in their formation. In isolation, the components of the latter ideophones are considered meaningless, as indicated by the asterisk.

(188) a. plé → pléplé
'early' 'quickly/fast'
b. dúmɔ́ → dúmɔ́ dúmɔ́
'a state of being slow' 'slowly'
(189) a. *fèlè → fèlèfèlè 'silky'
b. *trɔ̀ → trɔ̀trɔ̀ 'smooth'
c. *pìà → pìàpìàpìà 'sweet'

An important morphological feature of Etulo ideophones is their ability to take the low tone nominalizing vowel prefix o-. Many ideophones take this prefix when they function as nominal modifiers. Just like adjectival verbs (verbs of quality), ideophones may modify nouns with the help of this affix.

(190) a. ènì òtétété 'dripping water'
water PREF.IDEO
b. ìkíé òtrɛ̀trɛ̀ 'bald head'
head PREF.IDEO
c. ànwúntò òfèlèfèlè 'silky cloth'
cloth PREF.IDEO
d. èwô òtrɔ̀trɔ̀ 'smooth body'
body PREF.IDEO
e. òngìâ ògígígí 'shivering woman'
woman PREF.IDEO
f. ṅgísɛ̀ òléngéléngé 'slim person'
person PREF.IDEO
g. ànwúntò òkplédédédé 'a very whitish cloth'
cloth PREF.IDEO
h. òfɛ̀ ògàdàgàdà 'bumpy road'
road PREF.IDEO
i. ènì òkíɔ́kíɔ́ 'falling water'
water PREF.IDEO
k. ènì àdé òpìàpìàpìà 'sweet palmwine'
palmwine PREF-IDEO

4.7.3 Towards a semantic classification of Etulo ideophones

Two or more ideophones may express the same or similar meanings. For instance, both *fèlèfèlè* and *ǹdrèǹdrè* refer to the silky texture of a cloth. An ideophone may also denote different but semantically related meanings. The ideophone *fílídìdìdìdì* refers to a depiction of quietness and patience. In many cases, it is particularly difficult to provide an adequate glossing of Etulo ideophones in English. In such cases, I simply use the abbreviation 'IDEO' and then give a tentative translation in English. Etulo ideophones are grouped into two classes on the basis of their semantic properties: those that denote sensory property concepts such as taste, colour, texture and those that denote manner. They are further illustrated in the examples below:

property concepts

(191) a. texture: fèlèfèlè 'silky'
 b. colour: plédédédé 'white'
 c. taste: pìàpìàpìà 'sweet'

manner

(192) a. dúmɔ́ dúmɔ́ 'slowly'
 b. flɔ́flɔ́flɔ́ 'shufffling sound'
 c. 'wúūūū 'sound of a car'

An ideophone may fall into one or both semantic classes depending on the syntactic construction.

4.7.4 Syntactic characterization of Etulo ideophones

There have been claims in the literature that ideophones are often restricted to a specific sentence type: namely, the affirmative. In individual languages such as Didinga (an Eastern Sudanic language), the occurrence of ideophones is indeed restricted to the affirmative declarative and imperative sentence types (cf. Jong 1999). Newman (1968) suggests that the restriction of ideophones to certain basic sentence types is possibly a common syntactic feature of ideophones in African languages. It has, however, been attested that ideophones do occur in all sentence types in languages such as Ewe (cf. Ameka 1999).

Etulo ideophones occur in most sentence types: declarative, imperative, interrogative and negated clauses (193–196). In negated clauses, ideophones are directly followed by the negation particle *bá*, as illustrated in (195). When an ideophone occurs in the sentence final position of interrogative constructions, the final vowel is lengthened to mark interrogation. Examples:

(193) èwó ḿgbán lè trɔ̀trɔ̀
body POSS.3SG is IDEO.smooth
'Her body is smooth.'

(194) èwò ḿgbī íɲánì lè trɔ̀trɔ̀ɔ́
body POSS PN is IDEO.smooth.Q
'Is Inyani's body smooth?'

(195) ànwúntò ḿgbí ánî lè bìùùù bá
cloth POSS 1SG is IDEO.black NEG
'My cloth is not very black.'

(196) gbá áʃà ḿgbí ábû pàpàpà
flap wing POSS 2SG IDEO.sound.of.flapping.wings
'Flap your wing.'

Etulo ideophones perform four basic syntactic functions. They function as verb modifiers (adverbs), nominal modifiers (adjectives) and nominals in argument positions. They also have a predicative function as illustrated in (199–200). As an adverb, the ideophone is directly preceded by the verb which it modifies. In (197a), the ideophone *flɔ́flɔ́flɔ́* 'depiction of shuffling sound made with the feet' modifies the motion verb *kìkíè* 'walk', indicating the manner in which the event of walking is accomplished, while in (197b), the ideophone *kpùkpùkpù* describes the manner of sound which a grinding machine makes.

(197) a. àdì lé kìkíé flɔ́flɔ́flɔ́
PN PROG walk IDEO.sound.of.shuffling
'Adi is walking noisily.'

b. índʒìnê lè gbádù kpùkpùkpù
engine PROG sound IDEO
'The grinding machine is making a *kpukpukpu* sound.'

Ideophonic adjectives perform both attributive and predicative functions. In attributive function, the ideophones take the nominalizing low tone vowel prefix *o-* as illustrated below:

(198) a. ánî dí ànwúntò ò-fèlèfèlè
1SG:SUBJ see cloth PREF-IDEO.silky
'I saw a silky cloth.'

b. ánî gíá ènìàdè ò-pìàpìàpìà
1SG:SUBJ buy palmwine PREF-IDEO.sweet/sugary
'I bought a very sweet wine.'

In predicative function, Etulo ideophones are preceded by the low tone morpheme *le*.[20] This morpheme serves as a copula, linking the NP subject and the ideophone. Note that the use of *le* with ideophonic adjectives is in contrast with the use of the *li* copula in constructions involving simple adjectives or qualificatives (nouns) such as *àdì lì m̀màfà* 'Adi is young', *ìɲànì lì ìnwíndà* 'Inyani is beautiful'. The use of the *li* copula with ideophonic adjectives is ungrammatical. This is illustrated in the following examples:

(199) a. *àdì   lì   léŋgéléŋgé
            PN   COP   IDEO.slim
            'Adi is slim.'

       b. àdì   lè   léŋgéléŋgé
            PN   is   IDEO.slim
            'Adi is slim.'

(200) a. *ànwúntò nê   lì   ǹdrèndrè
            cloth   this   COP   IDEO.silky
            'This cloth is silky.'

       b. ànwúntò   nê   lè   ǹdrèndrè
            cloth   this   is   IDEO.silky
            'This cloth is silky.'

Similarly, the *lè* morpheme though compatible with ideophonic adjectives, is incompatible with other qualificatives (simple adjectives and nouns). The varying use of both morphemes may serve as a yardstick for differentiating between simple adjectives and ideophonic adjectives in predicative function.

There are marginal cases where some ideophones may serve as nominals via the affixation of the nominalizing prefix. Some of such ideophones occur as the NP$_1$ in genitive constructions (201 and 202). They may also co-occur with demonstratives (typical of nouns) such as *nê* 'this' or *nâ* 'that'.

(201) ò-pìàpìàpìà ḿgbí èniàdé   tíʃì
        PREF-IDEO   of   palmwine be.good
        'The sweetness of palmwine is good.'

(202) ò-fèlèfèlè   ḿgbí ànwúntò nê   tíʃì
        PREF-IDEO   of   cloth   this   be.good
        'The silkiness of this cloth is good.'

---

20 Note that the *lè* morpheme which precedes ideophones in a predicative context is homophonous with the progressive marker le. However, unlike the progressive marker which takes no affix and is tonologically conditioned, this le morpheme bears an inherent low tone. It also takes the nominalizing low tone prefix just like other verbs and copulas in Etulo (see Section 5.5.3 and Section 7.3.1).

4.7.5 The categorial status of Etulo ideophones

From the available data, one readily observes that Etulo ideophones do not constitute a distinct grammatical category. They rather cut across other word classes such as adjectives, adverbs and nouns, since one may find ideophones in all three functions. As demonstrated in previous examples, ideophones such as *plédédédé* 'white', *fèlèfèlè* 'silky', *bùùùù* 'black' etc. are characterized by a variety of syntactic functions. For instance, *plédédédé* 'white' in (203a and 203b) serves as an adjective in attributive and predicative functions and also as an ideophonic adverb modifying the verb *tundzɛ* 'be white' in (203c).

(203) a. ànwúntò ḿgbí ánî lè plédédédé Adj (predicative)
cloth POSS 1SG is IDEO.white
'My cloth is very white.'

b. ánî gíá ànwúntò ò-plédédédé Adj (attributive)
1SG:SUBJ buy cloth PREF-IDEO.white
'I bought a white cloth.'

c. ànwúntò ḿgbí ánî túndzē plédédédé adverbial function
cloth POSS 1SG be.white IDEO.white
'My cloth is very white.'

Note however, that there are a number of ideophones whose identifiable syntactic function restricts them to a single grammatical category. Such ideophones include *tùùù* 'depiction of a bad smell', *wúūū* 'sound of a moving car'. They only perform an adverbial function. The table below shows a number of Etulo ideophones and their possible grammatical functions.

Table 4.14 Categorial status of Etulo ideophones

Ideophones	Gloss	Nominal	Adjective	Adverb
pàpàpà	'depiction of the flapping of a bird'	✓		✓
gìgìgì	'depiction of shivering'	✓		✓
kwɔ́kwɔ́kwɔ́	'depiction of a manner of movement (walking noisily-shuffling)	✓		✓
flɔ́flɔ́flɔ́	'depiction of a manner of movement (noisily-shuffling)	✓		✓
lèbèlèbè	'depiction of a manner of action (sluggish)'	✓	✓	✓
trètrè	'description of baldness'	✓	✓	

Ideophones	Gloss	Nominal	Adjective	Adverb
trɔ̀trɔ̀	'smooth'	✓	✓	
tétété	'sound of dripping water'	✓		✓
kplédédédé	'depiction of whiteness'	✓	✓	✓
bíùùù	'depiction of darkness'		✓	✓
tùùù	'depiction of a horrible smell'			✓
wúūū	'sound of a car'			✓
ǹdrɛ̀ndrɛ̀	'texture of a cloth (silky)'	✓	✓	
fèlèfèlè	'texture of a cloth (silky)'	✓		✓
gàdàgàdà	'describable in terms of bumpiness and rowdiness'	✓	✓	
dúmɔ́ dúmɔ́	'slow'			✓
ɲáɲáɲá	'depiction of a manner of movement (walking arrogantly)'			✓
ʃílídìdìdì	'quiet'	✓	✓	✓
pìàpìàpìà	'very sweet/sugary'	✓	✓	✓
wúwúwú	'sound of a grinding machine'	✓	✓	✓

4.7.6 Conclusion

To recapitulate, Etulo has a large ideophone class. These ideophones are phonologically characterized by a uniform tone pattern and vowel lengthening. Morphologically, they are characterized by reduplication. Etulo ideophones may take the nominalizing *o-* prefix which derives a noun-modifying form. They may be classified semantically and syntactically. Semantically, they express sensory property or manner. Syntactically, they can be distinguished by their distribution and function, as verbal and nominal modifier or argument (with the nominalizing prefix) and predicate. Etulo ideophones do not form a distinct word class but rather cut across different word classes.

4.8 The numeral system

Languages adopt different strategies in building up numeral systems. In a cross-linguistic study, Comrie (2005) groups numeral systems into six types. Among them are the decimal, vigesimal, hybrid vigesimal-decimal and extended body part system. The most common of these systems is the decimal. English and Mandarin, for instance, present a decimal system. This is also the case for many languages of Europe. Other languages such as Yoruba, Igbo (West African) and Chukchi (Siberia) operate with a vigesimal system (cf. Comrie 1999). In the traditional system, Etulo adopts the vigesimal system. However, in modern usage, many Etulo speakers (especially the young generation) use numeral terms attested in other dominant languages such as Hausa and English, which are spoken alongside Etulo in the Benue speech community. As for semantics and function, numerals are classified into the cardinal, ordinal and distributive types. Depending on the language, ordinals may be derived from cardinals via morphological and syntactic means (cf: Stolz and Veselinova 2005).

This section examines the numeral system of Etulo with focus on the distinction between cardinal, ordinal and distributive numerals. The phonological, morphological and syntactic properties of these numerals are described. The most common way of deriving higher numerals in Etulo is by compounding or by periphrastic strategies.

4.8.1 Cardinal numerals

Traditionally, Etulo presents a vigesimal system. Base twenty is used consistently, such that forty is expressed as two twenties and hundred as five twenties. In modern usage however, hundred is alternatively expressed by the basic form *ìdèlí* 'hundred' which is borrowed from Hausa. Cardinal numerals in Etulo consist of simple and complex forms. The former include the numerals 1–10, and 20. Below are some examples:

(204) óɲíī   'one'
       èfà   'two'
       ètá   'three'
       éné   'four'
       èdá   'five'
       ègín   'six'
       ègíàfà   'seven'
       ègíátá   'eight'
       ègíànè   'nine'
       ìjúó   'ten'
       òsù   'twenty'

Cardinal numerals realized as complex forms are derived by either compounding or addition. For numbers such as 50, 70, 90, and other higher numerals, both strategies are involved.

4.8.1.1 Cardinal numerals formed by compounding

Some numerals are derived by combining two numerals without a linking element. For instance, the numeral *ònwúsɔ̀ èfà* 'forty' is derived by combining 'twenty' *ònwúsɔ̀* and *èfà* 'two'. In compounding, *òsù* 'twenty' is realized as *ònwúsɔ̀* 'twenty'.[21] It is not yet clear what sort of process (phonological/morphological) is involved. The literal translation of forty in Etulo would thus be 'two twenties'. In actual speech, there is assimilation of the final vowel of *ònwúsɔ̀* by the initial vowel of *efa* or any other numeral that follows. With regressive assimilation, *ònwúsɔ̀ èfà* becomes *ònwúsè èfà* 'forty'. The tone of the assimilated vowel is retained. Below are some examples of cardinal numeral compounds:

(205) a. ònwúsɔ̀   èfà   'forty'
         twenty   two
     b. ònwúsɔ̀   ènè   'eighty'
         twenty   four
     c. ònwúsɔ̀   ètá   'sixty'
         twenty   three
     d. ònwúsɔ̀   èdá   'one hundred'
         twenty   five

4.8.1.2 Cardinal numerals formed by addition

Some numerals are formed by adding any numeral to a base of ten or twenty. This is achieved by the use of the verb *dɔ́* 'add'. This verb is sometimes replaced by its variant *dɔ́n* especially in the derivation of numerals above forty (206a–e). The numerals 11–19, for instance, are formed by the addition of lower numerals to a base of ten, while 21–39 are derived by adding lower numerals to a base of twenty. In actual speech, the vowel of the verb assimilates to the following vowel.

Table 4.15 Cardinal numerals 11–39

11–19	Gloss	21–30	Gloss	31–39	Gloss
ìjúó dɔ́ óɲíí ten add one	'eleven'	òsù dɔ́ óɲíí twenty add one	'twenty one'	òsù dɔ́ íjūō dɔ́ íjūō óɲíí twenty add ten add ten one	'thirty one'
ìjúó dɔ́ èfà ten add two	'twelve'	òsù dɔ́ èfà twenty add two	'twenty two'	òsù dɔ́ íjūō dɔ́ íjūō èfà twenty add ten add ten two	'thirty two'
ìjúó dɔ́ ètá ten add three	'thirteen'	òsù dɔ́ ètá twenty add three	'twenty three'	òsù dɔ́ íjūō dɔ́ íjūō ètá twenty add ten add ten three	'thirty three'
ìjúó dɔ́ èné ten add four	'fourteen'	òsù dɔ́ ènè twenty add five	'twenty four'	òsù dɔ́ íjūō dɔ́ íjūō ènè twenty add ten add ten four	'thirty four'

---

21 In the derivation of cardinal numerals, some native speakers prefer using *nwúsò* in place of *ònwúsò* for 'twenty'. Examples: *nwúsò èfà* 'forty', *nwúsò ètá* 'sixty'.

11–19	Gloss	21–30	Gloss	31–39	Gloss
ìjúó dɔ́ è dá ten add five	'fifteen'	òsù dɔ́ èdá twenty add five	'twenty five'	òsù dɔ́ íjūō dɔ́ íjūō èdá twenty add ten add ten five	'thirty five'
ìjúó dɔ́ ègín ten add six	'sixteen'	òsù dɔ́ ègín twenty add six	'twenty six'	òsù dɔ́ íjūō dɔ́ íjūō ègín twenty add ten add ten six	'thirty six'
ìjúó dɔ́ ègíàfà ten add seven	'seventeen'	òsù dɔ́ ègiàfà twenty add seven	'twenty seven'	òsù dɔ́ íjūō dɔ́ íjūō ègíàfà twenty add ten add ten seven	'thirty seven'
ìjúó dɔ́ ègíátá ten add eight	'eighteen'	òsù dɔ́ ègiátá twenty add eight	'twenty eight'	òsù dɔ́ íjūō dɔ́ íjūō ègíátá twenty add ten add ten eight	'thirty eight'
ìjúó dɔ́ ègíànè ten add nine	'nineteen'	òsù dɔ́ ègiànè twenty add nine	'twenty nine'	òsù dɔ́ íjūō dɔ́ íjūō ègíànè twenty add ten add ten nine	'thirty nine'
		òsù dɔ́ íjūō twenty add ten	'thirty'		

4.8.1.3 Cardinal numerals formed by compounding and addition

Other numerals are derived by compounding and addition. They generally have a base of twenty and include numerals above forty. Tens based on odd numerals such as fifty, seventy and ninety fall under this group. They are constructed with the pattern XN + Y = Z where XN is the compound numeral, Y the added lower numeral and Z the resulting numeral. Consider the following examples:

(206) a. ònwúsɔ̀   èfà   dɔ́n   ɔ́ɲíī   'forty one'
         twenty   two   add   one
      b. ònwúsɔ̀   èfà   dɔ́n   íjūō   'fifty'
         twenty   two   add   ten
      c. ònwúsɔ̀   ètá   dɔ́n   íjūō   'seventy'
         twenty   three add   ten
      d. ònwúsɔ̀   ènè   dɔ́n   íjūō   'ninety'
         twenty   four   add   ten
      e. ònwúsɔ̀   èdá   dɔ́n   ègíátá   'hundred and eight'
         twenty   five   add   eight

When the borrowed numeral term *ìdèlí* is used, numerals such as *ìdèlí ètá dɔ́ íjūō* 'three hundred and ten (literal: three hundreds add ten)', *ìdèlí ɔ́ɲíī dɔ́n ègíátá* 'one hundred and seven' are obtained. Following the traditional numeral system of Etulo, one could possibly count (in hundreds) up to six hundred in a fairly simple way using a base of twenty. Numerals (in hundreds) above six hundred are more complex. This is probably one of the reasons why native speakers now resort to *idèlí* in the expression of hundreds. The table below provides the illustration.

Table 4.16 Traditional vs modern counting system

Traditional counting system	Gloss	Modern counting sytem	Gloss
ònwúsɔ̀ èdá twenty five	'one hundred'	ìdèlí óɲíī hundred one	'one hundred'
ònwúsɔ̀ ìjúó twenty ten	'two hundred'	ìdèlí èfà hundred two	'two hundred'
ònwúsɔ̀ ìjúó dɔ́n èdá twenty ten add five	'three hundred'	ìdèlí ètá hundred three	'three hundred'
ònwúsɔ̀ òsù twenty twenty	'four hundred'	ìdèlí ènè hundred four	'four hundred'
ònwúsɔ̀ òsù dɔ́n èdá twenty twenty add five	'five hundred'	ìdèlí èdá hundred five	'five hundred'
ònwúsɔ̀ òsù dɔ́n íjūō twenty twenty add ten	'six hundred'	ìdèlí ègín hundred six	'six hundred'

4.8.2 Ordinal numerals

Stolz and Veselinova (2005) observe that in many languages, ordinal numerals are derived from cardinal numerals. Etulo is one of such languages. Ordinal numerals are derived from cardinal ones by the addition of the morpheme *ònwí*.[22] For instance, the ordinal *ònwí ònwúsɔ̄ èfà* 'fortieth' is derived from *ònwúsɔ̄ èfà* 'forty'. The form of ordinal derivation that involves the use of *onwi* is applicable to most Etulo ordinals with the exception of *óvúlè* 'first'. The ordinal numeral 'first', is realized by two suppletive forms: *óvúlè* and *àbábɔ̀*. *Óvúlè* is exclusively used for kinship terms and functions syntactically as a nominal modifier (constituent of a NP) but does not co-occur with *onwi*. On the

---

22 The morpheme *onwi* used in deriving ordinal numerals, coincides with the relative pronoun. Etulo ordinals have the structure of a noun phrase. In the formation of the ordinals from 'two' upwards, the relative pronoun *onwi* is modified by the numeral. For instance, *onwi efa → onwufan* is loosely translated as the 'second one / one which is second'. The use of the Etulo relative pronoun in this context is not subject to the animacy distinction (see, by contrast, Section 4.1.6 on the relative pronoun).

other hand, *àbábɔ̂* applies to other animate [-human] and inanimate entities, co-occurs with *ònwí* and is also realized as a constituent of a NP. The use of both ordinals is illustrated below:

(207) a. ìɲànì   lì   ònwè   óvúlē ḿgbí ánî
         PN   COP   child first POSS 1SG
         'Inyani is my first child.'

   b. nénê   lì   àjàtù ḿgbí ánî   ònwí ábābɔ̂
      this   COP   car   POSS 1SG   REL.P first
      'This is my first car.'

   c. m̀dà   ònwí   ábābɔ̂ nwí   ánî   gíá   mà   kwúlú wà
      car   REL.P first REL   1SG:SUBJ buy   the die   PERF
      'The first cow that I bought is dead.'

   d. ǹgísè̀   ònwí   ábābɔ̂
      person   REL.P first
      'the first person'

In the formation of ordinals 2–9, a phonological change is observed. The word initial vowel and tone of the numeral is deleted after *ònwí* and the harmonic vowel [u] is inserted. As an example, *ònwí* + *èfà* realizes *ònwúfà* 'second'. Other examples are listed in Table 4.17 below.

Table 4.17 Ordinal numerals

1st–9th and 20th	Translation	10th–upwards	Translation
óvúlè/àbábɔ̂	'first'	ònwí íjūō one ten (tenth one)	'tenth'
ònwí + èfà → ònwúfàn	'second'	ònwí ósú dɔ̄ íjūō one twenty add ten	'thirtieth'
ònwí + ètá → ònwútā	'third'	ònwí ónwúsɔ̄ èfà one twentieth two	'fortieth'
ònwí + ènè̀ → ònwúnè̀	'fourth'	ònwí ónwúsɔ̄ èfà dɔ́n íjūō one twentieth two add ten	'fiftieth'
ònwí + èdá → ònwúdá	'fifth'	ònwí ónwúsɔ̄ ètá one twentieth three	'sixtieth'
ònwí + ègín → ònwúgīn	'sixth'	ònwí ónwúsɔ̄ ètá dɔ́n íjūō one twentieth three add ten	'seventieth'
ònwí + èglàfà → ònwúgīāfà	'seventh'	ònwí ónwúsɔ̄ ènɛ́ one twentieth four	'eightieth'

1st–9th and 20th	Translation	10th–upwards	Translation
ònwí + ègíátá → ònwúgīātā	'eighth'	ònwí ónwúsɔ̄ ènè dón íjūō one twentieth four add ten	'ninetieth'
ònwí + ègíànè → ònwúgīānè	'ninth'	ònwí ónwúsɔ̄ èdá one twentieth five	'hundredth'
ònwí + òsù → ònwúsû	'twentieth'		

4.8.3 Cardinal and ordinal numerals as modifiers

In Etulo, cardinal and ordinal numerals may modify the noun in the expression of quantity and hierarchy/position. Etulo falls in the group of languages in which cardinal numerals undergo no change when used as nominal modifiers. As constituents of a noun phrase, the numerals are preceded by the modified noun. In other words, they are postnominal. Their position relative to the noun changes when they co-occur with other modifiers in an NP. For instance, when a cardinal numeral co-occurs with an adjective, it is directly preceded by the adjective (moves farther away from the noun) as in the phrase: àjàtù òfùfè (ŋí) èfà 'three new cars' (N→Adj→Num). By contrast, in a NP such àjàtù (ŋí) èfà ńtónéní̌ 'These three cars', where the cardinal co-occurs with another modifier (a demonstrative), it is directly preceded by the noun (N→Num→Dem). If both the adjective òfùfè 'new' and the demonstrative ńtónéní̌ are involved as in: àjàtù òfùfè ŋí ètá ńtónéní̌ 'These three new cars', the order is N→Adj→Num→Dem. The linking element ŋi is optionally used in NPs comprising numerals in modifying function. More examples are given below:

(208) a. àfɛ̀ òsù
        book twenty
        'twenty books'
    b. àjàtù òsù dɔ́ íjūō dɔ́ íjūō óɲīī
        car twenty add ten add ten one
        'thirty one cars'
(209) a. ònwɛ̀ ònwúgīn
        child sixth
        'sixth child'
    b. m̀dà ònwútā
        cow third
        'third cow'

4.8.4 Distributive numerals

According to Seth (2012), distributive numerals are a derived numeral class which indicates that the modified NP 'is distributed over' some other entity or event. Thus, it is usually translatable into English as '*n* NPs each', '*n* at a time' or '*n* by *n*' (where *n* stands for any numeral). Distributive numerals denote a numerically specified category. They typically answer the question: *how many each?* Etulo distributive numerals are derived by full reduplication of the cardinal numeral. Consider the following examples:

(210) éjî ɣá ángwó mà ènè énè
     1PL:SUBJ share yam the four RED
     'We shared the yam four by four.'

(211) èmgbé ùmákárántá kwúdzê èfà èfà
     children school stand two RED
     'The students stood in twos.'

(212) á kīē ítsè mà ìjúó íjūō
     3PL:SUBJ carry chair the ten RED
     'They carried the chairs ten each.'

4.8.5 Arithmetic operations

In this subsection, I briefly examine the manner in which arithmetic operations such as addition, subtraction, multiplication and division are realized in Etulo.[23] As shall be seen in the following subsections, these operations are mostly expressed by verbs, except for multiplication. The result of an arithmetic operation is generally introduced by the copula *lì* 'be'.

4.8.5.1 Addition

Addition is expressed by the verb *tú* 'meet'. The use of this verb for addition seems to be common with older speakers. Younger Etulo speakers of Etulo prefer the verb *békè* 'join/merge'. Examples:

---

23 Some variations are observed in the realization of arithmetic operations by Etulo native speakers. For addition, some speakers use the verb *bɛkɛ* 'join/merge' together with the preposition *jì* 'with' while others use the verb *tu* 'meet'. The use of *bɛkɛ* is illustrated below:

i) èdá béké jì èdá jē ìjúó
   five join with five become ten
   'Five plus five equals ten.'

For introducing the corresponding sum realized from arithmetic operations, some informants use the copula *lì* 'be', while others prefer the use of the verb *jɛ* 'become'.

(213) a. ójñíí   tú   èfà   lì   età
           one   meet   two   COP   three
           'One plus two equals three.'
      b.   èdá   tú   èdá   lì   ìjúó
           five   meet   five   COP   ten
           'Five plus five equals ten.'

4.8.5.2 Subtraction

Subtraction is realized by the verb *dúrú* 'remove'. The result is introduced by the copula *lì* 'be' in alternation with the verb *sísí* 'remain'.

(214) a. ènè   dúrú   èfà   lì   èfà
           four   remove   two   COP   two
           'Four minus two equals two.'
      b.   ìjúó   dúrú   èdá   sísí   èdá
           ten   remove   five   remain   five
           'Ten minus five equals five.'

4.8.5.3 Division

Division is expressed by the verb *yá* 'share/divide. It co-occurs with the preposition *mì* 'in' in contexts where the dividend precedes the divisor as in (215a). It, however, functions independently of any other morpheme when the divisor precedes the dividend (see 215b).

(215) a. ènè   yá   mì   èfà   lì   èfà
           four   share   in   two   COP   two
           'Four divided by two equals two.'
      b.   èfà   yá   ènè   lì   èfà
           two   share   four   COP   two
           'Two divide four equals two.'

4.8.5.4 Multiplication

Multiplication involves the use of the noun *àkpé* 'a number of times'. It's semantics in an arithmetic operation connotes the cumulation of the multiplied number in a group of one, two, three or more. In spoken form, there is always assimilation of the final vowel of *àkpé* before a numeral. For instance, *àkpé óɲíí* becomes *àkpó óɲíí* 'once'. The resulting sum is introduced by the copula *lì* or the verb *jɛ* 'become'.

(216) a. ìjúó   àkpé   ètá   lì   òsù.dɔ́.íjūō
         ten   times three COP   thirty
         'Ten times three equals thirty.'
     b. èfà   àkpé   èfà   lì   ènè
         two   times two   COP   four
         'Two times two equals four.'

4.8.5.5 Fractions

Fractions are expressed by means of the preposition phrase *mi ikie* 'from head' and by qualificatives and nouns such as *àjé* 'half', *àngájî* 'half', *ítsítsî* 'short' The last three are specifically involved in the realization of 'half' as a fraction. The choice is conditioned or determined by the semantic feature of the noun.

(217) a. ánî   gíá   ìtístsí óbā   ísíkápá
         1SG   buy   short   bag   rice
         'I bought half bag of rice.'
     b. àjè   mbúábā kwúlúū
         half   animal die
         'Half of the animals died.'
     c. àdì   kíé   àngájî   ìbrédî nū   ánî
         PN   take   half   bread   give 1SG
         'Adi gave me half a loaf of bread.'

For other fractions, the prepositional phrase is used, as illustrated below:

(218) àdì   jí   úmí   óɲíī   mì   ìkíé   íjūō   ángwɔ́ ḿgbí ánî
       PN   steal theft one   from head   ten   yam   POSS 1SG
       'Adi stole one tenth of my yam.'

4.8.6 Conclusion

The foregoing discussion shows that the traditional numeral system of Etulo which adopts the base of twenty is vigesimal, much like what is observed in other West African languages such as Igbo and Yoruba. Some numerals are formed by compounding and other periphrastic means. The ordinal numerals are derived from the cardinal numerals by the use of the expression *onwi*. The Etulo vigesimal system is, however, relatively restricted and not very user-friendly. Deriving numerals above two hundred becomes quite complex with this system. This has motivated the tendency to borrow from other languages. In particular, in order to express higher numerals (hundreds, thousands, millions), a modern numeral system seems to be evolving, which utilizes numerals borrowed from Hausa, such as *ideli* 'hundred', and *idubu* 'thousand'.

5. Aspects of Etulo Syntax

5.0 Introduction

This chapter gives a description of various aspects of Etulo syntax such as negation, interrogatives, coordination, subordination, copular construction, numeral system and word order. Section 5.1 examines the structure of negative construction and identifies the strategies for marking negation. In Section 5.2, the two basic interrogative types, polar (yes/no) and content question are discussed. In Section 5.3, a distinction is made between overt (syndetic) and covert (asyndetic) coordinate constructions. The syndetic coordinate construction comprises the monosyndetic (a single coordinator) and the bisyndetic (two or more coordinators) types. A total of seven coordinators are identified and classified into three groups: conjunction markers, disjunction markers and the adversative marker. In Section 5.4, three types of subordinate clauses are discussed: complement, relative and adverbial. I describe their structure, as well as the features of the subordinators or markers associated with each clause type. Section 5.5 describes the three copulas attested in Etulo: *le, lì* and *dzè*. The copula *le* occurs with ideophone predicates. The copula *lì* takes specificational and predication complements (noun and adjectival phrases). It also allows a pro-drop subject. The copula *dzè* is used in locative clauses. In Section 5.6, I examine the order of constituents in basic sentences, possessive/genitive constructions and phrases. I also discuss how the Etulo word order conforms to or deviates from the cross-linguistic generalizations of word order correlations.

5.1 Negation

Negation is a language universal category. According to Crystal (2003: 310), negation is a construction in grammatical and semantic analysis which typically expresses the contradiction of some or all of a sentence's meaning. In a cross-linguistic study, Dahl (1979) observes that most languages of the world exhibit either morphological or syntactic negation. Syntactic negation involves the use of particles and auxiliaries, while morphological negation involves the use of affixes. A distinction is often made between standard negation (i.e. main clause negation) and other forms of negation (Payne 1985). In line with this view, Miestamo (2005) defines standard negation as the basic method a language has for negating declarative verbal main clauses. Thus, while standard negative markers are associated with basic declarative sentences, non-standard negative markers are associated with the prohibitive/imperative sentences, non-verbal clauses, polar questions and so on (cf. Miestamo 2005, Kahrel 1996). In lgbo and Yoruba, for instance, different markers are used in the negation of declarative vs imperative/prohibitive constructions. Specifically, the Igbo negative prefix *-ghi* is used in simple declarative constructions, while the negative prefix *-la* occurs in imperative constructions. As for Yoruba, Hewson (2006: 10) singles out the two negative particles *kò* and *má*: the former appears in main clauses while the latter appears in prohibitions or subordinate clauses.

This section focuses on the structural and functional properties domain of the Etulo negative markers. Emphasis is put on the phonological properties (tone and vowel lengthening) of the negative markers. The following constructions are explored: simple declarative, imperative, anticipative or future, perfectal and interrogative (polar questions). Also discussed is the negation of monoverbal, multiverbal and complex clauses.

5.1.1 Negation of basic declarative constructions

Basic sentences in Etulo are here exemplified with the simple present-referring, future-referring and perfectal constructions. In these constructions, negation is expressed by the high tone negative particle *bá*, which mainly occurs in sentence-final position regardless of the preceding word. These negated constructions contrast with their affirmative counterparts only because the presence of the negator *bá*. Examples:

(1) a. ánî lì ìnwíndà
    1SG:SUBJ COP beauty
    'I am beautiful.'
  b. ánî lì ìnwíndà bá
    1SG:SUBJ COP beauty NEG
    'I am not beautiful.'
(2) a. èmí òká ánî kà nwɔ́ m̀dà
    PL friend 1SG FUT kill cow
    'My friends will kill a cow.'
  b. èmí òká ánî kà nwɔ́ m̀dà bá
    PL friend 1SG FUT kill cow NEG
    'My friends will not kill a cow.'

(3) a. èmgbɛ́ lɛ́ ólē̄ wà
children play play PERF
'The children have played.'
b. èmgbɛ́ lɛ́ ólē̄ wà bá
children play play PERF NEG
'The children have not played.'

Just like mono-verb clauses, negation is marked only once in multi-verb constructions. In serial verb constructions, for instance, the sentence-final negative marker has scope over the whole clause.

(4) a. ìsèsɛ́ kà kíé ènì fúé èsɛ́
PN FUT take water spread floor
'Isɛsɛ will sprinkle water on the floor.'
b. ìsèsɛ́ kà kíé ènì fúé èsɛ́ bá
PN FUT take water spread floor NEG
'Isɛsɛ will not sprinkle water on the floor.'

5.1.2 Negation of imperatives

For imperative negative clauses, Etulo uses two morphemes: the high tone preverbal morpheme *ká* and the postverbal negative particle *bá*. In the negation of plural imperatives, *bá* is followed by the plural imperative marker *náà* (6b and 8b). Negative imperative constructions contrast with their affirmative counterparts on two counts: the dedicated preverbal morpheme and a negative particle. Consider the following examples:

(5) a. fà
swear
'Swear!'
b. ká fà bá
PTCL swear NEG
'Don't swear!'
(6) a. fà náà
swear PL
'Swear!'
b. ká fà bá náà
PTCL swear NEG PL
'Don't swear!'

(7) a. sò   àngìà
       pound   millet
       'Pound millet!'
    b. ká   sò   àngìà   bá
       PTCL   pound   millet   NEG
       'Don't pound millet!'
(8) a. sò   àngìà   náà
       pound   millet   PL
       'Pound millet!'
    b. ká   sò   àngìà   bá   náà
       PTCL   pound   millet   NEG   PL
       'Don't pound millet!'

5.1.3 Negation of interrogatives (polar questions)

The polar question in Etulo is distinct from other constructions. It is characterized by lengthening of the last vowel of the sentence-final word. For instance, the noun *ángwɔ́* 'yam' becomes *ángwɔ́ɔ̀* when it occurs as the last word in a polar question. The extra mora introduced as a result of vowel lengthening bears a low tone. Vowel lengthening and low tone therefore underlie the formation of polar questions in Etulo. Negation of polar questions involves the use of the lengthened negative marker *lóò*.[1] Let us observe the difference between the negation of polar questions and their variants. In the (a) examples of (9 and 10), the polar question is marked by vowel lengthening in the words *àtsúbōò* 'pepper' and *wàà* 'perfective marker' in sentence-final position. In the negated variant, instead, vowel lengthening shifts to the negative particle. Apart from this, all negative morphemes have two things in common: their structural domain and their nature as particles. Examples:

(9) a. ìɲànì   kpā   àtsúbōò
       PN   grind   pepper.Q
       'Did Inyani grind pepper?'
    b. ìɲànì   kpā   àtsúbō   lóò
       PN   grind   pepper   NEG.Q
       'Didn't Inyani grind pepper?'

---

1   The analysis of the negative particle *lo* given here differs slightly from the analysis proposed in Ezenwafor C. I. (2011), where the tone of the negative particle is analysed as a glide.

(10) a. ò   lú   wàà
        3SG:SUBJ go   PERF.Q
        'Has he gone?'

    b. ò   lú   wà   lóò
        3SG:SUBJ go   PERF NEG.Q
        'Hasn't he gone?'

5.1.4 Negation of complex clauses

In complex clauses such as focus constructions, negation is marked by the negative particle *bá*. At the surface level, the scope of the negative marker in focus constructions seems ambiguous. The negation of the focused constituent and of the main predicate is equally marked by the post-sentential negative particle, as respectively shown by (11 and 12). Examples:

(11) lì   ánî   nwí   àdì   tá   ánî   àfè   bá
     COP   1SG   REL   PN   slap 1SG   slap NEG
     'It is not me that Adi slapped.'

(12) lì   ánî   nwí   àdì   tá   ánî   àfè   bá
     COP   1SG   REL   PN   hit   1SG   slap NEG
     'It is me that Adi did not slap.'

In a complex construction involving two clauses, the scope of negation may be partial or full. Negation is marked once when only one clause in a complex construction is negated, but is doubly marked when both clauses are negated. In example (13), for instance, negation is marked once and it only has scope over the first clause. When the speaker wants to negate both clauses, as in (14), Etulo adopts the use of multiple negation-marking, which is indicated by the negator *bá* and the preverbal negative morpheme *jàmá*.[2] The latter directly precedes the verb of the first clause. In addition, the negative marker *ba* is marked twice. This is, however, optional.

(13) àdì   jé   gbĕē   ìɲànì   ná   úná   bá
     PN   know   COMP   PN   sleep sleep NEG
     'Adi did not know that Inyani slept.'

---

2   Besides the use of multiple negation in complex clauses, *jàmá* may also indicate negative emphasis as in the following construction:

   (i) àdì   ká   jàmá   ná   úná   bá
        PN   FUT   NEG   sleep sleep NEG
        'Adi will never sleep.'

(14) éjî   jàmá jé   gběē àdì ná   úná   (bá) bá
     1PL   NEG   know COMP PN   sleep sleep NEG   NEG
     'We did not know that Adi did not sleep.'

Etulo makes no formal distinction between sentential and constituent negation. The scope of the latter is restricted to constituents such as nouns (***No dogs** are allowed*) and adverbs (*not long ago*). Klima (1964) points out that constituent negation can be characterized in some languages by the use of negative affixes, such as the English *un-* prefix in *unintelligent*. Etulo does not only lack negative affixes for constituent negation, it also does encode the structural distinction between the negation of a sentence and of a focused constituent (see 11 and 12). Other negative morphemes or words attested in Etulo are discussed in the following section.

5.1.5 Negative words

In Etulo, negative words such as *ńkábá* 'nothing', *wùbá* 'never/no more', *Eeee* 'no' are attested. From a synchronic perspective, the first two negative words are considered lexicalized forms derived from two morphemes. *Ńkábá* is derived from the noun *ńká* and the negative particle *bá*, while *wùbá* is derived from the morpheme *wù* (which has no identifiable meaning in isolation) and the negator *bá*.[3] In different contexts, *ńkábá* loosely translates into English as nowhere or nothing (see 15a and 15b). As for the negative word *éè*, it is basically used to answer yes/no questions. Its syntactic position is preclausal (see 17b). The following examples are illustrative:

(15) a. lì   ńkábá
         COP   nothing
         'It is nothing.'
     b. ábû   lè   ké   ńkábá
         2SG:SUBJ PROG   go   nowhere
         'You are going nowhere.'
(16) a. ò   lè   fé   ánî   wùbá
         3SG   PROG   wait 1SG   no.more
         'He is no longer waiting for me.'
     b. àdì   kà   ʃá   íʃá   wùbá
         PN   FUT   laugh laugh never
         'Adi will never laugh.'

---

3   In Etulo, the negative word *nkaba* is commonly used as a response to traditional greetings. In such contexts, it is roughly the equivalent of the English words 'fine/not bad'. For instance, the typical response to the Etulo greeting *ò kɨɔ sínèé* 'How are you doing?' would be *ńkábá*, which literally means 'nothing'.

(17) a. ábû   kɪ̀ɔ̀   ùnwógīē
　　　　 2SG   cook   food
　　　　 'You cooked food.'

　　 b. éè   ábû   kɪ̀ɔ̀   ùnwógīē   bá
　　　　 no   2SG   cook   food   NEG
　　　　 'No, you did not cook food.'

5.1.6 Conclusion

In summary, two negative particles are attested in Etulo: *bá* and *lóò*. Declarative clauses are negated by the negative particle *bá* in clause-final position. Imperatives are negated in the same way, except that the plural marker *náà* follows the negative particle *ba* to indicate plural addressees. Negation of a polar interrogative involves the negative particle *loo* in clause-final position. Etulo makes no formal distinction between sentential and constituent negation. It falls among the languages that make use of particles for syntactic negation. It makes a distinction between the standard (*bá*) and non-standard (*lóò*) negative marker. In clausal sequences, negation can be marked either once clause-finally, taking scope over the main verb, or twice, with each instance taking scope over its respective verb.

5.2 Interrogatives

Interrogatives are constructions that seek the confirmation of a proposition or information. The three types of cross-linguistically identified questions include: polar, content and alternative questions. Different strategies are used to mark the different interrogative types across languages. In a cross-linguistic study, Dryer (2005) identifies various means of marking polar questions. The use of interrogative particles, verb affixes and intonation are the most common strategies.

In this section, I discuss the different types of interrogatives attested in Etulo. The polar question (Yes/No) is discussed in (Section 5.2.1), the content question and the alternative question are discussed in (Section 5.2.2). The strategies used to mark these interrogatives include: question words (as associated with content questions), and vowel lengthening/tone.

5.2.1 Polar questions

Polar questions are answered with a simple yes/no. They are typically used to enquire about the truth or falsity of the proposition (Konig and Siemund, 2007).

Polar questions are marked in Etulo via phonological means: vowel lengthening and pitch lowering. The last vowel of the sentence-final word is lengthened. The lowered pitch is realized as a low tone on the lengthened vowel. Polar questions differ from their declarative counterparts only on the basis of these phonological features. In the following examples, polar questions are placed beside their declarative counterparts:

(18) a. ò lú wàà
       3SG:SUBJ go PERF.Q
       'Has she gone?'
    b. ò lú wà
       3SG:SUBJ go PERF
       'She has gone.'

(19) a. òkà ánî ʃì ìfúéè
       friend 1SG dance dance:Q
       'Did my friend dance?'
    b. òká ánî ʃì ìfúé
       friend 1SG dance dance
       'My friend danced.'

Comparison of polar questions and the corresponding declarative sentences shows no difference in the pitch of words, except for the sentence-final word. For negative polar questions, this same strategy is utilized except that the lengthened vowel is always that of the negative particle *lóò* (see Section 5.1.3)

5.2.2 Content questions

Content questions are also referred to as WH questions in English or information questions. Unlike polar questions, they elicit answers that provide specific information. The expression of content questions involves the use of interrogative/question words or phrases. Dryer (2005) observes that all languages have a set of interrogative words, although the inventory varies across languages. In Section 4.1.5, I gave a list of four interrogative words which I described as interrogative pronouns. They include *èmé* 'who', *èkíé* 'what', *òlé* 'where' and *èngá* 'when'. In addition to these four interrogative pronouns, other interrogative words exist in Etulo. A list of all the identified interrogative words is given below:

(20) a. èmé   'who'
     b. èkíé   'what'
     c. (mì)   òlé   'where/
                                 which'
        PREP   where

d.	kɔ́			'where'
e.	èngá			'when'
f.	sīnēē̄			'how/what'
g.	kíɔ́	sìnèé		'why'
	do	how		
h.	èmìnè			'how many'
i.	(lì)	àlí	(ɔ̀nɔ̀)	'when, what'
	COP	which	time	

The interrogative word for 'why' is derived through a combination of the verb *kìɔ̀* 'do' and *sīnēē̄* 'how'. This combination (*kíɔ́ sìnèé*) could be shortened to *kíɔ́nê*. Some of the interrogative words realize more than one meaning. For instance, the interrogative form *(mi) ole* stands for 'where' and 'which', while *sīnēē̄* stands for 'what' and 'how'. Conversely, some of these interrogative meanings are realized via more than one means. For instance, 'where' is expressed by *(mì) òlé* and *kɔ́* depending on the context, and *when* is expressed as *èngá* and *àlí ɔ̀nɔ̀* ('which time'). In the following sections, I focus on the syntactic distribution of interrogative words, their function and semantic realizations.

5.2.2.1 Syntactic distribution of interrogative words

Across languages, interrogative words are known to occur in clause-initial or clause-final positions or both. In Etulo, these interrogative words are used in either simple or complex (cleft-like) constructions, and correspondingly occupy different syntactic positions depending on the specific word used.

5.2.2.2 Interrogative words in simple clauses

Interrogative words in Etulo are used *in situ*[4]. They mostly occur in clause-final position, excluding *kíɔ́nĕ/kíɔ́ sìnèé* 'why', whose syntactic position is clause-initial. In simple sentences, interrogative words occur in an object argument slot, i.e. a postverbal position (see examples 21–27). Observe that the occurrence of the preposition *mi* with the interrogative *òlé* is optional (see 23a and 23b). In (23c) the morpheme *kɔ́* is used as an alternate form for the interrogative word *mi ole* 'where'. The interrogative form *kɔ́* is compatible with animate entities. As stated earlier, interrogative words may have more than one semantic reading depending on the context. Take, for instance, the question word *sīnēē̄* which

---

[4] Wh-in-situ is a type of question where the interrogative word (such as the wh-question words in English) stays in its original position, instead of being moved to the front of a sentence.

is interpreted as *how* in (25a) and as *what* in (25b). Consider the following examples:

(21) ábû   lì   èmɛ́?
     2SG:SUBJ COP   who
     'Who are you/You are who?'

(22) á   kwúlúū   èngá?
     3PL:SUBJ die   when
     'When did they die?'

(23) a. ábû   lá   (mì)   òlé?
        2SG:SUBJ lie   in   where
        'Where did you sleep?'

     b. ábû   kè   òlé?
        2SG:SUBJ go   where
        'Where did you go?'

     c. ò   kɔ́?
        3SG:SUBJ   where
        'Where is he?'

(24) ábû   mìná   òlé?
     2SG:SUBJ want   which
     'Which one do you want?'

(25) a. á   kwúlú   sínèɛ́?
        3PL:SUBJ die   how
        'How did they die?'

     b. lì   sīnēē̄
        COP   how
        'How much?'

     c. ùmìà   sīnēē̄?
        price   how
        'Price, how much?'

(26) a. nénê   lì   èkíɛ́ ?
        this   COP   what
        'What is this?'

     b. ó   kìɔ̀   sìnèɛ̀?
        3SG:SUBJ do   what
        'What did he do?'

(27) ábû   mìná   èmìnè?
     2SG:SUBJ want   how.many
     'How many do you want?'

The interrogative word *kíɔ́ sìnèé/kíɔ́nĕ* 'why' seems to be the only one that may occur in a clause-initial position. The shortened and full form are used interchangeably as illustrated in (28a) and (28b):

(28) a. kíɔ́nè   nwí   ábû   mà   àkwɔ̀?
         why   REL   2SG   cry   cry
         'Why did you cry?'
     b. kíɔ́   sìnèè   nwí   ábû   mà   àkwɔ̀
         do   how   REL   2SG   cry   cry
         'Why did you cry?'

Some Etulo interrogative forms may function as NP determiners. Two of such interrogative words are *òlé* 'which' and *àlí* 'what/which'. See Section 4.2.4 on determiners for further discussion.

5.2.3 Interrogative complex clauses

Interrogative words are used in an emphatic complex clause similar to a cleft construction. The emphatic complex interrogative clause comprises two clauses: a matrix and a dependent clause. The matrix clause is introduced by the fronted *lì* copula which focuses on interrogative words.[5] The dependent clause may be introduced by the relative marker *nwí*. The following examples are illustrative:

(29) lì   èmé   kíɔ́   ùnwɔ́   nê?
      COP   who   do   thing   this
      'Who did this?'
(30) lì   èkíé   nwí   ó   kíɔ̀?
      COP   what   REL   3SG   do
      'What did he do?'
(31) lì   mì   òlé   nwí   ábû   lè   kéè̀?
      COP   in   where   REL   2SG   PROG   go
      'Where are you going to?'
(32) a. lì   èngá   nwí   ábû   lúū?
         COP   when   REL   2SG   go
         'When did you go?'
     b. lì   àlí   ɔ̀nɔ̀   nwí   á   kwúlúū?
         COP   which   time   REL   3PL   die
         'When did they die?'

---

5   In a cleft construction such as *lì àjàtù nwí ótsó ánî gīā* 'It is a car that my father bought', the low tone copula *lì* is fronted to focus on the noun *àjàtù* 'car'. When the copula is fronted in interrogative constructions, it is the interrogative word that is focused on.

(33) lì   èmìnè   nwí   ábû   mìná?
    COP how.many REL   2SG   want
    'How many do you want?'

An alternative question presents two or more possible options and presupposes that only one of the presented alternatives is true. In Etulo, alternative questions involve coordinated structures. They comprise phrases or clauses that are conjoined by linking elements such as *náádí* or *náá* (shortened form). Like polar questions, they are marked by vowel lengthening and a lowered pitch on the final word of the sentence. The following examples are illustrative:

(34) ábû   mìná   ò-ʃí   áʃí   náádí   ò-ʃí   ìfúéè
    2SG:SUBJ want   PREF-sing   song   or   PREF-dance dance
    'Do you want to sing or dance?'

(35) lì   ìɲànì   náádí   ìsèsé   ká   kìɔ   ùnwógíéè
    COP PN   or   PN   FUT   cook   food
    'Is it Inyani or Isɛsɛ that will cook food?'

(36) á   mìná   ò-bá   náádí   à   mìná   bá
    3PL:SUBJ want   PREF-come   or   3PL:SUBJ want   NEG
    'Do they want to come or not?'

5.2.4 Conclusion

Three types of interrogatives have been presented: polar, content and alternative questions. Polar and alternative questions are marked by vowel lengthening and a lowered pitch on the final word of the sentence. As for content questions, Etulo is characterized by *wh-in-situ*. About eight interrogative words have been identified: *èmé* 'who', *èkíé* 'what', *èngá* 'when', *sīnēē* 'how/what', *èmìnè* 'how many', *kɔ́* 'where', *òlé* 'where/which', *kíɔ́ sìnèé/kíɔ́nĕ* 'why'. In addition, two interrogative determiners are attested. They include: *òlé* 'which' and *àlí* 'what/which'.

5.3 Coordination

Coordination is a common syntactic feature that joins two or more constituents or units of the same type into larger units. According to Haspelmath (2004: 1), 'A construction [A B] is considered coordinate if the two parts A and B have the same status…' Across languages, coordination is overtly marked by a connecting morpheme (conjunction) or covertly marked by juxtaposition of the coordinands/conjuncts.

In this section, I discuss the process of coordination and how it is marked in Etulo. Both overt (syndetic) and covert (asyndetic) marking of coordination are attested. The latter is mostly associated with the coordination of clauses. The syndetic coordinate construction in Etulo comprises the monosyndetic (a single coordinator) and the bisyndetic (two or more coordinators). Seven coodinators have been identified: *jì, mà/mân, dí* 'and' (conjunction markers), *ónā, náá, náádí* 'or' (disjunction markers), *kpàâ* 'but' (adversative marker). A distinction is observed between noun phrase and verb phrase conjunctions.

In a typological study on noun phrase conjunctions, Stassen (2000) proposes a basic distinction between languages which use a different marker for noun phrase conjunction and comitative phrases (*and-languages*) and those in which the markers for noun phrase conjunction and comitative phrases are the same (*with-languages*). This study shows that Etulo belongs to the category of *with-languages*.

5.3.1 Coordination types

Coordination in Etulo can be classified on the basis of two criteria: linguistic coding and syntactic structures. With respect to syntactic structure, a distinction is made between phrasal and clausal coordination. In terms of linguistic coding, a distinction is made between overt and covert coordination. Overt coordination also known as syndetic, involves the use of morphemes to join two grammatical units (see (37)). Covert coordination, otherwise called asyndetic, expresses coordination via the juxtaposition of coordinands (38a). In Etulo, covert marking is peculiar to clauses and is optional (compare 38a and 38b), while overt marking of coordination is applicable to both phrases and clauses. Examples:

(37) òngìùlɔ́ nê jì òtsó ánî lì òkà
man this and father 1SG COP friend
'This man and my father are friends.'

(38) a. óbúé lí gíé ḿbúé òbàgwù lí gíé ágbūgbɔ̀
dog HAB eat meat monkey HAB eat banana
'Dogs eat meat and monkeys eat banana.'

b. óbúé lí gíé ḿbúé mà òbàgwù lí gíé ágbūgbɔ̀
dog HAB eat meat and monkey HAB eat banana
'Dogs eat meat and monkeys eat banana.'

In the following subsections, I examine the different coordinators and their usage in phrases and clauses.

5.3.2 Conjunction markers

As stated earlier, three conjunction markers exist in Etulo: *jì/béjì*, *dí* and *mà*, all translated as the English 'and'. Their choice depends on the syntactic structure of the coordinands.

5.3.2.1 The coordinator *jì*

The coordinator *jì* is a low tone morpheme that is strictly employed in the linking of noun phrases, including nouns (3a and 3b), pronouns (3c), and interrogatives (3d). It is used interchangeably with the form *béjì*. Its position is between the coordinands.

(39) a. àdì   jì   iɲànì   ké   òkwɔ̀
        PN   and   PN   go   farm
        'Adi and Inyani went to the farm.'
     b. ánî   dí   ǹdɔ̀   béjì   m̀dà
        1SG:SUBJ   see   goat   and   cow
        'I saw a goat and a cow.'
     c. ónwú   béjì/jì   ánî   bá   údé   ḿgbí   ábû
        3SG   and   1SG   come   house   POSS   2SG
        'He and I came to your house.'
     d. lì   èkíé   jì   èkíé   nwí   ábû   gíá
        COP   what   and   what   REL   2SG   buy
        'What and what did you buy?'

The *jì* marker is also used in comitative phrases where it denotes accompaniment (in company with/together with).[6] In a comitative function, the *jì* morpheme directly precedes the accompanying referent (40a and 40b). One can easily infer that the coordinating function was a diachronical product of the comitative function. The dual functions of this marker may be jointly expressed in a complex clause (see 40c). Besides semantics, another way of differentiating the conjunctive and the comitative use of the *jì* marker is by structural position: between the coordinands or before the accompanee.

---

6 The occurrence of the *jì* marker in comitative phrases illustrates its prepositional use. In addition to the notion of accompaniment expressed in the examples above, it may also express an instrumental meaning, as illustrated below:

(i) èmgbé   lè   lé   ólɛ̄   jì   ùbô
    children   PROG   play   play   with   ball
    'The children are playing with a ball.'

(40) a. àdì   kɛ́   òkwɔ̀   jì   iɲànì
         PN   go   farm   with   PN
         'Adi went to farm with Inyani.'

    b. àdì   ká   dzè   jì   ánî
        PN   FUT   stay   with   1SG
        'Adi will stay with me.'

    c. ónɔ́   ánî   jì   ánî   lɛ́   ólē   jì   èkà
        mother 1SG   and   1SG   play   play   with   each.other
        'My mother and I played together.'

5.3.2.2 The coordinator *dí*

The coordinator *dí* is a high tone morpheme that mostly links verb phrases. Just like the nominal conjunctive marker, its occurrence is obligatory for coordination. Its position is between coordinands (two or more verbs/verb phrases). In (41a–c), the linked verb phrases share the same subject. Apparently, Etulo makes a distinction between same subject vs different subject in the use of the coordinate marker *dí*; compare (41) and (42):

(41) a. àdì   dí   dí   kwū   iɲànì   èlâ
         PN   see   and   call   PN   voice
         'Adi saw and called Inyani.'

    b. ɛ̀mgbé   ḿgbí   éjî   lè   ʃá   íʃá   dí   lè   lɛ́   ólē
        children POSS   1PL   PROG   laugh   laugh   and   PROG   play   play
        'Our children are laughing and playing.'

    c. ótsó   éjî   lì   m̀nwàzá   dí   dzè   jì   àlùdù
        father 1PL   COP   handsome and   COP   with   wealth
        'Our father is handsome and wealthy.'

There are also a few instances where *dí* conjoins clauses. In (42a), for instance, two clauses with different subjects are joined by *dí*. In contrast with (41a and 41b), *dí* occurs in the preverbal position of the second clause rather than between the clausal coordinands. Example (42b) is considered ungrammatical because of the position of the coordinating marker.

(42) a. àdì   gíá   m̀tsà   á   dí   gīē
         PN   buy   mango   3PL:SUBJ   and   eat
         'Adi bought mangoes and they ate.'

    b. *àdì   gíá   m̀tsà   dí   á   gīē
         PN   buy   mango   and   3PL:SUBJ   eat
         'Adi bought mangoes and they ate.'

5.3.2.3 The coordinators mà/mân

The coordinator *mân* is specifically used in the linking of clauses with different subjects (43a–c), while the low tone coordinate marker *mà* is sometimes used where it links clauses with shared subjects (43c). Unlike the noun phrase and verb phrase conjunctive markers, the use of the *mân* marker is optional (covert coordination/juxtaposition). It may also be substituted by another conjunctive marker for the same function, namely the morpheme *sí* 'and' (not included in the above list of coordinating markers due to a lack of sufficient data).[7] Conversely, the low tone variant *mà* may be substituted by the verb phrase conjunctive marker *dí*. Consider the following examples:

(43) a. àdì gíá m̀tsà mân á gīē
PN buy mango CORD 3PL:SUBJ eat
'Adi bought mangoes and they ate.'

b. ánî kè ùdé mân òkà ánî kíé ánî ùnwógīē gíé
1SG:SUBJ go home CORD friend 1SG take 1SG food eat
'I went home and my friend ate my food.'

c. ń kà tóɲā mân ń kà wá lú-bā ìgbùdù
1SG:SUBJ FUT rest CORD 1SG:SUBJ FUT come go-come main.road
'I will rest then I will go to the main road.'

(44) àdì ʃígbô mà fíú ńfíú
PN be.tall and be.fat fatness
'Adi is tall and fat.'

The alternation of *mân* with *mà* or vice versa results in a different semantic interpretation (45a–b) or in ungrammaticality (46a–b). Further investigation is needed to fully ascertain the determining factors and scope of usage of both markers.

(45) a. àdì gíá m̀tsà mân á gīē
PN buy mango and 3PL eat
'Adi bought mangoes and they ate.'

b. ?àdì gíá m̀tsà mà á gīē
PN buy mango and 3PL eat
'Adi bought the mangoes they ate.'

---

7 Here is an example:
(i) àdì gíá m̀tsà sí á gīē
PN buy mango and 3PL eat
'Adi bought mangoes and they ate.'

(46) a. àdì ʃígbô mà fíú ńfíú
       PN   be.tall and be.fat fatness
       'Adi is tall and fat.'
    b. *àdì ʃígbô mân fíú ńfíú
       PN   be.tall and be.fat fatness
       'Adi is tall and fat.'

5.3.3 Disjunction markers

The disjunctive markers are used to express a choice between two or more possibilities or options. They connect noun phrases, verb phrases and clauses. One major disjunctive marker *náádí*, is identified in Etulo as corresponding to the English 'or'. It has two shortened variants realized as *ónā/náá* with which it may be interchanged. The coordinators *ónā* and *náá* link VPs and NPs in (47a and 47b), and *náádí* connects the same phrases in (47c and 47d).

(47) a. ìɲànì mìná ò-ʃí áʃí ónā/náá ʃì ifúé
       PN   want INF-sing song or   dance dance
       'Inyani wants to sing or dance.'
    b. ìɲànì ónā/náá ìsèsé ká kìɔ̀ ùnwógīē
       PN   or   PN   FUT cook food
       'Inyani or Isɛsɛ will cook food.'
    c. ábú mìná ò-ʃí áʃí náádí ʃì ifúéè?
       2SG:SUBJ want INF-sing song or dance dance-Q
       'Do you want to sing or dance?'
    d. lì ìɲànì náádí ìsèsé nwí ká kìɔ̀ ùnwógīē
       COP PN   or   PN   REL FUT cook food
       'It is Inyani or Isɛsɛ that will cook food.'

5.3.4 Adversative marker

The adversative marker expresses some sort of opposition or contrast in the overall meaning of a complex clause. It denotes the denial of an expectation. Etulo has the adversative marker *kpàâ* 'but' which links verb phrases (48a) and clauses (48b and 48c). Its position is usually between the conjoined units. Consider the following examples:

(48) a. ìɲànì ʃígbâ kpàâ fíú ńfíú
       PN   be.tall but be.fat fatness
       'Inyani is tall but fat.'

b. ìɲànì   lì   ìnwíndà   kpàâ   ádíɲá   tímbī
    PN   COP   beauty   but   PN   be.ugly
    'Inyani is beautiful but Adinya is ugly.'

c. àdì   kìɔ̀   ùnwógīē   bá   kpàâ   éjî   gíé
    PN   cook   food   NEG   but   1PL:SUBJ   eat
    'Adi did not cook food but we ate.'

5.3.5 Single vs multiple coordinate marking

When more than two coordinands are conjoined, coordination maybe marked once or multiple times, depending on the number of coordinands involved. The multiple marking of coordination is only applicable to phrasal conjunctive markers such as *jì* and *dí*. The choice of single or multiple marking is entirely dependent on the speaker. Examples (49a–b) and (50a–b), illustrate both types of coordinate marking:

(49) a. ánî   àdì   ìsèsé   jì   ádíɲá   gìè   ùnwógīē
        1SG   PN   PN   and   PN   eat   food
        'I, Adi, Isɛsɛ and Adinya ate food.'

b. ánî   jì   àdì   jì   ìsèsé   jì   ádíɲá   gìè   ùnwógīē
    1SG   and   PN   and   PN   and   PN   eat   food
    'I and Adi and Isɛsɛ and Adinya ate food.'

(50) a. ìɲànì   ká   kìɔ̀   ùnwógīē   gíé   ná   únâ   dí   lúū   ìdû
        PN   FUT   cook   food   eat   sleep   sleep   and   go   market
        'Inyani will cook food, eat, sleep and go to market.'

b. ìɲànì   ká   kìɔ̀   ùnwógīē   dí   gíé   dí   ná   únâ   dí   lúū   ìdû
    PN   FUT   cook   food   and   eat   and   sleep   sleep   and   go   market
    'Inyani will cook food and eat and sleep and go to market.'

5.3.6 Conclusion

Three types of coodinators have been described: conjunction markers, disjunction markers and the adversative marker. Etulo uses different conjunction markers for NPs, VPs and clauses. The conjunctions *jì/béjì* link NPs and are also used in comitative constructions; the conjunction *dí* mostly links VPs, while *mân* links clauses with different syntactic subjects. One major disjunction marker *náádí* is identified alongside its shortened variants: *ónā/náá*. As adversative marker, Etulo uses *kpàâ* 'but' which connects both VPs and clauses. From a typological viewpoint, it is evident that Etulo belongs to the category of *with-languages* (according to the terminology introduced by Stassen 2000), for it adopts the same marker for noun phrase conjunction and comitative phrases.

5.4 Subordination

In this section, I discuss the different types of subordinate clauses identified in Etulo. They include the complement clause (Section 5.4.1), the relative clause (Section 5.4.2), and the adverbial clauses (Section 5.4.3). I describe the structure of these subordinate constructions and the nature of the subordinators/markers associated with each of them. In Etulo, subordinate clauses are marked by special subordinating morphemes, one of which involves the grammaticalization of a verb.

5.4.1 Complement clause

A complement clause is a type of subordinate clause that fills an argument slot in the structure of another clause (cf. Dixon, 2010). In Etulo, the complement clause may function as the subject or object argument of the predicate. The three complementizers so far identified include: *gbĕɛ̄*, *dí*, and *dàfí*. They have the same grammatical function and are therefore often used interchangeably. There are, however, instances where they combine with each other as well as with other markers, such as *nì* and *ikíé* in the introduction of complement clauses. The time reference of the complement clause may differ from that of the main clause. Three major criteria have been used to define a complement clause in Etulo:

- the existence of a construction that comprises two clauses (a main and a dependent one);
- the dependent clause serves as the syntactic subject or the object argument of the main clause and is introduced by a complementizer;
- the complement clause has its own subject argument which always follows the complementizer.

So far, a limited set of verbs have been identified which take a complement clause. They include *fó* 'hear', *dí* 'see', *mà àkwɔ̀* 'cry', *gbúálú* 'decide', *tsɛ́wɛ́* 'think', *nù òjèjè* 'believe', *wɛ́* 'remember', *jé* 'know', *dífūī* 'observe/understand', *kwú ámbéɛ̀* 'notice', *gbɔ̀* 'talk', *ɲá* 'tell', *gbìlímɔ̌* 'forget', *kɪ̀ɔ̀ ìtíngá* 'be angry' etc. In the following subsections, I discuss the use of the three complementizers.

5.4.1.1 The complementizer *dí*

This section focuses on how the complementizer *dí* functions to introduce the dependent clause in an object argument position. The *dí* marker which occurs in the Etulo complement clause is identical in form and tone with the coordinator *dí* used in the linking of verb phrases (see Section 5.3.2.2). It is, however, obvious that these two markers occur in different syntactic constructions and perform different grammatical functions. The complementizer *dí* is a high tone marker which introduces the complement clause. As stated earlier, it is used interchangeably with the other two complementizers: *gbɛ̌ɛ̄* and *dàfí*. In many cases, it optionally combines with the complementizer *gbɛ̌ɛ̄* (see Section 5.4.1.5).

(51) a. á   ɲá   ánî   dí   ábû   bā
        3PL:SUBJ tell   1SG:OBJ COMP   2SG:SUBJ come
        'They told me that you came.'

   b. àdì tsɛ́wɛ́   dí   éjî   lè   ná   únâ
       PN   think   COMP 1PL:SUBJ PROG sleep sleep
       'Adi thought that we were sleeping.'

5.4.1.2 The complementizer *gbɛ̌ɛ̄*

The complementizer *gbɛ̌ɛ̄* derives from the speech verb *gbɛ̌ɛ̄* 'say'. This grammaticalization process may be seen as incomplete, considering that *gbɛ̌ɛ̄* occasionally takes an infinitive verb form *ò-gbɛ̌ɛ̄* 'to say' when introducing a complement clause in a subject argument position (see Section 5.4.1.5). I illustrate below the use of *gbɛ̌ɛ̄* as a complementizer. In all of the examples (52a–c), the complement clause fills the object slot.

(52) a. éjî   jé   gbɛ̌ɛ̄   á   kà   bá
        1PL:SUBJ know   COMP   3PL:SUBJ FUT   come
        'We know that they will come.'

   b. iɲànì   dí   gbɛ̌ɛ̄   ánî   kɪ̀ɔ̀   ìtíngā
       PN   see   COMP   1SG:SUBJ do   anger
       'Inyani saw that I am angry.'

   c. àdì   wé   gbɛ̌ɛ̄   ìsèsé   lì   ònwúnɔ́   ánî
       PN   remember   COMP   PN   COP   brother 1SG
       'Adi remembered that Isɛsɛ is my brother.'

5.4.1.3 The pairing of gbĕē and dí

Gbĕē and dí can optionally combine to introduce a complement clause. Either of them can be deleted without altering the meaning of the clause. The individual use of these two complementizers, as well as their joint use, makes up the equivalent of the English *that* complementizer. Consider the following examples:

(53) a. iɲànì   jé   gbĕē   dí   éjî   dí   ónwú   bá
        PN   know   COMP   COMP   1PL:SUBJ   see   3PL:SUBJ NEG
        'Inyani did not know that we saw him.'

   b. àdì   tsɛ́wɛ́   gbĕē   dí   éjî   lè   ná   únâ
      PN   think   COMP   COMP   1PL:SUBJ   PROG   sleep   sleep
      'Adi thought that we were sleeping.'

5.4.1.4 Pairing of gbĕē and nì

The combination of *gbĕē* and *nì* introduces a type of complement clause which expresses the potentiality of the subject of the complement clause to be involved in an activity or state. It yields a rough equivalent of the English *to* complement clause. Recall that in Etulo, the subject of the complement clause is directly preceded by the complementizers.

(54) a. ánî   mìná   gbĕē   nì   àdì   ʃí   áʃí
        1SG:SUBJ   want   COMP   SUBR   PN   sing   song
        'I want Adi to sing.'

   b. àdì   wó   iɲànì   òlà   gbĕē   nì   ò   lú   údɛ́
      PN   put   PN   law   COMP   SUBR   3SG:SUBJ   go   home
      'Adi ordered Inyani to go home.'

5.4.1.5 The complementizer dàfí

This morpheme has different grammatical functions.[8] As a complementizer, it directly precedes the complement clause and obligatorily co-occurs with the clause-final particle *mànì*. This is in contrast with the use of other complementizers for which no sentence-final particle is required. Its function is restricted to introducing the complement clause in an object argument position. It is also mostly compatible with stative predicates.

---

8   Besides its function as a complementizer, the morpheme *dàfí* serves as a subordinator which introduces a type of time adverbial clause (see Section 5.4.3.2). It is also used in a comparative manner adverbial clause.

(55) a. éjî   jé   dàfí   á   kà   bā   mànì
       1PL:SUBJ know   COMP   3PL:SUBJ FUT   come   PTCL
       'We know how they will come.'
    b. ìɲànì   dí   dàfí   ánî   kìɔ̀   ìtíngā mànì
       PN   see   COMP   1SG:SUBJ do   anger   PTCL
       'Inyani saw how angry I am.'

5.4.1.6 Complement clause in the subject argument position

Two major strategies are utilized in the realization of the complement clause in the subject argument position of cleft sentences: the pairing of *gběē* and *ìkíé* and the pairing of the infinitive form *ò-gběē* and *dí*.

The complementizer *gběē* pairs with the preposition *ikie* when introducing a complement clause in the subject argument position, as illustrated in (56a and 56b).[9] The verbs which allow the joint use of both markers within a complement clause include *gbìlímɔ̀* 'forget', *jí úmí* 'steal', *dí* 'see' etc. There are, however, some Etulo verbs that are clearly incompatible with the combination of these two markers as complementizers in the subject argument slot. Such verbs adopt an alternative strategy (see 57a–b). Example (56c) shows that the use of *gběē* and *ìkíé* as complementizers in a complement clause comprising the verb *nwɔ́* 'kill' results in ungrammaticality. Perhaps, *ìkíe gběē* requires non-eventive verbs (or at least non-fully eventive ones).

(56) a. ìkíé   gběē   àdì   gbìlímɔ́ gběē ánî   kwún   èlá   nê   tíʃí   bā
       COMP   COMP   PN   forget   COMP 1SG   call.3SG voice   this   be.good NEG
       'That Adi forgot I called him is not good.'
    b. ìkíé   gběē   ánî   dí   ìɲànì   ínɛ̆   nū   má   kìɔ̀   ìtíngā
       COMP   COMP   1SG:SUBJ   see   PN   eye   make   3PL:OBJ do   anger
       'That I saw Inyani made them angry.'
    c. *ìkíé   gběē   ábû   nwɔ́   àdì   lì   òtítí
       COMP   COMP   2SG:SUBJ   kill   PN   COP   truth
       'That you killed Adi is true.'

The infinitive form of the verb *gběē* combines with the complementizer *dí* to introduce a complement clause in the subject position. In (57a and 57b), the verbs *nwɔ́* 'kill' and *gbìlímɔ́* 'forget' are the predicates within the complement clause. For some verbs, the *ìkíé gběē* pair can be replaced by *ògběē dí* in a

---

9 The combination of these two markers has two other functions in Etulo: to introduce the adverbial clause of reason and the purpose clause in an argument slot (see Section 5.4.3). The morpheme *ikíé* independently functions as a preposition expressing reason (because of) and a benefactive meaning (see Chapter 4).

complement clause without triggering a change in meaning. This is the case of the verb *gbìlímɔ́* which is introduced by *ìkíé gbɛ̆ɛ̄* in (56a) and alternatively by *ògbɛ̆ɛ̄ dí* in (57b). On the contrary, the verb *nwɔ́* 'kill' bars the use of *ìkíé gbɛ̆ɛ̄* in (56c) but allows the use of *ògbɛ̆ɛ̄ dí* in (57a).

(57) a. ò-gbɛ̆ɛ̄ dí ábû nwɔ́ àdì lì òtítí
INF-say COMP 2SG kill PN COP truth
'That you killed Adi is true.'

b. ò-gbɛ̆ɛ̄ dí àdì gbìlímɔ́ èlâ nwú ánî kwún nê ì tíʃí bā
INF-say COMP PN forget voice REL 1SG call.3SG this 3SG be.good NEG
'That Adi forgot I called him is not good.'

5.4.1.7 Speech verbs

Three speech verbs can be identified in Etulo: *gbɛ̆ɛ̄* 'say', *ɲá* 'tell' and *gbɔ̀* 'talk/speak'. The speech verb *gbɛ̆ɛ̄* 'say' which is the base of one of the complementizers does not allow a complement clause introduced by *gbɛ̆ɛ̄*. In (58a) the verb *gbɛ̆ɛ̄* takes a complement clause introduced by *dí*. As indicated by the bracket, the use of the complementizer *dí* is not obligatory since its deletion does not alter the meaning of the construction. The use *gbɛ̆ɛ̄* in the complement clause of the speech verb *gbɛ̆ɛ̄* results in ungrammaticality (58b). On the contrary, the other two verbs *ɲá* 'tell' and *gbɔ̀* 'talk/speak' like other verbs are compabitble with complement clauses introduced by all of the complementizers (*dí*, *gbɛ̆ɛ̄* and *dàfì*) in the object argument slot. In contrast with the verb *gbɛ̆ɛ̄* 'say', the complementizer cannot be omitted with other speech verbs (see 59b and 60b). I illustrate the use of both verbs with the complementizer *gbɛ̆ɛ̄* in (59a and 60a).

(58) a. ùtɔ̀ gbɛ̆ɛ̄ (dí) àdì kà bā
king say COMP PN FUT come
'The king said Adi will come.'

b. *ùtɔ̀ gbɛ̆ɛ̄ gbɛ̆ɛ̄ àdì kà bā
king say COMP PN FUT come
'The king said Adi will come.'

(59) a. àdì gbɔ̀ gbɛ̆ɛ̄ ónwú jé má
PN talk COMP 3SG know 3PL:OBJ
'Adi said that he knows them.'

b. *àdì gbɔ̀ ónwú jé má
PN talk 3SG know 3PL:OBJ
'Adi said that he knows them.'

(60) a. á   ɲá   ánî   gběē   ábû   bā
         3PL:SUBJ tell 1SG   COMP   2SG:SUBJ   come
         'They told me that you came.'

     b. *á   ɲá   ánî   ábû   bā
         3PL:SUBJ tell 1SG   2SG:SUBJ   come
         'They told me that you came.'

5.4.2 The relative clause

A relative clause is a subordinate clause which delimits the reference of an NP by specifying the role of its referent in the given situation. Etulo makes no grammatical distinction between restrictive and unrestrictive relative clause. Since no such distinction is made, I only provide examples of the restrictive type, pointing out its distinguishing features such as: position within a NP, relative clause-final particles, semantic and syntactic features of the relativizers and the relative pronouns. The relative clause is mainly marked by two relativizers: *nwí* and *nwú*. It may also be marked by the relative pronouns *ònwí* and *ònwú*, as well as the high tone syllabic nasal *ŋ́*.

5.4.2.1 Syntactic and semantic functions of the relativizers

The relativizers *nwú* and *nwí* are respectively characterized by the feature [+ human] and [-human], as shown in (61–64). The two relative markers are occasionally substituted by the relative pronouns *ònwú* and *ònwí* (see Section 5.4.2.3). The head of the relative clause can be a subject, an object, an indirect object, and a possessor.

(61) ánî   jé   ònwè   òngìùlô nwú   kíé   m̀tsà   gíé   mànì
     1SG:SUBJ know   child man   REL   take   mango   eat   the
     'I know the boy who ate the mango.'

(62) òngìùlô nwú   ánî   lé   gbò   ódzé   mà   lì   èmúmì
     man   REL   1SG:SUBJ PROG   talk   talk   the   COP   thief
     'The man that I was talking to is a thief.'

(63) òngìâ   nwú   ònwàn   kwúlú   mà   ánî   dún
     woman   REL   child.3SG   die   the   1SG:SUBJ see.3SG
     'I saw the woman whose child died.'

(64) àfè   nwí   ábû   nū   ánî   nê   lì   ògbùgbè
     book   REL   2SG:SUBJ   give   1SG:OBJ this   COP   old
     'This book that you gave me is old.'

The homorganic high tone syllabic nasal *ŋ́* can replace the two main markers to introduce a relative clause. Whether this marker is derived from *nwi* and *nwu* remains unclear. It is however obvious that it has a restricted usage. In example (66) for instance, its use results in ungrammaticality possibly because of some phonological factors. Further investigation will ascertain the context in which this marker is preferably used.

(65) ání jé ònwè ń kà gíé m̀tsà nâ mànì
1SG:SUBJ know child REL FUT eat mango that the
'I know the child who will eat that mango.'

(66) * ánî dí àfè ń ábû gíá mànì
1SG:SUBJ see book REL 2SG buy the
'I saw the book that you bought.'

5.4.2.2 Position of the relative clause

The Etulo relative clause is externally headed. With respect to the head, the relative clause is postnominal. In other words, it is directly preceded by the head, which is usually a noun or pronoun. Any attempt to inverse this order results in ungrammaticality. The relative clause modifies the head in both the subject and object argument positions (67a–b).

(67) a. iɲànì nwú lì ìnwíndà nâ bā m̀mènénǐ
PN REL COP beauty that come here
'That Inyani, who is beautiful, came here.'

b. ánî dí iɲànì nwú lì ìnwíndà
1SG see PN REL COP beautiful
'I saw Inyani, who is beautiful.'

5.4.2.3 A note on the relative pronoun

The two relative pronouns (ònwú and ònwí) attested in Etulo are derived from the two relative markers by the prefixation of a low tone vowel o-. In a relative clause, both relative pronouns perform the dual function of a pronominal and a relative marker. Just like the head noun of a relative clause, the relative pronoun is modified by the definite article mànì 'the', which usually occurs in the clause-final position of a relative clause. The relative pronouns can replace the head noun and the relative marker in a relative clause. This is evident when one compares examples (18a) with (68b) and (69a) with (69b). In both cases, the relative pronoun ònwú substitutes ŋgìsé nwú 'person that' while ònwí substitutes ùnwɔ́ nwí 'thing that'.

(68) a. éjî dí ònwú gíé éjî ùnwógīē mànì
1PL:SUBJ see REL.P eat 1PL food the
'We saw who ate our food.' (Lit: 'We saw the one who ate our food.')

b. éjî dí ǹgísè̀ nwú gíé éjî ùnwógīē mànì
1PL:SUBJ see person REL eat 1PL food the
'We saw who ate our food.' (Lit: 'We saw the person who ate our food.')

(69) a. ánî gíá ònwí ánî mìná mànì
1SG:SUBJ buy REL.P 1SG want the
'I bought what I want.' (Lit: 'I bought the one I want.')

b. ánî gíá ùnwô nwí ánî mìná mànì
1SG:SUBJ buy thing REL 1SG want the
'I bought what I want.' (Lit: 'I bought the thing that I want.')

The relative pronouns may also co-occur with the head noun in a relative clause. In such instances, they serve as the relative markers and introduce the relative clause. In (70), the head noun òngìâ 'woman' is directly followed by the relative pronoun ònwú while in (71), the head noun m̀dà 'cow' is followed by ònwí.

(70) ánî dí òngìâ ònwú tá òngìùlɔ́ àfè
1SG:SUBJ see woman REL.P hit man slap
'I saw a woman who slapped a man.'

(71) ánî dí m̀dà ònwí àdì ʃé ŋà
1SG:SUBJ see cow REL.P PN be.big surpass
'I saw a cow that Adi is bigger than.'

5.4.2.4 The relative clause-final morphemes

The relative clause-final morphemes comprise determiners including the definite article *mà* and the demonstratives *nâ* 'that', and *nê* 'this'. The head noun of the relative clause is usually modified by these markers, showing that the relative clause has the shape of a determinate NP with an embedded clause. There are, however, few instances where the NP is indeterminate (70–71). In any determinate NP involving the Etulo relativizers, the determiner is separated from the relativized head by other constituents. Its position is clause-final. An alternation is observed in the form of these clause-final articles. When the relative clause precedes the main clause, the markers are realized as *mâ, nâ* or *nê*. In contrast, when the relative clause is preceded by the main clause, the markers are realized as *mànì, nánǐ* or *néní.*[10] This alternation in form is, however, not a peculiar feature of their use in the relative clause, but rather a general feature of articles and demonstratives in the grammar of Etulo (see Section 4.1.7).

5.4.3 The adverbial clause

In the following subsections, I discuss six adverbial clauses in Etulo. They include the adverbial clause of cause, manner, time, purpose, condition and concession.

5.4.3.1 The causal clause

A causal adverbial clause states the motivation for a given action or state. In Etulo, this clause is marked in two ways: by the subordinate morpheme *ìkékíé* or the *ìkíé-gběē* pair. The subordinator *ìkékíé* is exclusively used when the causal clause is preceded by the main clause (72a–b), and vice versa for the *ìkíé-gběē* pair (73). An exchange in the usage of these markers, (*ìkékíé* and *ìkíé-gběē*) yields ungrammatical constructions.

(72) a. ánî jèdɔ́ ìkékíé nénê lì ùdé ḿgbí ánî
       1SG:SUBJ return SUBR this COP house POSS 1SG
       'I returned because this is my house.'

   b. àdì fúá ò-kpà ìkékíé ò dzè jì údzà bá
      PN refuse PREF-pay SUBR 3SG:SUBJ COP with money NEG
      'Adi refused to pay because he had no money.'

(73) ìkíé gběē àdì gbó òmbàdí èwó nê ò kà ké
     because COMP PN fail to.test body this 3SG:SUBJ FUT go
     ùmákárántá bá
     school NEG
     'Because Adi failed the exam, he will not go to school.'

5.4.3.2 Time adverbial clause

A time adverbial clause expresses the temporal relationship existing between two events. In Etulo, this clause type is marked by single words such as *dúúséè* 'before', *ɔ̀nɔ̀*

---

10 There are instances where the morpheme *mànì* occurs in sentence-final position but not as a nominal modifier. Its specific meaning is still unclear in such constructions. Its use is illustrated in the following example:

(i) éjî jé dàfí á kà bá mànì
    1PL:SUBJ know COMP 3PL:SUBJ FUT come PTCL
    'We know that they will come.'

'time' and *dàfí* 'as'. Some temporal adverbial clauses have a relative clause structure that features a combination of the noun *ɔ̀nɔ̀* 'time' and the relative marker *nwí*.

The subordinator *dúúséè* 'before' is used to mark temporal clauses that correspond to the English *before* and *after* clauses (74–75). This subordinator may alternate with its shortened form *see* 'before'. Etulo has no direct equivalent of the subordinator 'after'.[11] As an example, the English clause *They slept after eating* would be realized in Etulo by the use of the verb *ǹgíé* 'finish' and *dúúséè* 'before'. The event of eating is described as having ended before the event of sleeping. The invariable order is main clause followed by dependent clause.

(74) a. éjî   jé   àdì   nwɔ́n   dúúséè ábû   ɲá   éjî
        1PL:SUBJ know   PN   kill.3SG before 2SG:SUBJ tell   1PL:OBJ
        'We knew Adi killed her before you told us.'

    b. ó   ná   únâ   dúúséè ó   giè   ùnwógīē
        3SG:SUBJ sleep   sleep before 3SG:SUBJ eat   food
        'He slept before he ate food.'

(75) á   gīē   ùnwógīē ǹgīē   dúúséè ná   únâ
        3PL:SUBJ eat   food   finish before sleep sleep
        'He finished eating food before sleeping./He slept after eating.'

In expressing temporal reference, three other subordinators may introduce an adverbial clause: *ɔ̀nɔ̀*, *nwí* and *ɔ̀nɔ̀ nwí*. The subordinators *ɔ̀nɔ̀* and *ɔ̀nɔ̀ nwí* translate 'when', while *nwí* translates 'when' and 'as'. The temporal clause introduced by these markers may precede or be preceded by the main clause. When it is preceded by the main clause as in (76a and 76b), the subordinators, *ɔ̀nɔ̀* and *ɔ̀nɔ̀ nwí* are used interchangeably. If, on the other hand, the temporal clause precedes the main clause, the subordinator *nwí* and *ɔ̀nɔ̀ nwí* are used interchangeably (77a and 77b). In this context, however, native speakers prefer the use of *ɔ̀nɔ̀ nwí* (rather than *nwí*) to avoid ambiguity. Their preference is attributed to the fact that two semantic interpretations (*when* and *as*) are possible with *nwí* in such position or context.

(76) a. àdì   ʃá   íʃá   ɔ̀nɔ̀   nwí   í   kíɔ́   mànì
        PN   laugh laugh   time   REL   3SG:SUBJ do   the
        'Adi laughed when it happened.'

---

11 An alternative way of realizing the English *after* clause is by using the verb *ǹgíé* and the adverbial *ɔ̀nɔ̀ nwí*. In the following example, the event of singing is described as having ended before the event of playing.

(i) ánî   lɛ́   ólē   ɔ̀nɔ̀   nwí   ánî   ʃí   áʃí   ǹgīē   mànì
    1SG:SUBJ play play   time REL   1SG:SUBJ sing   song   finish DET
    'I played when I finished singing/I played after I sang.'

	b.	á	tsán	ɔ̀nɔ̀	ó	lè	tsɛ́	ɔ̀ɲà	mànì
		3PL:SUBJ	shoot.3SG:OBJ	time	3SG:SUBJ	PROG	run	race	the

'They shot him when he was running.'

(77) a. nwí ánî dí iɲànì ò lé gbɔ̀ òdzé pléplé
     SUBR 1SG:SUBJ see PN 3SG:SUBJ PROG talk talk fast
     'When I saw Inyani, she was speaking very fast.'

   b. ɔ̀nɔ̀ nwí ánî dí iɲànì ò lé gbɔ̀ òdzé pléplé
      time REL 1SG:SUBJ see PN 3SG:SUBJ PROG talk talk fast
      'When I saw Inyani, she was speaking very fast.'

To indicate that a sub-event occurs simultaneously with the main event, two subordinators are used: *nwí* 'as' and *dàfí* 'as'. When a temporal clause is introduced by *nwí*, it may be preceded by the main clause. An inversion of this order is however possible (see 78a–c). With the subordinate marker *dàfí*, the main clause obligatorily precedes the temporal adverbial clause (79). An inversion of the order is not possible.

(78) a. àdì dí iɲànì nwí ó lúū mànì
     PN see PN SUBR 3SG:SUBJ go PTCL
     'Adi saw Inyani as she left.'

   b. á tsān nwí ò lè fá ájàtù mànì
      3PL:SUBJ shoot.3SG:OBJ SUBR 3SG:SUBJ PROG drive car PTCL
      'They shot her as she drove off.'

   c. nwí ò fá ájàtù lúū èmúmí mà tsán
      SUBR 3SG:SUBJ drive car go thief the shoot.3SG:OBJ
      'As she drove off, the thieves shot her.'

(79) àdì dí iɲànì dàfí ò lè lúū údē
     PN see PN SUBR 3SG:SUBJ PROG go home
     'Adi saw Inyani as she was going home.'

5.4.3.3 The conditional clause

The Etulo conditional clause is characterized by the high tone marker *ní* and the clause-final particle *jɔ́*. [12] This clause may precede or follow the main clause. The

---

12   Some Etulo speakers use the form nú interchangeably as conditional marker in conjunction with the clause-final particle *jɔ́*. A conditional clause introduced by *nu* either precedes the main clause or follows it. The following examples are illustrative:

(i)   nú má bā jɔ́ éjî kà gíé
      if 3PL:OBJ come PTCL 1PL:SUBJ FUT eat
      'If they come we will eat.'

(ii) éjî kà gíé nú má bā jɔ́
      1PL:SUBJ FUT eat if 3PL come PTCL
      'We will eat if they come.'

subordinator *ní* introduces both the factual conditional clause in (80a–b) and the counterfactual conditional clause in (81a–b).

(80) a.
ní	á	bā	jɔ̄	éjî	kà	gíé
if	3PL:SUBJ	come	PTCL	1PL:SUBJ	FUT	eat

'If they come we will eat.'

b.
éjî	kà	gíé	ní	á	bā	jɔ̄
1PL:SUBJ	FUT	eat	if	3PL:SUBJ	come	PTCL

'We will eat if they come.'

(81) a.
ní	ábû	kí	kà	bā	jó	éjî	kí	kà	ké	ùmákárántá
if	2SG:SUBJ	MOD	FUT	come	PTCL	1PL	MOD	FUT	go	school

'If you had come we would have gone to school.'

b.
éjî	kí	kà	ké	ùmákárántá	ní	ábû	kí	kà	bā	jó
1PL:SUBJ	MOD	FUT	go	school	if	2SG:SUBJ	MOD	FUT	come	PTCL

'We would have gone to school if you had come.'

Etulo has a type of concessive conditional clause which is marked by the conditional marker *ní* and a repetition of the verb root.

(82) a.
ń	kà	bá	bá	ní	ábû	kwú	kwú	ánî	èlâ
1SG:SUBJ	FUT	come	NEG	if	2SG:SUBJ	call	RED	1SG:OBJ	voice

'I will not come even if you call me.'

b.
ní	ábû	kwú	kwú	ánî	èlâ	ń	kà	bá	bá
if	2SG:SUBJ	call	RED	1SG:OBJ	voice	1SG:SUBJ	FUT	come	NEG

'Even if you call me I will not come.'

5.4.3.4 The purpose clause

The purpose clause expresses the motivation of an event which is still unrealized at the time of the main event. This clause type is marked by a string of three morphemes, namely: *ìkíé*, *gbɛ̌ɛ̄* and *nì*.[13] A combination of these three morphemes loosely translates as 'so that' or 'in order to'. The main clause must precede the dependent clause. Their respective position cannot be reversed. Consider the following examples:

---

13 The *ìkíé* marker can independently introduce the purpose clause if its covert subject is shared by the main clause.

(i)
àdì	kìɔ̀	ùnwógīē	ìkíé	ò-gíé
PN	cook	food	in.order	INF-eat

'Adi cooked in order to eat.'

(83) a. àdì kɨ̀ɔ ìdɔ̀ kpákpá ìkíé gbɛ̌ɛ̄ nì ónwú jɛ̌ álūdù
       PN do work INT SUBR COMP MOD 3SG:SUBJ become wealth
       'Adi worked very hard so that he became rich.'
   b. àdì kíé fálū òkwɔ̀ ìkíé gbɛ̌ɛ̄ nì ónwú kīē ètò kíà
       PN take clear farm SUBR COMP MOD 3SG:SUBJ take seed plant
       'Adi cleared the farm so that he can plant seed.'

5.4.3.5 Adverbial clause of manner

The manner clause expresses the way or manner in which an event is carried out. It answers the question *how*. The Etulo adverbial clause of manner is marked by the subordinate marker *dàfí*. It corresponds to English 'like/as' and has multiple functions. In examples (84a and 84b), the manner clause is introduced by *dàfí* and is preceded by the main clause.

(84) a. kíé   ònwè èjéjí nê   dàfí   ánî̀   ɲá   ábû   mànì
       carry child blood this SUBR 1SG:SUBJ tell 2SG PTCL
       'Carry this baby like I told you.'
   b. á   kɨ̀ɔ   ánî̀   ùnwógīē dàfí òtsètsé gbɔ̀   mànì
       3PL:SUBJ cook 1SG food SUBR teacher talk PTCL
       'They cooked food for me like the teacher said.'

5.4.3.6 The concessive clause

The concessive clause expresses an event that is in some way contrary to the event expressed by the main clause. The concessive clause in Etulo is realized by a combination of two markers: the subordinate marker *nwí* and the adversative marker *kpàâ* 'but'. Their combination translate as 'although/even though'. The *nwí* marker introduces the concessive clause while *kpàâ* occurs in the clause-final position. The concessive clause precedes the main clause. The following examples are illustrative:

(85) a. nwí   ánî̀   gbɔ̀ òtsítsí kpàâ ónɔ́   ánî̀ gbó ánî̀ ònìtsé
       SUBR 1SG:SUBJ talk truth but mother 1SG beat 1SG:OBJ cane
       'Even though I told the truth my mother flogged me.'
   b. nwí ànwúntò ŋ́gbí ánî̀ ʃímbī kpàâ ò sá má bá
       SUBR cloth POSS 1SG be.dirty but 3SG:SUBJ wash 3PL:OBJ NEG
       'Even though my clothes were dirty she did not wash them'

5.4.4 Conclusion

Etulo allows both subject and object complement clauses. It has two declarative complementizers for object clauses, *gbə̌ə̄* and *dí*. Both complementizers may occur independently or together. Complement clauses can also be introduced by *dàfí*, which requires a clause-final article *mànì*. For some predicates, subject complement clauses are introduced by a combination of *ìkíé* and *gbə̌ə̄*. The infinitive form of the grammaticalized complementizer *ò-gbə̌ə̄*, is also used to introduce subject clauses. Relative clauses are introduced by the relative markers *nwú* [+human] and *nwí* [-human]. Both relativizers can occasionally be substituted by the relative pronouns *onwu* and *onwi*. Relative clauses are post nominal and are externally headed.

5.5 The copula construction

This section discusses the characterization of the Etulo copula. Three copulas have been identified: *lì* 'be', *lè* 'be' and the existential copula *dzè* 'be there'. A copula verb is often analyzed as a dummy element or as being semantically empty, in practice serving as support for the TAM (tense-aspect-mood) markers (Hengeveld 1992). This is certainly appropriate for the *lì* and *lè* copulas, but not for the *dzè* copula.

In some languages, copula constructions consist of a verb that links a subject (NP) with a predicate complement, which can be a noun phrase, an adjective and a clause. The semantics of a copula construction may be predicational or specificational. According to Declerck (1988: 55), 'A specificational sentence is one whose semantic function is to specify a value for a variable. In contrast, a predicational sentence rather predicates a property of the subject NP.' Declerck also proposes a further distinction between the specificational type and similar sentence types such as the identificational and identity statements. However, the latter appears to be a specifically pragmatic use of the former. Identity statements express a relation of identity between two entities. It may be paraphrased as NP_1 is the same as NP_2 in a referential way.

In this work, the terms 'inclusive' and 'identifying' are used to characterize the functions of copula constructions in place of Declerck's 'predicational' and 'specificational' proposition. The inclusive function predicates the inclusion of the referent into a set characterized by a specific property, while the identifying function predicates the substantial identity of two alternative designations of a given referent. The constituents of a copula construction are usually subject, copula and complement. The identified Etulo copulas are characterized as verbal. They are compatible TAM markers and have the morphological form of the verb, that is, they take the infinitive prefix much like Etulo verbs. A description of the three copulas is given below.

5.5.1 The copula *lì*

The *lì* copula is a low tone morpheme that establishes a link between an NP subject and its complement (a noun, noun phrase or adjective). The *lì* copula lacks a semantic content. It assigns value to the NP subject in an identifying sentence (86a–b) and assigns a specific property to the NP subject in an inclusive sentence (87a–c). Etulo makes no formal distinction between the identifying and inclusive sentence types. In examples (86–87), the *lì* copula functions as a linking element between the NP subject and the complements which are realized as nouns and adjectives. Identifying copula constructions in Etulo serve as answers to the question, *who is X?*, while inclusive copula constructions answer the question, *what is X?*

(86) a. ótsó   ánî   lì   ùtɔ̀
        father   1SG:POSS   COP   chief
        'My father is a chief.'

     b. àdì   lì   èmúmī   mànì
        PN   COP   thief   the
        'Adi is the thief.'

     c. àdì   lì   íngíú
        PN   COP   PN
        'Adi is Ingyu.'

(87) a. ànwúntò   ḿgbí   ánî   lì   óndzúndzé
        cloth   POSS   1SG   COP   white
        'My cloth is white.'

     b. àjàtù   nâ   lì   ófúfê
        car   that   COP   new
        'That car is new.'

The copula *lì* allows subject pro-drop (88). It takes the low tone nominalizing vowel prefix *o-* in its infinitive form just like Etulo verbs (89a). It also cooccurs with the temporal markers such as *nose* 'before' and the future marker *ká* (89b–c).

(88)   lì   àbá   óbūē   ò-lá-lā
        COP   teeth   dog   NOM-bite-RED
        'It is a dog bite.'

(89) a. ánî   mìná   ò-lì   ìnwíndà
        1SG:SUBJ   want   INF-COP   beauty
        'I want to be beautiful.'

	b.	ánî	lì	ìnwíndà	nósē
		1SG:SUBJ	COP	beauty	before
		'I was beautiful.'			
	c.	ò	ká	lì	ìnwíndà
		3SG:SUBJ	FUT	COP	beauty
		'I will be beautiful.'			

There are instances where the *lì* copula may be replaced with the morpheme *dí*. Such replacement is only possible in copula constructions where the proper name or identity of an individual is specified. Further investigation is needed on the characterization of the *dí* morpheme in copula constructions. Consider the following examples:

(90)	a.	ìjí	ánî	lì	ìɲànì
		name	1SG	COP	PN
		'My name is Inyani.'			
	b.	ìjí	ánî	dí	ìɲànì
		name	1SG	COP	PN
		'My name is Inyani.'			

5.5.2 The semi copula *dzè*

The low tone morpheme *dzè* is a verb that realizes a variety of meanings. It expresses a locative/existential meaning, a possessive meaning and a lexical meaning 'stay/live'. As a locative, it answers the question 'where is X'? Unlike the *lì* copula, *dzè* has a semantic content, hence it is not a copula in the true sense of this word. One might call it a semi-copula. Examples (91–93) illustrate the nuances of meaning associated with *dzè*. In (91), *dzè* functions as a locative indicating the location of the NP subject. An existential meaning is expressed in (92) by *dzè* in combination with the particle *mà*. In (93), *dzè* expresses the lexical meaning 'live/stay'. The English translations in (91–93) might suggest an ambiguity in the semantic reading of *dzè*. For instance, two interpretations are possible (91): 'Adi is here' or 'Adi stays/lives here', and an alternative interpretation of (93) would be 'I am with my mother'. Note, however, that for the native speakers, this is mere vagueness.

(91)	àdì	dzè	m̀mènénî
	PN	COP	here
	'Adi is here.'		
(92)	ìmgbàʃò	dzè	mà
	god	COP	DET
	'There is a God.'		

(93) ánî   dzè   jì   ónɔ́   ánî
      1SG:SUBJ live/stay with   mother 1SG
      'I live/stay with my mother.'

When *dzè* expresses a locative meaning, it agrees in number with the NP subject. If the NP subject is a singular noun or pronoun, the locative *dzè* is obligatorily used, but may be replaced by the suppletive form *tó* when the subject is plural (94 and 95).¹⁴

(94)   ánî   dzè   m̀mènénǐ
         1SG:SUBJ COP   here
         'I am here.'

(95) a. á   tō   ùmákúrdí
         3PL:SUBJ LOC:PL   PN
         'They are in Makurdi.'

     b. á   dzè   ùmákúrdí
         3PL:SUBJ COP   PN
         'They are in Makurdi.'

Etulo lacks a verb corresponding to the English verb of possession *have*. To express possession, a combination of the semi-copula *dzè* and the preposition *jì* is used.

(96) a. éjî   dzè   jì   óbūē
         1PL:SUBJ COP   with   dog
         'We have a dog./We own a dog.'

---

14 The suppletive number distinction/agreement associated with the locative verb/ semi-copula (*dzè tó*) is also observed in complex predicates that denote the location or position of an object. In the examples below, the complex predicate involves a combination of the verb *wó* 'put' and the locatives *dzè* and *tó*. In (i), *wó+dzè* agrees with the singular NP subject in number while *wótō* agrees with the plural NP subject in (ii). In this context, Etulo depends on the predicate rather than the subject for the indication of number. Note that the tone of these locatives changes in a complex predicate. The tone of *dzè* changes from low to a mid tone, while that of *tó* changes from high to a mid tone. The occurrence of a preposition in these constructions is optional, as indicated by the brackets.

(i)   àfè   wó-dzē   (mì)   ígbé
      book   put-LOC:SG   in   bag
      'A book is in a bag/ There is a book in a bag.'

(ii) àfè   wó-tō   (mì)   ígbé
      book   put-LOC:PL   in   bag
      'There are books in a bag.'

	b.	ìɲànì	dzè	jì	àfè		
		PN	COP	with	book		
		'Inyani has a book./Inyani owns a book.'					

Just like other Etulo stative verbs, *dzè* has a default present reading but may assume a past reading in appropriate contexts. In examples (97a and 97b), the time adverbial *téjî* disambiguates the present and past temporal reference of *dzè*. It co-occurs with the preverbal future marker in (97c). The *dzè* semi-copula is compatible with the habitual marker *lí* but hardly with the progressive marker. In the few instances where it occurs with the progressive marker, a future rather than a progressive meaning is realized.

(98)	a.	àdì	dzè	ùmákúrdí			
		PN	COP	PN			
		'Adi is in Makurdi.'					
	b.	ánî	téjî	dzè	ùmákúrdí		
		1SG:SUBJ	before	COP	PN		
		'I was in Makurdi.'					
	c.	ánî	kà	dzè	m̀mànánǐ		
		1SG:SUBJ	FUT	COP	there		
		'I will be there.'					
	d.	ó	lí	dzè	m̀mènê	àlí	ɔ̀nɔ̀	dúú
		3SG:SUBJ	HAB	COP	here	every	time	all
		'He is always here.'					

A summary of the semantics of *dzè* is highlighted in the diagram below.[15]

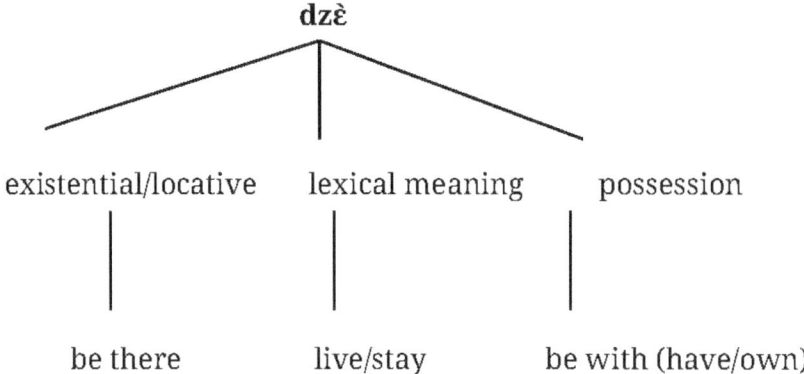

Fig. 5.1 A summary of the semantics of *dzè*. Drawn by the author (2025)

---

15 The sketch above does not necessarily include all the possible denotations of the verb *dzè* in Etulo. It rather focuses on a set of semantic interpretations of this verb that seem interrelated or linked to the notion of *being* in its broadest sense.

5.5.3 The copula *lè*

The *lè* copula is a low tone morpheme which links the subject NP with a complement. The complement is usually an ideophone which describes or assigns a specific property to the subject NP in a predicational sentence (99a–b). Just like the *lì* copula, the *lè* copula is semantically empty. Even though both copulas share similar features, both occur in mutually exclusive contexts. The *lè* copula also takes the low tone nominalizing prefix as illustrated in (100).

(99) a. ànwúntò ḿgbí ánî lè plédédé
cloth POSS 1SG COP IDEO (white)
'My cloth is very white.'

b. àdi lè léŋgéléŋgé
PN COP IDEO (slim)
'Adi is slim.'

(100) àdì mìná ò-lè léŋgéléŋgé
PN want INF-COP IDEO (slim)
'Adi wants to be slim.'

From the foregoing, one can deduce that all identified copulas in Etulo are verbal; just like verbs, they take the nominalizing low tone prefix and are compatible with TMA markers.

5.5.4 Conclusion

To summarize, Etulo has two verbal copulas: *lì* and *lè* plus the locative/existential semi-copula *dzè*, also used in possessive constructions. The copula *lì* can be used in both 'inclusive' and 'identifying' clauses. It allows subject pro-drop. The locative/existential verb has the singular *dzè* and the plural *tó* forms that agree with the subject. The copula le occurs with ideophone predicates. These three lexemes may take the nominalizing *o-* prefix and may co-occur with TAM particles.

5.6 Constituent order

One of the common means of the typological classification of languages is based on word and constituent order in the sentence, clause and phrase. The term 'basic word order', as often used, refers to the preferred word order of a language. Word order typology feeds the idea that one could make correlations or predictions on the features of a language based on word order characteristics. For instance, one could predict that languages with VSO (verb-subject-object) order are prepositional or that in languages with prepositions, the genitive tends to follow the governing noun, while in languages with postpositions, it almost always precedes. This is captured in Greenberg's implicational universals. In his work on word order typology, Greenberg (1963) identifies three language types; SVO, SOV, VSO and describes the other three possibilities (VOS, OVS, OSV) as being rare. In more recent studies, these rare types have been attested in a few languages. There are also languages that have a variable word order, i.e. without a predominant or preferred word order. Dryer (2005) identifies 172 such languages. In German, the order is SVO in main clauses without an auxiliary, but VSO in subordinate clauses without an auxiliary (Nebel 1948 in Dryer 2005). Similarly, in Miya (a Chadic language spoken in Nigeria), both SVO and VOS are found in main clauses, while in subordinate and relative clauses, only the VOS word order is attested (cf. Schuh 1998). In many Niger Congo languages, the predominant word order is SVO. Heine (2008) observes that the proportion of languages with SVO constituent order is much higher in Africa than globally. It is the word order of approximately 71% of African languages. SOV order, though less common, is attested in some Niger Congo languages like Mande, Dogon and Tegem (cf. Williamson & Blench 2000, Heine 1976).

In the following subsections, I examine the order of constituents in basic sentences (declarative and interrogative constructions), possessive/genitive constructions, phrases (noun phrase, preposition phrase and verb phrase), relative clause and comparative construction. I also comment on how the Etulo word order conforms to cross-linguistic generalizations on word order correlations.

5.6.1 Basic order of subject, object and verb

The basic order of constituents in a sentence is determined by the position of the subject, object and verb in relation to each other. The terms 'subject' and 'object' are often used in a syntactic sense, or semantically to refer to agent-like and patient-like arguments in a transitive construction. Recall that, as described in Section 4.3.2, the semantically intransitive constructions in Etulo may allow a complement (mostly a noun) in what would be the syntactic object position in a transitive clause. The order of constituents in intransitive constructions may thus be SVO if the noun complement of the verb is taken as a syntactic object. In other words, semantically intransitive constructions in Etulo may contain not only the subject and the verb, but also a noun complement. Etulo exhibits a rigid SVO pattern in the ordering of constituents in a sentence. The grammatical function of the arguments is not morphosyntactically marked. Word order is therefore crucial in establishing the argument functions. An alternate ordering in a sentence brings about a meaning change.[16] In transitive and intransitive constructions, the verb is preceded by the subject and followed by the object (see 100a and 100b). Note however, that some semantically intransitive constructions do not require a noun complement in the object slot as illustrated in (100c). In both declarative (see 100a–d) and interrogative sentences (see 101a and 101b), the SV(O) order is maintained. Contrary to the VO-OV word order alternation attested in many Niger Congo languages, (as conditioned by finiteness or temporal aspectual properties), finite or aspectual constructions do not affect the basic SVO order in Etulo. By contrast, in the relevant Niger Congo languages, the presence of TAM auxiliaries in a sentence leads to a change in word order, from SVO to S- AUX-OV (cf. Aboh 2004, Zeller 2011, Marchese 1986). All Etulo tense-aspect morphemes directly precede the verb, except for the perfect marker which mostly occurs in sentence-final position.

(100) a. éjî   nwɔ́   m̀dà   SVO
          1PL:SUBJ   kill   cow
          'We killed a cow.'

      b. àdì   ʃá   íʃá   SVO
          PN   laugh   laugh(n)
          'Adi laughed.'

      c. ádíɲá   kwúlú   wà   SV
          PN   die   PERF
          'Adi has died.'

      d. àdì   lè   gbɔ́   ódzân   SVO
          PN   PROG   read   about.3SG:OBJ
          'Adi read about it.'

---

16 A deviant order of constituents is however, observed with predicates such as *kpā* 'like/love', which belongs to the set of the so-called *psych*-verb that have a notoriously peculiar behaviour cross-linguistically. A declarative sentence with this verb shows an order where the perceived object precedes the verb yielding an OVS order. The stimulus argument occurs in the preverbal position while the experiencer argument occurs in the postverbal position (i). A reversal of the order of the constituents gives a different meaning (ii):

(i) ìɲànì   kpā   àdì   OVS   (ii) àdì   kpā   ìɲànì   OVS
     PN   like   PN   PN   like   PN
     'Adi likes Inyani.'   'Inyani like Adi.'

Other psychological verbs such as *mìò* 'fear', instead, maintain the basic SVO word order, while a flexible word order is observable with some stative verbs such as *kìɔ̀ ìtíngā* 'be angry', *dɔ́ ótsē* 'be sick'. For example:

(iii) àdì   lé   kìɔ̀   ìtíngā   (iv) ìtíngā   lé   kìɔ̀   àdì
      PN   PROG   do   anger   anger   PROG   do   PN
      'Adi is feeling angry.'   'Adi is feeling angry.'

(101)	a.	ábû	gìè	ùnwógīē	ínēè?		SVO
		2SG:SUBJ	eat	food	today.Q		
		'Did you eat food today?'					
	b.	ò	kà	kìɔ̀	ùnwógīèè?		SVO
		3SG:SUBJ	FUT	cook	food.Q		
		'Can you cook (food)?'					

5.6.2 Order of tense-aspect particles relative to the verb

Tense-aspect particles which are similar to auxiliaries may either precede or follow the verb in languages where they are present. According to Dryer (2006), they tend to precede the verb in both OV and VO languages, but follow the verb slightly more often in OV languages. He, however, notes that the correlation between verb-particle and OV word order is weak. His claim coincides to some extent with Greenberg's proposition on the order of TA auxiliaries in relation to the verb. Greenberg (1963) proposes that SOV languages have their auxiliary following the verb, while verb-initial languages have the main verb following their auxiliary. In Etulo, tense-aspect particles (the future *ká*, habitual *lì* and progressive *lè* morphemes), with the exception of the perfect morpheme *wà*, consistently precede the verb, giving the order: particle-verb (102–104). In the case of serial verb constructions, where more than one verb integrates the predicate, the progressive particle may precede the first or second verb (105a)-(105b). Either way, the Etulo order of tense-aspect particles coincides with the postulation of Dryer (2006) on the correlation between VO and the order of tense aspect auxiliaries in relation to the verb.

(102)		á	kà	kíé	ìkínākpà	tsé	ɔ̀nɔ̀
		3PL:SUBJ	FUT	take	maize	spread	sun
		'They will dry the maize.'					
(103)		àdì	lè	ʃí	áʃí		
		PN	PROG	sing	song		
		'Adi is singing a song.'					
(104)		ò	lí	ná	úná	mì	ákwúló
		3SG:SUBJ	HAB	sleep	sleep	on	bed
		'She sleeps on the bed.'					
(105)	a.	àdì	lè	kíé	ànwúntò	ṁgbán	gīā
		PN	PROG	take	cloth	POSS:3SG	sell
		'Adi is selling his clothes.'					
	b.	àdì	kíé	ànwúntò	ṁgbán	lè	gíá
		PN	take	cloth	POSS:3SG	PROG	sell
		'Adi is selling his clothes.'					

5.6.3 Order of copula and predicate

The order of copula and predicate often correlates with the order of verb and object in many languages. This applies in Etulo where the copulas *lì* and the quasi-copula *dzè* are followed by their predicate and therefore correlate with the VO order. Below are some examples:

(106) a. ìɲànì   lì   ìnwíndà
         PN   COP   beauty
         'Inyani is beautiful.'

   b. àdì   dzè   ùmákúrdí
         PN   COP   PN
         'Adi is in Makurdi.'

5.6.4 Order of adposition

Etulo adpositions precede the noun and are therefore realized as prepositions. Preposition is used here to refer to words that govern a noun and may (but not always) express a spatial or locative meaning. I illustrate the order of the adposition and the noun category using four Etulo prepositions: *m̀bí* (directional-to/towards), *mì* (locative- 'in', 'on', 'at'), *ìkíé* 'for', *jì* 'with'. Observe, in examples (107–111), that the aforementioned prepositions are sometimes preceded by the verb, but are followed by the noun or noun phrase, with which they form the prepositional phrase.

(107) ìsèsé   fúé   èní   mì   èsé
      PN   sprinkle   water   on   floor
      'Isese sprinkled water on the floor.'

(108) ánî   lè   tsɛ́   èní   mì   èkìô
      1SG:SUBJ   PROG   swim   water   in   river
      'I am swimming in the river.'

(109) ánî   lé   dzè   jì   ònɔ́   ánî
      1SG:SUBJ   PROG   stay   with   mother   1SG
      'I am staying with my mother.'

(110) àdì   lé   kpà   ìkíé   ánî
      PN   PROG   pay   for   1SG
      'Adi is paying for me.'

(111) àdì   lè   dɔ́   ésó   bā   m̀bí   éjî
      PN   PROG   send   message come   to   1PL:OBJ
      'Adi is sending a message to us.'

5.6.5 Order within a noun phrase

In this section, I focus on the order of NP constituents that consist of numerals, adjectives/qualificative nouns, demonstratives and quantifiers.

Creissels (2000) notes that in African languages, NPs whose nominal heads precede demonstratives, numerals and adjectives are more frequent than N-final NPs. In Etulo, numerals follow the head noun and may be optionally linked to the noun by the morpheme ŋi (112a–b). Demonstratives and quantifiers are also preceded by the noun in an NP (114a–d, 116a and 116d). For an NP comprising a noun and adjective, two possible constituent orders have been identified; head (N) initial and head (N) final.[17] The preference of one order over the other could be dependent on the context, and sometimes, the speaker's choice. In examples (113a–d), two orders are shown: N>Adj and Adj>N. They are used alternatively. Etulo has a consistent way of ordering nominal modifiers (Adj>Dem>Num) in relation to each other and the head noun. In a head-initial NP that includes these modifiers, the adjective directly precedes the numeral which is followed by the demonstrative: N>Adj>Num>Dem (115d). In cases where the adjective is prenominal, the order becomes Adj>N>Num>Dem. In the absence of the adjective, this order is retained. The demonstrative always occurs in the NP-final position. It is evident that Etulo predominantly allows head-initial order in NPs, except for some NPs consisting of noun and adjective.

(112) a. àfè (ŋí)[18] età   N>Num
         book PTCL three
         'three books'

      b. ájàtù (ŋí) èdá   N>Num
         car   PTCL hundred
         'one hundred cars'

(113) a. ájàtù òfùfè   N>Adj
         car   new
         'new car'

      b. òfùfè ájàtù   Adj>N
         new   car
         'new car'

      c. òngìâ inwíndà   N>Adj
         woman beautiful
         'beautiful woman'

---

17 In my discussion of the constituent order of the noun phrase, I use the term adjective/qualificative for both adjectives and nouns that perform adjectival functions.

18 The ŋí morpheme which is labelled as ptcl (particle) links the noun and the numeral. Its occurrence is optional.

	d.	ìnwíndà	òngìâ				Adj>N
		beautiful	woman				
		'beautiful woman'					
(114)	a.	àfè	né(nǐ)				N>Dem
		book	this				
		'this book'					
	b.	àfè	ná(nǐ)				N>Dem
		book	that				
		'that book'					
	c.	àfè	ńtóné(nǐ)				N>Dem
		book	these				
		'these books'					
	d.	àfè	ńtóná(nǐ)				N>Dem
		book	those				
		'those books'					
(115)	a.	ájàtù	òfùfè	(ŋí)	èfà		N>Adj>Num
		car	new	PTCL	two		
		'two new cars'					
	b.	ájàtù	ómbímbí	nâ			N>Adj>Dem
		car	black	that			
		'that black car'					
	c.	ájàtù	(ŋí)	èfà	ńtónénǐ		N>Num>Dem
		car	PTCL	three	these		
		'these two cars'					
	d.	óbúé	ómbímbí	(ŋí)	íjūō	ńtónénǐ	N>Adj>Num>Dem
		dog	black	PTCL	ten	these	
		'these ten black dogs'					
(116)	a.	ùndò	ámgbéká				N>Quantifier
		goat	some				
		'some goats'					
	b.	ájàtù	kwùbà				N>Quantifier
		car	many				
		'many cars'					

Table 5.1 Constituent order of the Etulo NP

A summary of constituent order in NP	
N>Num	head-initial
N>Adj/Adj>N	head-initial and head-final
N>Dem	head-initial
N>Quantifier	head-initial

A summary of constituent order in NP	
N>Adj>Num	head-initial
N>Adj>Dem	head-initial
N>Num>Dem	head-initial
N>Adj>Num>Dem	head-initial
Adj>N>Num>Dem	

5.6.5.1 Article and noun

In addition to demonstratives, Etulo has the definite article *mà* which makes reference to an entity identifiable by the participants in a discourse. Dryer (2006) states that definite articles have tendency to precede the noun in VO languages like English, but follow the noun in OV languages. In Etulo, however, the attested order is N-Art. The definite article or determiner follows the noun just like other nominal modifiers (demonstratives, numerals, quantifiers). Examples:

(117) a. àfè   mà
            book the
            'the book'
      b. m̀tsà mà
            mango the
            'the mango'

5.6.5.2 Plural word and noun

Pluralizarion of nouns in Etulo is achieved in different ways; by vowel substitution (especially with kinship terms), with the plural morpheme *èmí*, and occasionally with quantifiers (*kwùbà* 'many') and numerals. For many nouns, plural marking with the plural morpheme is not obligatory. The noun is always preceded by the plural morpheme in contrast with quantifiers like *kwùbà* which must be preceded by the noun. Examples:

(118) a. èmí   m̀dà
            PL   cow
            'cows'
      b. èmí   ájàtù
            PL   car
            'cars'

5.6.6 Order in possessive/genitive constructions

In this subsection, I focus on the constituent order of pronominal genitive (possessive constructions), which involve a combination of a pronoun and a noun, as well as the genitive construction (N+N combination). The order of constituents in a genitive construction has an implication for word order typology. Greenberg (1963) observes that languages with prepositions are harmonic with N>G (noun-genitive) constituent order, while languages with postpositions are associated with G>N (genitive-noun) constituent order. Dryer (2006) posits that SVO languages allow either order, N>G and G>N, as in English. In Etulo, possessive/genitive constructions are formed in two ways: by the use of the possessive morpheme *mgbi* as in (119a and 119b), or by juxtaposition or apposition of the constituents as in (120a) and (120b). Both strategies can be alternatively used in genitive constructions (121a–b). In examples (119a–121b), one can observe that the possessed noun is followed by the possessor or genitive noun. This is not surprising, considering that Etulo is a verb-initial (VO) language and adopts prepositions rather than postpositions. Examples:

(119)	a.	àfè	ḿgbí	ánî	possessed>possessor (N>Gen)
		book	POSS	1SG	
		'my book'			
	b.	àbɔ́	ḿgbí	éjî	possessed>possessor (N>Gen)
		hand	POSS	1PL	
		'our hand'			
(120)	a.	ónɔ́	ánî		possessed>possessor (N>Gen)
		mother	1SG		
		'my mother'			
	b.	ótsó	ábû		possessed>possessor (N>Gen)
		father	2SG		
		'your father'			
(121)	a.	ìkíé	(ḿgbī)	úndɔ̂	possessed>possessor (N>Gen)
		head	of	goat	
		'goat head'			
	b.	óbá	ísīkāpā		possessed>possessor (N>Gen)
		bag	rice		
		'bag of rice'			

5.6.7 Order of the relative clause and noun

Relative clauses are introduced by the relative markers; *nwí* [-animate], and *nwú* [+animate]. The *nwí* marker modifies inanimate head nouns while *nwú* modifies animate head nouns. Relative clauses are preceded by the head noun, resulting in the N-Rel word order. In (122a and 122b), the inanimate head nouns *àjàtù* 'car' and *m̀tsà* 'mango' precede the relative marker '*nwí*'. This also applies in (123a and 123b), where the animate head nouns (NPs) *ótsó éjî* 'our father' and *ongia* 'woman' are followed by the relative marker *nwú*. Below are some examples:

(122) a. àjàtù nwí ánî gíá jì àwújá m̀gbí ánî nê sùmsè
car REL 1SG buy with money POSS 1SG DEM be.beautiful
'This car which I bought with my money is beautiful.'

b. á kīē m̀tsà nwí ánî gíá mà gíé
3PL:SUBJ take mango REL 1SG buy the eat
'They ate the mango that I bought.'

(123) a. ótsó éjî nwú lé kìɔ́ ìdɔ́ mì òkwɔ̀ nâ gbò èsé
father 1PL REL PROG do work in farm DEM fall down
'Our father who is working in the farm fell down.'

b. òngìâ nwú lì òwán nâ lì ònwúnɔ́ ánî
woman REL COP wife.3SG:POSS DEM COP sister 1SG:POSS
'The woman who is his wife is my sister.'

5.6.8 Order in comparative constructions

Prepositional languages typically adopt the order Adj>marker>standard in comparisons of superiority while postpositional languages predominantly adopt the order standard>marker>Adj (Greenberg 1963). In Etulo, comparison is expressed by the verb *ŋa* 'surpass'. A comparative construction, as illustrated in (124), adopts the order Adj>marker>standard:

(124) àjàtù m̀gbī àdì lì òfùfè ŋā àjàtù m̀gbī ìɲànì
car POSS PN COP new surpass car POSS PN
'Adi's car is newer than Inyani's car'

5.6.9 Correlation with cross-linguistic generalizations

In this subsection, I briefly examine how the basic constituent order in Etulo conforms to universal tendencies of word order typology as discussed in Greenberg (1963) and Dryer (2006).[19] The basic word order of a sentence is crucial in predicting other characteristics of a language. Thus, it may be predicted that a

---

19 Dryer (1992, 2006) rejects the proposition of Greenberg (1963) on the order of noun and adjective. He instead claims that the constituent order of Adj>Noun shows no correlation with the basic order of sentences in both VO and OV languages.

language with SOV word order is predominantly postpositional while languages with SVO or VSO (verb-initial word order) are predominantly prepositional. Some prototypical correlations existing between verb-initial languages and other constituent orders as summarized in Dryer (2006) are listed below:

VO

- prepositions
- noun > genitive
- copula > predicate
- auxiliary > verb
- noun > relative clause
- article > noun
- plural word > noun
- adj > standard
- marker > standard

As noted earlier, Etulo has a SVO order in basic declarative and interrogative (yes/no, tag and content questions) constructions. In conformity with the typological tendencies of verb-initial languages (see below), Etulo uses prepositions (where the preposition is preceded by the verb and followed by the governed noun). It allows constituent orders where the copula precedes the predicate, the relative clause follows the noun and the genitive follows the noun. Contrary to the common pattern in SVO languages, the definite article is preceded by the noun, similar to the order attested in NPs involving N>Dem, N>Quantifier, N>Numeral. The assumption that adjectives follow the nouns they modify in SVO languages does not apply in Etulo. Both consitituent orders are attested: Adj>N and N>Adj. The following table lists the SVO consistent vs non-consistent patterns attested in Etulo.

Table 5.2 Correlating vs non correlating patterns

SVO CORRELATING PATTERNS	SVO NON-CORRELATING PATTERNS
preposition	noun > article
copula > predicate	noun > numeral
noun > relative clause	noun > demonstrative
plural word > noun	adjective > noun/noun > adjective
adj > marker > standard	
TA particles > verb	
noun > genitive	

From the foregoing, one can observe that Etulo exhibits a large number of features expected of an SVO language from a typological perspective.

5.6.10 Conclusion

Etulo is consistently SVO. TAM particles are preverbal, with the exception of the perfective marker which is 'sentence-final'. The copula precedes non-verbal predicate. Adpositions are realized as prepositions. Nominal dependents consistently follow the head, with the exception of qualificatives which may precede or follow, and the plural marker which precedes the NP. Etulo allows the N>Rel and the N>Gen order.

6. Valency, Transitivity and Serialization

6.0 Introduction

Across languages, one of the most common classifications made for the verb category is based on the number of arguments a verb takes. This chapter is split into three broad sections. In Section 6.1, the subcategorization frame of verbs in Etulo with respect to grammatical relations and semantic roles is examined. Etulo verbs are grouped into the following syntactic types: transitive, intransitive, ambitransitive and ditransitive. Following the classification of Etulo verbs into OCVs and non-OCVs (see Chapter 4), I further discuss the criteria for distinguishing between nouns that function as true direct objects as opposed to mere complements of a verb. In this connection, I describe the use of word order as the major argument marking strategy adopted in Etulo. In Section 6.2, I discuss the application of typical valence-increasing operations (such as causativization) and valence-decreasing operations (such as passivization) on Etulo verbs. In relation to argument structure, emphasis is laid on other predicate types such as serial verbs. In Section 6.3, a detailed description of verb serialization in Etulo is given. Each main section is followed by a concluding part.

6.1 A definition of valence

Valence is a grammatical feature that characterizes the verb category. It denotes the number of arguments or participants involved in the activity expressed by the verb. From a purely syntactic perspective, arguments of a verb are realized as subject, object and indirect object. From a semantic perspective, arguments match semantic roles such as agent, patient, theme, instrument and benefactive, amongst others. Grammatical relations are not always direct representations of semantic roles. Take, for instance, the grammatical subject, which may coincide with semantic roles such as agent, instrument, patient etc. This is illustrated with the following examples from English:

(1) a. George opened the door.   subject = AGENT
    b. This key opened the door.   subject = INSTRUMENT
    c. The wind opened the door.   subject = FORCE
    d. The door was opened by the wind   subject = PATIENT

(Payne 1997: 131).

In the following subsections, I focus on the characterization of intransitive, transitive, ditransitive and ambitransitive verbs in Etulo.

6.1.1 Intransitive verbs

From a semantic perspective, Etulo intransitive verbs denote an action or state that starts and ends with an NP (the subject). In Section 4.3, the Etulo verbs were classified into two broad groups: the obligatory complement verbs (OCVs) and the non-obligatory complement verbs (NCVs). This classification is extended to the domain of transitivity. A distinction is made between intransitive OCVs and intransitive NCVs. The intransitive OCVs comprise a subset of intransitive verbs that co-occur with two nouns. The preverbal noun functions as the subject and the postverbal noun as the complement. On the other hand, the intransitive NCVs comprise a subset of verbs which take only one NP (subject argument), and include the following: *bùlù* 'fly', *kwúlúū* 'die', *ǹdéē̄* 'be tired', *kúkú* 'crawl', *nwɔ́ɔ́* 'be dry' *gbélâ* 'agree' *kìà* 'rain', *m̀bùò* 'be full', *fé* 'be big', *kíē̄* 'be old', *tímbī* 'be bad', *sùndô* 'be heavy', *mámā* 'be sour', *kìkíɛ̀* 'walk' and *bùà* 'decay', amongst others. A few of the intransitive NCVs are illustrated in examples (2a–c). These verbs select only one subject NP argument.

(2) a. àdì   kwúlú   wà
       PN   die   PERF
       'Adi has died.'
    b. á   lē   kìkíɛ̀
       3PL:SUBJ   PROG   walk
       'They are walking.'
    c. ónɔ́   ánî   ǹdéē̄
       mother   1SG   be.tired
       'My mother is tired.'

In structural terms, intransitive NCVs of motion such as *bā* 'come', *lúū* 'go', *ké* 'go' may co-occur with postverbal nouns. These nouns are not categorized as direct objects of the verb. At the syntactic level, most of these nouns do not pass the pronominalization test associated with direct objects of transitive verbs.

From a semantic viewpoint, the postverbal NPs are not involved in the activity expressed by the verb. Etulo is unlike languages where such locative nouns are preceded by a preposition. Examples (3a and 3b) illustrate the occurrence of some motion verbs with the locative nouns ùmákárántá 'school' and ùdé 'home'.

(3) a. èmgbé   kɛ́   ùmákárántá
          children go   school
          'The children went to school.'

     b. àdì   lè   bā   údé
          PN   PROG come home
          'Adi is coming home.'

6.1.2 Intransitive OCVs

Intransitive OCVs are semantically one-place predicates. In other words, they have one argument which is the subject. These verbs are, however, followed by noun complements which further specify the meaning of the verbs. In contrast to transitive OCVs, intransitive OCVs do not co-occur with direct objects and their meaning specifiers do not perform a dual function. The meaning specifying nouns of intransitive verbs also fail the pronominalization test, which is one of the criteria for delimiting true objects in Etulo. Below is a list of some intransitive OCVs in Etulo:

(4) a. mà   àkwɔ̀   'cry'
     b. tá   élâ   'scream'
     c. gbò   èsɛ́   'fall'
     d. ná   únâ   'sleep'
     e. ʃá   íʃá   'laugh'
     f. lɛ́   ólē   'play'
     g. fíú   ńfíú   'be fat'
     h. fìà   ǹfìà   'be sweet'
     i. bɔ́   íbɔ́   'pray'

The following examples illustrate the OCV in sentential contexts.

(5) a. èmgbé   lɛ́   ólē   wà
          children play play PERF
          'The children have played.'

     b. òkà   ánî   fíú   ńfíú
          friend 1SG be.fat fatness
          'My friend is fat.'

c.	àdì	lè	ná	únâ
	PN	PROG	sleep	sleep
	'Adi is sleeping.'			
d.	èniàdɛ́	nê	fìà	ǹfìà
	palmwine	this	be.sweet	sweetness
	'This palm wine is sweet.'			

At the surface and structural level, the transitive and intransitive dichotomy for OCVs could be partially determined using the pronominalization test. For the intransitive OCVs, an application of the pronominalization test on the co-occurring nouns may result in ungrammaticality because these NPs are complements and not object arguments (see 6a–b). In other cases, an application of the pronominalization test on intransitive OCVs could be meaningful only in restricted contexts. In (7a–b), the pronominalized noun complement *àkwɔ̀* gives an emphatic reading.[1] The existence of complement verbs in Etulo makes it difficult to describe its transitivity in purely syntactic terms. Consider the following examples:

(6)	a.	òkà	ánî	fíú	ńfíú
		friend	1SG	be.fat	fatness
		My friend is fat.'			
	b.	*[2]òkà	ánî	fíún	
		friend	1SG	be.fat:SG:OBJ	
		*'My friend is fat it.'			
(7)	a.	éjî	mà	àkwɔ̀	èdɛ̌dɛ̌
		1PL:SUBJ	cry	cry	yesterday
		'We cried yesterday.'			
	b.	?[3]éjî	màn	èdɛ̌dɛ̌	
		1PL:SUBJ	cry.3SG:OBJ	yesterday	
		'We cried it yesterday./We really cried yesterday.'			

---

[1] The pronominalization test is a syntactic test used as a yardstick for differentiating between NPs that are categorized as meaning specifiers and as objects. I propose that an NP which is coterminous with the verb can only be fully pronominalized if it functions as an object or performs a dual function.

[2] The asterisk used before an example signals ungrammaticality.

[3] The question mark used before an example indicates that the meaning is questionable, or marginal. It also signals that the example may convey a meaning or structure somewhat different from what's intended.

6.1.3 Transitive verbs

Transitive verbs express an activity or state involving more than one participant. They are two place predicates (bivalent). In other words, they require two arguments; the subject and the object. These arguments are realized as nominals/pronominals. In Etulo, transitive verbs co-occur with one or two nominals. One of these nominals function as a meaning specifier while the other functions as the direct object. There are, however, instances where a nominal performs the dual role of a complement and direct object (see 8a). The subject of a verb occurs in preverbal positions while the object occurs in postverbal positions. Prototypical transitive verbs attested in Etulo include *nwɔ́* 'kill', *gíé* 'eat', *gíá* 'buy', *kpáā* 'grind', *sò* 'pound', *gbíkīē* 'break', *dzé* 'cut', *yá* 'divide', *fá* 'drive', *ʃέ* 'pluck', *búá* 'catch' and *fàwá* 'tear'. They are further illustrated in the following constructions:

(8) a. àdì sò àngìà wà
       PN pound millet PERF
       'Adi has pounded millet.'
    b. ótsó ḿgbí ánî nwɔ́ ùndɔ̀
       father POSS 1SG kill goat
       'My father killed a goat.'
    c. éjî ʃέ m̀tsà
       1PL:SUBJ pluck mango
       'We plucked mangoes.'

6.1.4 OCVs and transitivity

As noted earlier, Etulo has a subclass of verbs which obligatorily require a meaning specifier or complement (usually a noun). These complements are not necessarily synonymous with the direct object of verbs. In other words, although there are instances where they perform a dual function (as both complement and a direct object), there also are cases where the complement co-occurs with the direct object in syntactic constructions. Transitive OCVs therefore take either one or two nouns. When assigned a single noun, the complement and object argument functions are merged (10a and 10b). When a transitive complement verb is assigned two nouns, the two functions are split. In other words, one noun serves solely as a complement/meaning specifier and the other as the direct object (see 11a and 11b). When both nouns co-occur, the complement is usually displaced by the direct object. Some transitive OCVs are listed below:

(9) a. tá   ámgbá   'greet'
     b. tá   àfè   'slap'
     c. kíá   úkíá   'set trap'
     d. ʃò   èwô   'bath'
     e. jí   úmí   'steal'
     f. kpà   àkpà   'vomit'
     g. gbá   ángwɔ́   'peel (yam)'
     h. wá   ènì   'drink (water)'

The following examples illustrate the transitive OVC in sentential contexts.

(10) a. èmgbé   wá   ènì   wà
         children drink   water   PERF
         'The children have drunk water.'
     b. ánî   gbá   ángwɔ́   ńtónénǐ
         1SG:SUBJ peel   yam   these
         'I peeled these yams.'
(11) a. éjî   tá   òtsètsê ámgbā
         1PL:SUBJ greet   teacher greeting
         'We greeted the teachers.'
     b. àdì   lé   ʃò   ònwè   èwô
         PN   PROG   bath   child   body
         'Adi is bathing the child.'

In examples (10a–b), the transitive OCVs *wá* 'drink' and *gbá* 'peel' co-occur with the nouns *ènì* 'water' and *ángwɔ́* 'yam'. These nouns function as both the complement and the direct object. As stated earlier, one could further differentiate between the direct object and the complement by means of a pronominalization test. This syntactic test involves the substitution of the direct object with a pronoun. The noun complement of the transitive OCV cannot be substituted by a pronoun except it performs the dual function. In (12a) for instance, the direct object *òtsètsê* 'teacher(s)' illustrated in (10a) above is replaced by the 3rd person plural pronoun. Example (12b) shows that the substitution of the noun complement *èwô* 'body' by a pronoun results in ungrammaticality. Examples:

(12) a. éjî   tá   má   ámgbā
         1PL:SUBJ greet   3PL:OBJ   greeting
         'We greeted them.'
     b. *àdì   lé   ʃò   ònwèn
         PN   PROG   bath   child.3SG:OBJ
         'Adi is bathing the child.'

At the surface level, verb-complement combinations such as *támgbā* 'greet', *fùwó* 'bath' *ʃáʃí*, 'sing' etc. are easily misinterpreted as cases of compounding.[4] Such analysis is possibly motivated by phonological processes such as vowel elision and contraction which occurs at the word boundary of such combinations in speech. In syntactic constructions, however, there are pointers that prove that the Etulo verb-complement combinations are not cases of compounding. In transitive verbs for instance, the complement may co-occur with the direct object as in (10a). If the noun complement performs a dual function, it can be modified by a qualificative (see 13a). In the formation of derived nominals (gerunds), the morphological processes are enacted on the verb root alone (see 13b). Imperative constructions may allow the use of only the verb root (see Chapter 7). The noun complement can be substituted by another noun or pronoun only if it performs the dual function. For instance, the noun *ènì* 'water' which acts as both a complement and direct object in (10a) is replaced by the 3rd person singular pronoun in (13c) below.

(13) a. ánî   gbá   ángwɔ́   ófúfê
          1SG:SUBJ   peel   yam   new
          'I peeled a new yam.'
     b. úmì   ò-jí-jī   tíʃí   bā
          theft   PREF-STEAL-RED   be.good   NEG
          'Stealing is not good.'
     c. èmgbɛ́   wán   wà
          children   drink.3SG:OBJ   PERF
          'The children have drunk it'

6.1.5 Ditransitive verbs

Ditransitive verbs are three place predicates. They require three arguments: the subject and two objects. The subject is realized as the agent and the objects as recipient and theme. Ditransitive constructions in Etulo include double object construction and applicative construction. The latter is a type of valence-increasing mechanism. Etulo verbs involved in ditransitive constructions are *nū* 'give', *lɔ̀* 'write', *kwɔ́* 'fetch', *gíá* 'buy', *dó (èsɔ́)* 'send', *wó* 'wear' and *tsò* 'point/show'.

---

4 Considering the fact that Etulo has no standardized form yet, some native speakers write the verb-noun complement combinations as single words with respect to the applicable phonological processes. For the purpose of this work however, such combinations are written separately as individual words. This eliminates the inconsistency of realizing them in different ways across different syntactic construction. I therefore represent *fuwo* as *fo ewo* 'bath' *ʃaʃi* as *ʃi aʃi* 'sing', *tamgba* as *ta amgba* 'greet'.

6.1.5.1 Double object construction

Ditransitive verbs which occur in double object constructions include: *nū* 'give', *tsò* 'show', *wó* 'dress/wear.' These verbs require three arguments. The objects of the verbs which are realized as theme and recipient follow a specific order. The theme is preceded by the recipient. A reversal of the order results in ungrammaticality. In Etulo, no preposition or morphological marking is needed to introduce the recipient. The role of each argument is solely determined by word order. The subject/agent occurs in preverbal position while the objects (theme and recipient) occur in postverbal position. The verb *nu* 'give' is realized in two ways: as a ditransitive verb in a double object construction or as a serial verb construction, where it pairs with the verb *kíé* 'take'. The latter is illustrated with the following construction: *àdì kíé àfè nū ánî* 'Adi gave me a book' (literally: 'Adi take book give me'). Below are examples of ditransitive verbs in constructions:

(14) a. á tsò éjî ùdé ḿgbí ámá
 3PL:SUBJ show 1PL:OBJ house POSS 3PL:OBJ
 'They showed us their house.'
 b. àdì nū èmgbé àfè
 PN give children book
 'Adi gave the children a book.'
 c. ánî kà wó àdì ànwúntò
 1SG:SUBJ FUT wear PN cloth
 'I will dress Adi.'

6.1.5.2 Applicative construction

This type of ditransitive construction is mostly derived from a transitive one. Both transitive OCVs and transitive NCVs can become applicative. In Etulo, applicative constructions involve a subject (agent) and two objects realized as theme and benefactive. The applicative NP (object) expresses the entity on whose behalf the action denoted by the verb is carried out. Verbs involved in applicative constructions include *lò* 'write', *kwɔ́* 'fetch', *ʃí áʃí* 'sing', *sá* 'wash', *kɪɔ̀* 'do', amongst others. All of these verbs take one object in basic constructions. In applicative constructions, their valence is increased and the direct object (theme) is displaced by the indirect object (benefactive). In other words, the direct object is preceded by the indirect object.

(15) a. àdì   lè   kwɔ́   ánî   ènì
        PN   PROG   fetch   1SG:OBJ water
        'Adi is fetching me water./Adi is fetching water for me.'
    b. ìsèsé   kà   sá   àdì   ànwúntò
        PN   FUT   wash   PN   cloth
        'Isɛsɛ will wash clothes for Adi.'
    c. ónɔ́   éjî   kìɔ̀   éjî   ùnwógīē
        mother   1PL   do   1PL:OBJ food
        'Our mother cooked us food./ Our mother cooked food for us.'

The indirect object in an applicative construction may be introduced by a preposition. In such cases, there is a reversal of the beneficiary-theme word order. The direct object precedes the indirect object. This could be likened to a case of double object alternation or dative shift in languages like English. Note that not all verbs used in applicative constructions can be optionally introduced by a preposition. A further discussion of the dative shift in Etulo is given in Section 6.2.1.2.

(16) a. àdì   lè   kwɔ́   ènì   ìkíé   ánî
        PN   PROG   fetch   water   for   1SG:OBJ
        'Adi is fetching water for me.'
    b. ìsèsé   kà   sá   ànwúntò ìkíé   àdì
        PN   FUT   wash   cloth   for   PN
        'Isɛsɛ will wash clothes for Adi.'

6.1.6 Ambitransitive verbs

Etulo has a small subset of verbs which may be transitive or intransitive. They include *kwùlú* 'open', *fàwá* 'tear', *gbíkīē* 'break', *gbóbú* 'break' *túkwû* 'close' and *dzé* 'cut'. The subject of such verbs, when intransitive, corresponds to their direct object when transitive. In some languages, this group of verbs is referred to as ergative verbs. Examples (17–18) illustrate the transitive and intransitive use of these verbs.

(17) a. ònùfé   kwùlúū
        door   open
        'The door opened.'
    b. àdì   kwùlú   ònùfê
        PN   open   door
        'Adi opened the door.'

(18) a. ànwúntò   fáwā   wà
         cloth   tear   PERF
         'A cloth is torn.'
    b. àdì   fàwá   ànwúntō   wà
         PN   tear   cloth   PERF
         'Adi has torn a cloth.'

6.1.7 Argument marking

Numerous cross-linguistic studies on argument marking show that arguments can be morphologically marked, and this motivates some sort of flexibility. The arguments can be ordered in more than one way. Conversely, languages that lack such morphological marking resort to the use of word order as a major means of identifying the arguments' grammatical relations and their interpretation with respect to semantic roles. Etulo belongs to the second group of languages and heavily relies on strict word order as a crucial means of argument marking.

6.1.7.1 Word order

As stated earlier, the only means of identifying the arguments' grammatical relations in Etulo is by a rigid SVO word order.[5] The subject occurs to the left of the verb and the object to the right. A reversal of this order yields a different semantic reading (see 19a and 19b). There is however, a small subset of verbs in Etulo (symmetrical verbs) for which some form of alternation is possible (see Section 6.1.7). In relation to semantic roles, the preverbal argument is assigned a number of roles such as agent, experiencer, while the postverbal argument is assigned the role of patient/theme. Intransitive verbs take a grammatical subject which may be assigned the semantic role of agent or patient. In Etulo, as in most if not all languages, semantic roles do not always coincide with specific grammatical relations (subject and object).

---

5 In comparison with other verbs in Etulo, a peculiarity is observed in the interaction between the semantic roles and grammatical relations of the verb *kpà ìtúkwû* 'love'. The semantic role of experiencer is realized as the object argument while the participant for whom the event is experienced is realized as the syntactic subject. For other psychological verbs, however, the experiencer is usually the syntactic subject.

(i) àdì   kpā   ánî   ìtúkwû   (ii) ánî   kpā   àdì   ìtúkwû
    PN   like   1SG:OBJ   heart   1SG:SUBJ like   PN   heart'
    'I love Adi.'   'Adi loves me.'

(19) a. èmgbé   nwɔ́   òbúé
         children kill   dog
         'The children killed a dog.'

    b. òbúé   nwɔ́   èmgbé
        dog   kill   children
        'A dog killed the children.'

(20) a. àdì   lè   kwúlúū
         PN   PROG   die
         'Adi is dying.'

    b. ánî   lè   míò   ìmíò
        1SG:SUBJ PROG   fear   fear (N)
        'I am afraid.'

For three-place predicates, the order of the arguments or participants is Agent-Recipient-Theme.[6] An alternation of this order as Agent-Theme-Recipient is obtained in cases where the recipient or benefactor (indirect or oblique object) is introduced by a preposition or in serial verb constructions. In example (22a), the recipient precedes the theme of the ditransitive verb *nū* 'give'. Conversely, both NPs (recipient and theme) are realized as objects of the serial verbs *kíé* 'take' and *nū* 'give' in which case, the theme precedes the recipient (see 21b). In the applicative constructions of (22a), the recipient/benefactor *àdì* 'name of person' precedes the theme *ùnwógīē* 'food'. This order is however reversed in (22b) where the recipient is introduced by the preposition *ìkíé* 'for' and preceded by the theme. Consider the following examples:

(21) a. àdì   nū   ánî   àfè
         PN   give   1SG:OBJ   book
         'Adi gave me a book.'

    b. àdì   kíé   àfè   nū   ánî
        PN   take   book   give   me
        'Adi gave me a book.'

(22) a. ónɔ́   éjî   ká   kìɔ̀   àdì   ùnwógīē
         mother   1PL   FUT   do   PN   food
         'Our mother will cook Adi food.'

    b. ónɔ́   éjî   ká   kìɔ̀   ùnwógīē   ìkíé   àdì
        mother   1PL   FUT   cook   food   for   PN
        'Our mother will cook food for Adi.'

---

6 The term 'recipient' is used in a loose sense to include the benefactive role in applicative constructions.

With pronominal NPs, the rigid word order is maintained. Unlike nouns, some pronominals are realized in varying forms depending on their syntactic function (as nominative or accusative) while for others; one form is used in all syntactic functions. For instance, the 1st person plural pronoun *éjî* 'we', undergoes no change in form in both subject and object positions. Its grammatical relation is solely assigned on the basis of word order: subject in preverbal position and object in postverbal position. On the other hand, the 3rd person plural pronoun is realized as *a* 'they' in the nominative function and as *ma* in the accusative function. In either case, a strict word order is followed. (See Chapter 4 for a discussion of the Etulo pronominal forms.)

6.1.8 Symmetrical verbs

Symmetrical verbs encode a relationship *r* between two entities such that $X\,r\,Y$ entails $Y\,r\,X$ (Miller 1998). They are a group of verbs whose arguments (subject and object) can be switched. Etulo has a small subset of verbs that undergo the subject-object switch in constructions. They are mostly psychological verbs such as *kìɔ̀ ìtíngā* 'be angry', *dɔ́ ótsē* 'be sick', *wó ìmìò* 'be afraid'. The arguments linked to these verbs are a noun which undergoes the psychological state (experiencer) and another noun which refers to the psychological state. The switching of the arguments of symmetric verbs introduces a slight change in the semantic orientation of the constructions. In (23a, 24a and 25a), the subject is assigned the semantic role of 'experiencer' and the constructions are construed as being agent oriented. In contrast, the subject in (23b, 24b and 25b) is assigned the role of agent where the affectedness of the states of anger, sickness and fear on the human entity is emphasized. The constructions are construed as being patient oriented. A similar phenomenon is attested in other West African languages such as Igbo where it is described as SOS (subject-object switching) (see Uwalaka 1988, Uchechukwu 2007). It is often difficult to provide a literal English translation for some of these verbs. In the examples below, they are glossed as SYMV.

(23) a. ánî   lé   kìɔ̀   ìtíngā
          1SG:SUBJ PROG SYMV anger
          'I am angry.'

      b. ìtíngā lé   kìɔ̀   ánî
          anger   PROG SYMV 1SG:OBJ
          'I am angry.'

(24) a. àdì   kà   dɔ́   ótsē

(23) a. ánî   lé   kɩ̀ɔ̀   ìtíngā
         PN   FUT   SYMV   sickness
         'Adi will be sick.'
    b.   ìmíò   lè   wó   ánî
         fear   PROG   SYMV   1SG:OBJ
         'I am afraid.'

6.1.9 Conclusion

Etulo verbs are classified as transitive, intransitive, ambitransitive and ditransitive. The distinction made between OCVs and NCVs is extended to the domain of transitivity. Intransitive OCVs are distinguished from intransitive NCVs. The latter selects only one subject NP argument, while the former co-occurs with two nouns: the subject NP argument in the preverbal position and the noun complement (a specifier) in the postverbal position. The noun complements of intransitive OCVs are not analyzed as grammatical objects of the verb. The pronominalization test allows one to point out true direct objects in Etulo. The application of this test shows that only true objects of transitive verbs can be fully pronominalized, while the noun complements selected by intransitive OCVs cannot. Pronominalizing the noun complement of an intransitive OCV yields ungrammaticality or a restricted semantic reading.

6.2 Valence-adjusting operations

Languages adopt morphological, lexical or periphrastic means to adjust the valence of a predicate by reducing or increasing the number of its arguments. In the following subsections, I discuss the valence-increasing and decreasing mechanisms available in Etulo.

6.2.1 Valence-increasing operation

Valence-increasing operations involve syntactic processes that add an argument to the basic argument structure of a verb. The verb may be originally transitive or intransitive. The two most common valence-increasing devices are causatives and applicatives. The applicative construction was partially discussed in Section 6.1.5.2. In the following subsections, I focus on: (i) the Etulo causative, (ii) a form of dative argument alternation that characterizes applicatives and (iii) the realization of intransitive verbs in applicative constructions.

6.2.1.1 Causative

According to Haspelmath (2008), a causative construction denotes a situation which contains a causing subevent and a resulting situation. Etulo does not have a morphological process to mark causation. Causation is expressed analytically by means of the verb *nū* 'make/cause'. The causative process is applicable to both transitive and intransitive verbs. A new argument is introduced to serve as the causer/subject of the matrix verb. The original subject of the caused event fulfills a patient role for the matrix verb and an agentive role to the caused event. The following examples are illustrative:

(25) a. àwò né nū ìsèsé ná únâ
    breeze this make PN sleep sleep
    'This breeze made Isɛsɛ sleep.'
  b. ónɔ́ ánî lé nū àdì ʃí ífúé
    mother 1SG PROG make PN dance dance
    'My mother is making Adi dance.'

Lexical causation is expressed by lexical causatives. These are manifested by simple verbs such as *gbíkīē* 'break', *nwɔ́* 'kill' or complex/compound verbs such as *gbónwɔ́* 'kill by beating', *tsénwɔ́* 'kill by hitting'. The compound verbs typically denote cause-effect events. Examples (26a and 26b) illustrate the use of these verbs in expressing causation.

(26) a. Àdì nwɔ́ ìsèsé
    PN kill PN
    'Adi killed Isɛsɛ.'
  b. Àdì gbó-nwɔ́ ìsèsé
    PN beat-kill PN
    'Adi beat Isɛsɛ to death.'

In Table 6.1, I give a summary of the number of arguments realized in the analytical and lexical causatives. Note that the presence of the third argument is dependent on the transitivity class of the predicate.

Table 6.1 Valence features

Causative type	Causer (Argument 1)	Causee (Argument 2)	Object (Argument 3)
Analytic/ periphrastic	A	O/A	(O)
Lexical	A	O	-

6.2.1.2 Applicatives and object alternation (dative shift)

As discussed in Section 6.1.4.2, the applicative in Etulo is a valence-increasing operation which adds an indirect object argument (applicative NP) to the predicate. The indirect object argument is realized via different morphosyntactic means: as the object of a serial verb, as an oblique object introduced by a preposition and by juxtaposition where it precedes the direct object in a transitive clause.

Intransitive verbs are also used in applicative constructions. This adds an additional argument to one place predicates. The new argument is assigned a benefactive role as in (27). In some cases (i.e. for some verbs), however, the added argument denotes a participant to whom an action is directed (28). Consider the following examples:

(27) a. ìmgbàʃò   kwúlúū
         god   die
         'God died.'

     b. ìmgbàʃò   kwúlú   éjî
         god   die   1PL:OBJ
         'God died for us.'

(28) a. àdì   ʃá   íʃá
         PN   laugh   laugh
         'Adi laughed.'

     b. àdì   ʃá   ánî   íʃá
         PN   laugh   1SG:OBJ   laugh
         'Adi laughed at me.'

With transitive predicates, dative shift is observed when one of the direct objects is displaced by the applicative NP; compare (29a and 29b). For intransitive OCVs, it is the meaning specifier that is displaced; compare (30a and 30b). The prepositional constructions (29b and 30b) illustrate the shifted position of direct object and complement after the application of dative shift.

(29) a. àdì   lè   gíá   ánî   àfè
         PN   PROG   buy   1SG:OBJ   book
         'Adi is buying me a book.'

     b. àdì   lè   gíá   àfè   ìkíé   ánî
         PN   PROG   buy   book   for   1SG:OBJ
         'Adi is buying a book for me.'

(30) a. ónɔ́   ánî   bɔ́   ánî   íbɔ́
       mother 1SG   pray   1SG:OBJ prayer
       'My mother prayed for me.'

    b. ónɔ́   ánî   bɔ́   íbɔ́   ìkíé ánî
       mother 1SG   pray   prayer for   1SG
       'My mother prayed for me.'

6.2.2. Valence-decreasing operations

A valence-decreasing operation is a process that removes an argument from a verb valence pattern. The eliminated argument could be the object/patient or the subject/agent. The most common valence-decreasing operations in languages include passives, reciprocals, reflexives and anticausatives. While some of these operations are attested in Etulo, the passive construction is not.

6.2.2.1 Absence of passivization

Passivization is a grammatical process that typically applies to transitive verbs. It involves a shift in focus from the subject of a predicate to its object. Across languages, passive constructions are characterized by verb morphology, the elevation of the object to the position of a grammatical subject, the demotion of the subject to an oblique role, or its outright deletion, optional or obligatory depending on the language. For instance, in languages such as English, the verb is morphologically marked in passive constructions, the object is elevated and the demoted subject is optionally deleted.

Passivization is not attested in Etulo. In place of passive constructions, Etulo uses impersonal constructions, which do not require dedicated verb morphology and the promotion or demotion of arguments. The grammatical subject is substituted by an impersonal pronoun, which could be more or less interpreted as a non-referential or dummy subject.[7] The following examples are illustrative:

(31) a. ìsèsé   búa   ánî
       PN   catch 1SG:OBJ
       'Isɛsɛ caught me.'

    b. á   búa   ánî
       IMPRS catch 1SG:OBJ
       'They caught me./I was caught.'

---

[7] This pronoun is either realized as the 3rd person plural subject or as an impersonal pronoun. In (31b and 32b), the impersonal pronominal meaning is implied.

(32) a. àdì   nwɔ́   ǹgísè   ńanǐ
        PN   kill   person   that
        'Adi killed a man.'
    b. á   nwɔ́   ǹgísè   nánǐ
        IMPRS   kill   person   that
        'They killed a person./A person was killed.'

6.2.2.2 The reflexive construction

A reflexive construction is one in which the subject and object are co-referent. There are languages for which the reflexive is morphologically marked, so that only one argument (usually the subject) is expressed. From a semantic perspective, the reflexive construction reduces the valence of a transitive verb by specifying that one entity fulfils two semantic roles.

In Etulo, the reflexive construction does not fit into a prototypical mould as a valence-decreasing operation. An analytic means, involving the use of the noun *èwô* 'body' and a pronoun, is adopted. From a syntactic point of view, the two arguments (subject and object) are realized. Semantically however, both arguments make reference to the same entity. An anaphoric relationship exists between the object and the subject. Transitive verbs that are used in reflexive constructions typically denote activities; especially those revolving around grooming, body care etc. They include *fò èwô* 'bath', *sá* 'wash', *wó* 'dress/wear', *dzέ* 'cut', *nwó* 'kill', *tá àfὲ* 'slap' etc. Examples (33 and 34), illustrate the purely transitive and reflexive use of these verbs.

(33) a. ánî   sá   ànwúntò
        1SG:SUBJ wash   cloth
        'I washed clothes.'
    b. ánî   sá   èwó   ánî
        1SG:SUBJ wash   body   1SG
        'I washed myself.'
(34) a. á   nwɔ́   mà   wà
        3PL:SUBJ kill   3PL:OBJ PERF
        'They have killed them.'
    b. á   nwɔ́   èwó   má   wà
        3PL:SUBJ kill   body   3PL   PERF
        'They have killed themselves.'

6.2.2.3 The reciprocal construction

A reciprocal construction involves two arguments/participants that act on each other. The reciprocal is similar to the reflexive in the sense that the arguments involved are co-referential but for different reasons. In Etulo, reciprocal constructions are marked by the morpheme *èkà* which occurs in the object argument slot (see 35a–c). With the exception of inherently reciprocal verbs such as *tú* 'meet', most transitive verbs in Etulo can be used in reciprocal constructions. Consider the following example:

(35) a. éjî tú èkà wà
 1PL:SUBJ meet RECP PERF
 'We have met each other.'
 b. àdì jì ìsèsé tú èkà wà
 PN and PN meet RECP PERF
 'Adi and Isɛsɛ have met.'
 c. á nwɔ́ èkà
 3PL:SUBJ kill RECP
 'They killed each other.'

6.2.2.4 The anticausative

In an anticausative construction, the subject of the verb is assigned the semantic role of patient. The verb denotes an event that affects its subject but gives no syntactic indication of the cause of the event. According to Haspelmath (2005), anticausatives can only be formed from verbs expressing actions performed without any specific instruments or methods, so that they can be thought of as happening spontaneously. Etulo expresses anticausativity in the same way as English and some other languages, i.e. without morphological tools, but by simply omitting reference to any possible causer. Anticausative verbs in Etulo include *gbóbū/gbíkīē* 'break', *kwùlú* 'open', *fàwá* 'tear', *túkwû* 'close', *dɔ́ òdɔ̂* 'cook (soup)', *dzé* 'cut' etc. These verbs are labelled anticausatives when they are used intransitively.

(36) a. àfɛ̀ nâ fàwá wà
 book that tear PERF
 'That book has torn.'
 b. úgà ḿgbí ánî gbóbúū
 plate POSS 1SG break
 'My plate broke.'

6.2.3 The valence pattern of serial verbs

The serial verb construction is a core feature of the Etulo verbal system. Serial verbs are a sequence of verbs which act together as a single predicate, without an overt marker of co-ordination, subordination or syntactic dependency of any sort. The verbs that make up a serial verb construction may originally have the same or a different transitivity status. There are several combinatorial possibilities such as the transitive-transitive, transitive-intransitive, intransitive-intransitive and intransitive-transitive. Irrespective of the transitivity status of individual verbs, the transitive value of some serial verb constructions (like the asymmetric SVC) is determined by the main verb. I present below the different combinations:

(37) a. á kīē ànwúntò ǹtónê fàwá wà Transitive-transitive
3PL:SUBJ take cloth these tear PERF
'They have torn these clothes.'

b. àdì kíé ítsê mà lú òdzû Transitive-intransitive
PN carry chair the go house
'Adi carried the chair to the house.'

c. ìnwúnɔ̂ bùlù lú wà Intransitive-intransitive
bird fly go PERF
'The bird has flown away.'

d. á tā ēlā wó éjî Intransitive-transitive
3PL:SUBJ scream voice put 1PL:OBJ
'They screamed at us.'

e. ánî kà wá ʃé m̀tsà Intransitive-transitive
1SG:SUBJ FUT come pluck mango
'I am coming to pluck mango.'

6.2.4 Conclusion

For valence increase, Etulo allows applicatives and causatives via periphrastic and lexical means. Etulo has no special verb morphology for both construction types. For valency decrease, Etulo has no passive but allows the impersonal construction. The absence of passives is not peculiar to Etulo; it is a common feature of many West African languages. Also discussed were reflexives, reciprocals, anticausatives and the valence pattern of serial verbs. The term 'anticausative' is applied to ambitransitive verbs in constructions where the agent is omitted.

6.3 Verb serialization

In this section, I discuss Etulo serial verbs as a type of complex predicate using the typological criteria proposed in Aikhenvald (2006). Different types of serial verb constructions (SVCs) are established: the symmetric vs asymmetric, optional vs obligatory. The SVCs are further distinguished from a similar multiverb construction known as the 'consecutive construction'.

6.3.1 The typological criteria

Verb serialization has long been typologically established as an areal feature of many West African languages, especially of the Kwa, Benue Congo and Gur subgroups. It is equally attested in other language families like Oceanic and Australian. According to Aikhenvald (2006: 1) 'serial verb construction is a sequence of verbs which act together as a single predicate, without an overt marker of co-ordination, subordination, or syntactic dependency of any other sort. Serial verb constructions describe what is conceptualised as a single event...' This view of SVCs has come under criticisms by recent works by Baker and Harvey (2014), who view SVCs as being multi-predicational. They regard the conceptual structure of SVCs as one in which there are multiple events in a monoclausal construction. Supporting this view, Foley (2014) claims that SVCs are in no sense a unified phenomenon, but rather express diverse types of event structures ranging from simple to multiple or even more complex events. Notwithstanding the divergent views, it is generally agreed that SCVs obligatorily involve a sequence of verbs occurring in a single clause. I adopt here Aikhenvald (2006) typological framework for SVCs, which proposes a number of parameters for the classification of SVCs. These are based on the composition of the SVC components, on the contiguity vs non-contiguity of the components and on the wordhood of SVCs. With respect to the composition, a two-way split is made between the symmetric and asymmetric type. Symmetric SVCs involve verb combinations from an unrestricted semantic class and typically denote subevents following a temporal sequence. Asymmetric SVCs involve instead components from both restricted and unrestricted classes and typically denote single events. The verb from the closed (restricted class) often functions as a modifier in its occurrence with the main verb.

Below are some typical characterizations of SVCs across the worlds' languages as summed up by Aikhenvald:

- Monoclausality
- A sequence of two or more contiguous or non-contiguous verbs in a clause
- Absence of any marker of syntactic dependency
- The individual verbs can function as independent verbs in simple clauses
- Shared tense, aspect, mood, modality, negation
- Verbs share a single subject
- Components of SVCs cannot be questioned separately

The absence of any marker of syntactic dependency as a prototypical feature of SVCs can be problematic in some languages where there are other multi-verb structures such as consecutive, overlapping and even conjoined structures (existing alongside SVCs) that lack markers of syntactic dependency as well. This is evident in Goemai (a West Chadic language), in which syntactic dependency markers are absent in both SVCs and conjoined structures (cf. Hellwig 2006). This is also observed in Etulo, as briefly shown in Section 6.2.3. Such languages therefore adopt other language internal means for distinguishing SVCs from other multi-verb structures.

There are, however, instances where individual languages with SVCs exhibit features that contradict a few of these prototypical features. In Ewe (a West African language), Ameka (2006) observes that although components of an SVC cannot be individually marked for propositional questions, they can be separately questioned using the content question strategy. In the following example from Ewe, the verbs *da* 'cook' and *du* 'eat' are separately questioned. To question a VP or happening requires the phrase *nu ka* 'what' and the function verb *wɔ* 'do'.

(38) a. nu   ka   wo-da   nu-a   kɔ   wɔ
          thing   INTER   3SG-cook   thing-DEF   take   do
          'What did she cook the food and do?'
      b. nu   ka   wo-wɔ   du
          thing   INTER   3SG-do   eat
          'What did she do and eat?'

(Ameka 2006:140)

Besides this prototypical characterization of SVCs, individual languages may have additional criteria for identifying or characterizing SVCs which differ from one language to the other. SVCs express several nuances of meaning which include (but are not restricted to) direction, manner, comparison, benefactivity, causation, and resultativity. From a cross-linguistic perspective, certain serial verbs like *take* and *give* are considered more common than others. SVCs are briefly examined in the light of the above typological characterization.

6.3.2 The functional properties of SVCs

SVCs generally comprise a minimum of two verbs in Etulo but could contain as many as three verb series or more, especially in narrative contexts. The most frequently occurring serial verbs (as attested in our data) include *kíé* 'take', *nū* 'give', and directional motion verbs such as *kè*, *lúū* 'go', *wá*, *bā* 'come'. Below is an example taken from a narrative which gives an elaborate description of the subevents involved in the overall event of returning from church to one's home. Emphasis is on the main clause.

(39)	ní	àdúà	wá	ńgīē,	ánî	kà	tásê	jìdó	lú-bā	údé
	if	mass	come	finish	1SG:SUBJ	FUT	come. out	return	go-come	home

'If the mass ends, I will return home.'

Serial verbs may express benefactive (*nū* 'give'), instrumental (*kíé* 'take'), and comparative (*ŋà* 'surpass') meaning. They also express prepositional and adverbial notions indicating direction using the motion verbs listed above, etc. Note that any of these verbs could serve as the sole predicate in a grammatical construction. Consider the following examples:

(40)	ínwúnɔ́	bùlù	lú	wà			
	bird	fly	go	PERF			

'The bird has flown away.'

(41)	àdì	lè	dó	ésó	bā	m̀bí	éjî
	PN	PROG	send	message	come	to	1PL:OBJ

'Adi is sending a message to us.'

(42)	ánî	lè	dó	ésó	kè	m̀bó	má
	1SG:SUBJ	PROG	send	message	go	to	3PL:OBJ

'I am sending a message to them.'

(43)	ánî	kíé	ífà	lè	wó	má	ìmíò
	1SG:SUBJ	take	snake	PROG	put	3PL:OBJ	fear

'I am frightening them with a snake.'

6.3.2.1 Comparative and superlative meaning

Comparative and superlative meanings are expressed via the process of verb serialization using the verb *ŋà* 'surpass' in postverbal position. Example (44a) illustrates the use of *ŋà* as a comparative marker preceded by the main verb *gígíé* 'be sharp'. For the superlative construction, *ŋà* is used in combination with *dúú* 'all' (44b).

(44) a. èbà   ḿgbī   ìsèsé   gígíè   ŋà   ḿgbí   ánî
         knife   POSS   PN   be.sharp   surpass   POSS   1SG
         'Isɛsɛ's knife is sharper than mine.'

    b. èbà   ḿgbī   ìsèsé   gígíè   ŋà   dúú
         knife   POSS   PN   be.sharp   surpass   all
         'Isɛsɛ's knife is the sharpest.'

6.3.2.2 Completive aspect

The verb of completion *ǹgíé* 'finish' co-occurs with many verbs in SVCs to indicate the completion of an event. It shares same temporal values with the main verb. Consider the following examples:

(45) a. àdì   gíé   ùnwógīē   ńgīē   plé
         PN   eat   food   finish   early
         'Adi finished eating on time.'

    b. àdì   gíé   ùnwógīē   ńgīē   wà
         PN   eat   food   finsh   PERF
         'Adi has finished eating.'

6.3.2.3 SVCs and grammaticalization

There are two Etulo verbs that seem to be on a grammaticalization path; the speech verb, *gběē* 'say' and the motion verb, *kè* 'go'. The use of a verb meaning 'say' as a complementizer is a relatively common pattern in many West African languages (cf. Lord 1993, Aikhenvald 2007). It has been the practice of some linguists to analyze such verbs as a serial verb or as a grammaticalized verb depending on the language (cf. Yeung 2003, Matthew 2007). In Etulo complement clause, the verb *gběē* 'say' functions as a complementizer with a restricted number of predicates, such as *jé* 'know', *fó* 'hear', *dí* 'see' and in copula constructions.[8]

---

8   In addition, the morpheme *dàfī* 'like/as' may be used interchangeably with the grammaticalized speech verb *gběē* (complementizer), in some complement clauses (Section 5.4.1).

Apparently, it has been desemanticized (having lost its original meaning as a speech verb) and now assumes the grammatical function of introducing a clause. It is analyzed here as a complementizer rather than a component of a SVC, partly because its occurrence and grammatical function is not restricted to SVCs. In (46a and 46b), the verb *gbĕɛ̄* 'say' co-occurs with the stative verbs *jé* 'know' and *fó* 'hear' in constructions that seem like SVCs. In contrast, *gbĕɛ̄* occurs in a copula construction where its function as a complementizer is retained (see 10c). In all its occurrences, the original meaning is lost. Unlike the complementizer *gbĕɛ̄*, the motion verb *kè* 'go' largely retains its original meaning in SVCs. It tends to function in such contexts as a directional marker (see 47a and 47b).[9] Below are some examples:

(46) a. ìɲànì   jé   gbĕɛ̄   ò   kà   bā
         PN   know   COMP   3SG   FUT   come
         'Inyani knows that she will come.'

   b. án î   fó   gbĕɛ̄   á   nwɔ́   àdì
       1SG   hear   COMP   3PL:SUBJ   kill   PN
       'I heard that they killed Adi.'

   c. ìtíngā   ḿgbí   ánî   lì   ìkíé   gbĕɛ̄   ó   kwúlúū
       anger   POSS   1SG   COP   COMP   COMP   3SG:SUBJ   die
       'My anger is (about the fact) that he died.'

(47) a. àdì   gbó   ìɲànì   kè   íkwóngíè
         PN   beat   PN   go   death
         'Adi beat Inyani to death.'

   b. àdì   lí   kíé   ònwé   mà   kè   ùmákárántá
       PN   HAB   take   child   the   go   school
       'Adi takes the child to school every day.'

---

9   Note that the use of *kè* is not required in its causative counterpart. Compare the two examples below:

(i)   ánî   nū   àdì   gbó   ìsèsé   kè   íkwōngíè
      1SG:SUBJ make   PN   beat   PN   go   death
      'I made Adi beat Isɛsɛ to death.'

(ii) ánî   nū   àdì   gbó-nwɔ́   ìsèsé
      1SG:SUBJ make   PN   beat-kill PN
      'I made Adi kill Isɛsɛ.'

The possible grammaticalization of *kè* is even more evident in some compound verbs where its function shifts from denoting direction to indicating a location or position. Examples: *wókē* 'put in', *lákē* 'lie on'. In these examples, the motion verb *kè* 'go' functions as a locative (has a prepositional meaning) and seems to have no direct semantic link with its original meaning (see Section 4.6.5).

6.3.3 Monoclausality

SVCs in Etulo constitute a single clause with no marker of syntactic dependency. This however does not seem to be a peculiar feature of SVCs since some consecutive constructions lack an overt linker and can be easily confused with SVCs at a superficial level (see Section 6.3.8).With SVCs, the insertion of such marker of syntactic dependency as illustrated in examples (48a–c) yields ungrammatical sentences.[10] Even though an Etulo SVC may be defined in terms of monoclausality and the absence of a syntactic dependency marker, such characterization is not restricted to SVCs but may be extended to include a subset of consecutive constructions. In addition to the presence vs absence of a syntactic dependency marker, other distinctive parameters for distinguishing between both constructions are required.

(48) a. ??á   kīē   údzà   dí   lè   nū   m̀kpà
          3PL:SUBJ   take   money   CORD   PROG   give   credit
          'They are lending money.'

      b. *àdì   tá   élâ   dí   wó   éjî
          PN   scream   voice   CORD   put   1PL:OBJ
          'Adi screamed at us.'

      c. ??àdì   kíé   ánî   údzà   dí   tsé   òɲà   lúū
          PN   take   1SG:POSS money CORD   run   race   go
          'Adi ran away with my money.'

6.3.4 Optional and obligatory SVCs

There are many instances of optional and obligatory SVCs in Etulo, especially with *kíé* 'take' and other verbs like *nū* 'give'. The verb *kíé* functions both as a main and minor verb in different semantic contexts and always occupies the first slot in SVCs, while *nū* occupies the final verb slot. Example (49a) shows the optional occurrence of *kíé*. Its deletion in (49b) does not affect the meaning of the main verb *fúé*. The native speakers do not seem to perceive any semantic difference between such constructions. In the words of my informants, sentence (49b) is a shorter way of saying (49a). From a pragmatic point of view, however, it could be that the co-occurrence of the minor verb *kíé* with *fúé* indicates an elaborate breakdown or description of the event of sprinkling, which involves first the subevent of taking (scooping) water and then sprinkling it. This can likewise

---

10   The double question mark is used in some examples to specify that though the constructions do not count as SVCs, they may possibly receive a consecutive or coordinate interpretation. For instance, (12c) could be interpreted as *Adi took my money and ran away* rather than *Adi ran away with my money*. The first interpretation indicates that the verb series express two different but sequential events, while the second interpretation indicates a unified meaning.

account for the optional co-occurrence of *kíé* with nū in (50a and 50b). In contrast, the omission of the minor verb *kíé* in (51b) changes the meaning from *'sell'* to *'buy'*. The co-occurrence of *kíé* with *gíá* in a SVC is therefore obligatory for the realization of the meaning 'sell' (see 51a). The combination of *gbó ábɔ̂* 'clap' and *nū* 'give' in (51c) produces the idiomatic meaning 'beg' which can be re-interpreted as clap if one of the serial verbs (*nū* 'give) is deleted.

(49) a. ń   kà   kíé   ènì   fúé
        1SG:SUBJ FUT   take   water   sprinkle
        'I will sprinkle water.'

     b. ń   kà   fúé   ènì
        1SG:SUBJ FUT   sprinkle water
        'I will sprinkle water.'

(50) a. á   kīē   údzà   lè   nū   m̀kpà
        3PL:SUBJ take   money   PROG   give   credit
        'They are lending money.'

     b. á   lē   nū   m̀kpà   údzâ
        3PL   PROG   give   credit money
        'They are lending money.'

(51) a. àdì   kíé   ángwɔ́   gīā
        PN   take   yam   sell
        'Adi sold yams.'

     b. àdì   gíá   ángwɔ́
        PN   buy   yam
        'Adi bought yams.'

     c. àdì   lè   gbó   ábɔ̂   nū   ìsɛ̀sɛ́
        PN   PROG   clap   hand   give   PN
        'Adi is begging Isɛsɛ.'

6.3.5 The asymmetric and symmetric divide

Asymmetric SVCs in Etulo mostly encode single events expressed by a verb (main verb) as further modified by another verb (minor verb). The minor verb specifies direction, comparison, benefactive and instrumental role. Verbs that often occupy the minor slot in an asymmetric SVC include motion verbs (*lúū, kɛ̀* 'go', *bá, wá,* 'come', *zìtá* 'leave'), *nū* 'give' (benefactive), *ŋà* 'surpass' (comparative), *kíé* 'take/carry' (instrumental) etc. A peculiar feature of this closed set of verbs is their capacity to co-occur with a wide range of major verbs in the asymmetric context, functioning as modifiers. Some of these modifying verbs follow a fixed order; *lúū* and *ŋà* always follow the main verb, while *kíé* may occur as the first element in an asymmetric verb series. The transitivity value of the minor verb corresponds to that of the main verb, but this is not always the case. There are instances in which the components of an SVC have different transitivity values. Though the verb series of an asymmetric SVC may have different transitivity values, it is the transitive feature of the main verb that determines the transitivity value of the SVC as a whole. In (52) the main verb *gíá* 'buy' is modified by the minor verb *nū* 'give' for a benefactive meaning. Both verbs have transitive values.

Example (53) illustrates the co-occurrence of the major verb *kíé* 'carry' (transitive) and the motion verb 'go' (intransitive), which functions as a direction-indicating modifier; its transitive meaning stems from the main verb. In (54), one observes a combination of the intransitive main verb *tsé* 'run' and the transitive minor verb *ŋà* 'surpass', where the latter indicates comparison. The construction is however intransitive as a result of the point made earlier, i.e. that the transitivity value of an asymmetric SVC is derived from that of the main verb. The foregoing reasserts the view that verbs do not necessarily retain their original transitivity status when they form a SVC. A strict categorization of main and minor verbs as obligatory occupants of, respectively, the first and second verb slots does not seem to apply in Etulo. Thus, a main or minor verb could occur either as the first or second element in an asymmetric SVC. Observe that *kíé* the main verb appears as the V_1 in (53), while *nū* 'give', the main verb, occurs as V_2 in (55). Apparently, certain verbs are more likely to occur as the first element than the second element and vice versa. Besides, this possibility is not triggered by their function as main or minor verbs. Note also, that some of these minor verbs do not always function as modifiers in an SVC.

(52) àdì gíá àfè óɲíī nū ánî
PN buy book one give 1SG
'Adi bought me one book.'

(53) àdì kíé ítsè mà lú ódzû
PN carry chair the go house
'Adi carried the chair to the house.'

(54) àdì lí tsé òɲà ɲà iɲànì
PN HAB run race surpass PN
'Adi runs faster than Inyani.'

(55) á kīē údzà lé nū m̀kpà
3PL:SUBJ take money PROG give credit
'They are lending money.'

Symmetric SVCs encode more complex events that comprise sub events which occur sequentially and are semantically or pragmatically linked together. The components of a symmetric SVC come from an unrestricted class and have an equal status. A set of verbs that are now synchronically v+v compounds (see Section 3.5.3) used to belong to the class of symmetric SVC. Some of these verbs denote manner (cause-effect) as exemplified in (56) where V$_1$ *tsé* 'hit' encodes causation and V$_2$ *nwɔ́* 'kill' the result or effect of the event of hitting. Other symmetric verbs denote two consecutive aspects of an event as in (57), where the verbs *nū* and *kwúlésĕ* jointly mean 'stop'. These verb series may as well be reinterpreted as a causative construction. Components of symmetric SVCs can be contiguous or non-contiguous, and often share the same transitivity value. Such SVCs in Etulo might possibly be in the process of lexicalization considering their idiomatic inclinations in some contexts. Take for instance the idiomatic meaning of the SVC *àdì gbó ábɔ̂ nū isèsé* 'Adi begged Isɛsɛ' which has the literal interpretation: 'Adi clap hand give Isese' / 'Adi clapped for Isese'. These SVCs mostly share the same subject but not always the same object. Consider these examples:

(56) àdì   tsé-nwɔ́   isèsé
     PN   hit-kill   PN
     'Adi killed Isɛsɛ.'

(57) ánî   nù   má   kwúlésĕ
     1SG   make   3PL:OBJ   stop
     'I stopped them./ I made them stop.'

(58) á   kīē   ìkínākpà   lè   tsé   ɔ̀nɔ̀
     3PL:SUBJ   take   maize   PROG   spread   sun
     'They are drying the maize.'

6.3.6 Wordhood and contiguity

The components of an SVC in Etulo may be contiguous or non-contiguous. With the exception of lexicalized serial verbs (now compounds), which form a single grammatical word made up of two phonological words, Etulo SVCs consist of multiple (separate) words. Multi-word serial verbs refer to separate individual words that function jointly as a single SVC. They may be separated by other constituents such as prepositions, direct objects, complements etc. Example (59) illustrates two identical SVCs that involve different positioning of the serial verbs. In sentence (59a), the SVC comprises two contiguous verbs, *kíé* 'take' and *fàwá* 'tear'. In (59b), these same verbs are separated by the direct object *ànwúntò* 'cloth' and are therefore non-contiguous. The contiguity of serial verbs in such cases is relatively optional. In example (60a), however, the non-contiguity of the serial verbs *tá* 'scream' and *wó* 'put' is obligatory. Both verbs are separated by the nominal complement *èlâ* 'voice'. The direct juxtaposition of both verbs results in ungrammaticality (60b).

(59) a. á kīē fàwá ànwúntò ńtónê wà
       3PL:SUBJ take tear cloth these PERF
       'They have torn these clothes.'
  b.   á kīē ànwúntò ńtónê fàwá wà
       3PL:SUBJ take cloth these tear PERF
       'They have torn these clothes.'
(60) a. á tā élâ wó éjî
       3PL:SUBJ scream voice put 1PL:OBJ
       'They screamed at us.'
  b.   *á tā wó élâ éjî
       3PL:SUBJ scream put voice 1PL:OBJ
       'They screamed at us.'

6.3.7 Argument sharing

Argument sharing is a core feature of Etulo serial verbs. Both subject and object arguments may be shared. While subject sharing is applicable to both transitive and intransitive verbs, object sharing is restricted to transitive verbs.

6.3.7.1 Subject sharing

Subject sharing is the most common form of argument sharing in Etulo. In a SVC, the verbs (whether transitive or intransitive) obligatorily share the same subject. This is illustrated in (61a and 61b).

(61) a. àdí kìkíè lúū wà
       PN walk go PERF
       'Adi has walked away.'
  b.   ánî kà tásɛ́ jìdɔ́ lú-bā údé
       1SG:SUBJ FUT come.out return go-come home
       'I will return home.'

6.3.7.2 Object sharing (same subject-same object)

Object sharing is a feature of some transitive verbs in SVCs. In (62a), for instance, the verbs *kíé* 'take and *fúé* 'sprinkle' share the object argument *ènì* 'water'. This is also shown in (62b).

(62) a.
	ìsèsé	kíé	ènì	lè	fúé
	PN	take	water	PROG	sprinkle

'Isɛsɛ is sprinkling water.'

b.
	ń	kà	kíé	fàwá	àfè	ḿgbí	ámá
	1SG:SUBJ	FUT	take	tear	cloth	POSS	them

'I will tear their clothes.'

6.3.7.3 Arguments and switch function

A possible instance of switch function, where the perceived object of V$_1$ is interpreted as the subject of the V$_2$ is exemplified in (63).[11] Here, two subevents are identified, 'push' and 'open', where the object of V$_1$ *tsàmú* 'push' functions syntactically as the subject of V$_2$ *kwùlúū* 'open'. Note that V$_2$ is intransitive in and by itself as in *ònùfé mà kwùlúū* 'the door opened'. As observed in Section 6.1.7, core arguments are not morphologically marked in Etulo, but rather specified by constituent order.

(63)
	ó	tsàmú	ònùfé	mà	kwùlúū
	3SG:SUBJ	push	door	DET	open

'He pushed the door open.'

6.3.8 Differentiating SVCs from consecutive constructions

In many verb serializing languages of West Africa, such as Igbo, Ewe and Akan, one finds a group of roughly similar constructions, all involving the occurrence of verb sequences. Aikhenvald (2008) adopts 'multi-verb construction' as an umbrella term for such constructions. They include serial, consecutive and overlapping constructions.

Two forms of multi-verb constructions are identified in Etulo: consecutive and serial.

Basically, consecutive constructions involve two or more verbs that express related events which may occur in succession or simultaneously, while SVCs involve a sequence of verbs that may jointly serve as a single predicate, denoting a unified event or related phases of an event. The consecutive constructions of (64a and 64b) express a series of related events that occur sequentially, such as steal-run and fetch-wash.

---

[11] In Etulo, the causative construction may be understood as an example of switch function, whereby the object of V$_1$ (causative verb) functions as the subject of V$_2$ (main verb) as in *àdì nū ánî mà àkwɔ́* 'Adi made me cry'. The causative is formed by the causative verb *nū* and the main verb (see Section 6.2.2.1). The stative form of the dynamic verb *kwùlúū* 'open' is realized by the stative verb *la* 'lie/lay' and the adjective *ásísá* 'open. Thus one can say *ònùfê lá ásísá* 'the door is open'.

(64) a. àdì   jí   úmí   ánî   údzà   dí   kíé   tsé   òɳà   lúū
         PN   steal theft 1SG:POSS money   CORD   take   run   race   go
         'Adi stole my money and ran away.'

    b. ábû   mùà   ènì   nwù   íné   wà
       2SG:SUBJ   fetch   water   wash   face   PERF
       'You have fetched water and washed your face.'

Both construction types share a lot of similarities which can be somewhat misleading. Tey have in common the sequence of two or more verbs in a single clause, shared arguments, and shared temporal values. They, however, differ in several ways. One of the major distinctions between the consecutive and serial verb constructions in Etulo is the optional occurrence of the linking element or connector *dí* in some consecutive constructions. Such linking element is obligatorily absent in SVCs (see 65a–b). Other points of divergence stem from the different inherent nature of the event expressed by both constructions, and the optionality of jointly vs multiple marking of tense-aspect values (This will be discussed in Section 6.3.8.1).

(65) a. àdì   kíé   ítsè   mà   lú   ódzū   wà
        PN   take   chair   the   go   home   PERF
        'Adi has taken the chair home.'

    b. á   kà   gíé   ùnwógīē   (dí)   ná   únâ
       3PL:SUBJ FUT   eat   food   CORD   sleep   sleep
       'They will eat and sleep.'

6.3.8.1 TAM values of SVCs and consecutive constructions

The TAM values of SVCs are jointly marked. In other words, the preverbal or postverbal particles that express TAM are marked just once in an SVC. Each of these particles has its peculiar distribution or occurrence pattern in relation to V_1 and V_2. The future morpheme *kà* is linked to the first verb in a verb series. If, on the other hand, the future marker directly precedes V_2, there is a change in meaning. In the latter case, the construction changes from a SVC to a consecutive construction. Unlike SVCs, verb series in a consecutive construction may have the same or different temporal or aspectual values. In (66a), the future marker precedes V_1 (*kíé*, 'take') and has scope over the whole construction. In (66b), where it directly precedes V_2 (*fúé*, 'sprinkle') the first verb (V_1) receives a past interpretation, thereby restricting the scope of the future morpheme to V_2.[12] The

---

[12] Multiple marking using the progressive morpheme (having the progressive morpheme precede each verb in an SVC) seems possible in Etulo but sounds unnatural. A construction such as *á kīē íkínákpà lé tsē ònɔ* 'they are drying maize' is natural and preferred over *á lē kīē íkínákpà lé tsē ònɔ*.

perfect marker occurs in sentence final position of any SVC and has scope over the entire construction. Any change in its position of occurrence yields ungrammatical constructions (see 67a and 67b). In both symmetric and asymmetric SVCs, the habitual morpheme *lí* can only be linked to the first verb (see 68a). Ungrammatical constructions are realized when it is directly followed by the second verb in a verb series, as illustrated in (68b). For the progressive, the preverbal particle *le* directly precedes the main verb in some asymmetric SVCs, especially directional SVCs (see 33a). With comparative (asymmetric) and most symmetric SVCs, it may directly precede either one of the verbs (see 69b and 69c). SVCs occur with all existing TAM categories and in all moods without restrictions. In English, for instance, an imperative construction such as *go eat* looks like a SVC at the surface level. However, one readily observes that such constructions are restricted to the imperative mood. Thus one cannot possibly say *I went eat*. Such restrictions are not characteristic of SVCs in Etulo and in languages where they occur. No temporal or aspectual contrast has been observed in Etulo SVCs in relation to the individual verb components. Serial verbs basically share the same TAM values. The reverse is the case in languages like Ewe, where in addition to being marked for the same categories, components of a SVC can also be marked for different categories to the extent that semantic compatibility is fulfilled.

(66) a. ìsèsé kà kíé ènì fúé
       PN   FUT take water sprinkle
       'Isɛsɛ will sprinkle water.'

   b. ìsèsé kíé ènì kà fúé
       PN   take water FUT sprinkle
       'Isɛsɛ took water to sprinkle.'

(67) a. á kīē ànwúntò ńtónê fàwá wà
       3PL:SUBJ take cloth these tear PERF
       'They have torn these clothes.'

   b. *á kīē ànwúntò ńtónê wà fàwá
       3PL:SUBJ take cloth these PERF tear
       'They have torn these clothes.'

(68) a. àdì lí kíé ànwúntò ḿgbán gīā
       PN HAB take cloth POSS:3SG sell
       'Adi sells his clothes.'

   b. *àdì kíé ànwúntò ḿgbán lí gīā
       PN   take cloth POSS:3SG HAB sell
       'Adi sells his clothes.'

(69) a. ínwúnɔ̂ lé bùlù lúū
       bird   PROG fly go
       'The bird is flying away.'

b. àdì   lè   kíé   ànwúntò   ḿgbán   gīā
   PN   PROG   take   cloth   POSS:3SG   sell
   'Adi is selling his clothes.'

c. àdì   kíé   ànwúntò   ḿgbán   lè   gíá
   PN   take   cloth   POSS:3SG   PROG   sell
   'Adi is selling his clothes.'

For non-finite constructions (like the infinitive), the low tone prefix which marks the infinitive always attaches to the first verb in both symmetric and asymmetric SVCs.

(70) a. ínwúnɔ́   nâ   mìná   ò-bùlù   lūú
        bird   that   want   INF-fly   go
        'That bird wants to fly away.'

     b. àdí   mìná   ò-kíé   ànwúntò   ḿgbán   gīā
        PN   want   INF-take   cloth   POSS:3SG   sell
        'Adi wants to sell his cloth.'

The similarities and differences of multi-verb constructions can be summarized as in the table below:

Table 6.2 Distinguishing SVCs from consecutives

Features	Consecutive	SVCs
Shared argument (subject)	Yes	Yes
Monoclausal interpretation	Yes	Yes
Marker(s) of syntactic dependency	(Optional)	No
Shared temporal frame	Possible	Yes
Single marking of tense-aspect	Yes (optional)	Yes
Express a unified event	No	Yes
Individual verbs can function as independent verbs in simple clauses (in same form)	Yes	Yes

6.3.9 Conclusion

The serial verb construction is clearly a productive grammatical device in Etulo. It expresses a variety of semantic notions. Some of its semantic functions make up for the paucity of other grammatical categories. In many ways, the identified features of the Etulo SVCs correspond with the cross-linguistic characterization of SVCs. The functional motivation for the common occurrence of SVCs in Etulo is partly tied to the speakers' need to connect events considered to be closely related for pragmatic or cultural reasons. Some symmetric SVCs comprise verb sequences that give rise to an idiomatic meaning rather than designating unified or related subevents. This may be understood in relation with the grammatical process of lexicalization. SVCs differ from consecutive constructions on the basis of some crucial parameters: the former do not allow co-ordinating conjunctions, while the latter do, the former share a single TAM while the latter need not.

7. Tense, Aspect and Modality

7.0 Introduction

This chapter discusses the strategies involved in expressing tense, aspect and modality (TAM) in Etulo. In the typological literature on tense and aspect, it is often asserted that many African languages (see for instance, Igbo and Yoruba) have aspect as a grammaticalized category. Bhat (1999), states that languages could be typologically classified on the basis of the prominence given to one or more of the TAM categories. How this assumption applies to Etulo needs to be ascertained. The idea of tense adopted here is inspired by the notion of absolute vs relative tense proposed by Comrie (1976). For the aspectual category, emphasis is laid on the basic distinction, perfective vs imperfective.

7.1 An overview of tense and aspect

Tense is the grammaticalized expression of location in time (Comrie 1976). It is a grammatical category that locates an event or situation in time relative to the speech time (deictic) or to some other reference point given in the utterance (non-deictic). The terms deictic and non-deictic correspond respectively to absolute and relative tense. Comrie (1985: 58) equally states that 'the difference between absolute and relative tense is not that between the present moment versus some other point in time as a reference point, but rather between a form whose meaning specifies the present moment as reference point and a form whose meaning does not specify that the present moment must be the reference point.' For absolute tense, a three-way distinction is made between the past, present and future as in languages like English. Past time reference denotes an event or situation that occurred prior to the speech time, present denotes an event that coincides or occurs simultaneously with the speech time, and future denotes an event located after the speech time. The distinction, remote vs distant, is morphologically expressed in some languages, with a further distinction between recent and remote past, and/or between immediate and distant future. Future time reference is often said to involve elements of prediction and/or intention. However, as Dahl (1985) observes, intention more often than not is not a necessary condition for the use of the future. The future category in mood prominent languages falls in the irrealis class rather than tense. As for relative (or non-deictic) tenses, the reference point for the location of a situation is some point in time given by the context, not necessarily the moment of discourse, as in the case of absolute tense.

The grammaticalization of tense distinctions implies the morphological coding of tense by means of affixation, auxiliaries, particles or clitics. The grammatical markers of tense are in some languages derived from verbs of movement like 'go', 'come' etc. Though all human languages have some way to indicate time reference, there are languages that are described as tenseless, i.e. languages that lack any grammaticalized expression of tense. For such languages, aspect or mood may be more prominent. Time adverbials (yesterday, today, tomorrow) are of course utilized for time distinction in all languages.

Aspect essentially embodies the temporal makeup of an event or situation as either ongoing or completed. It is inherently non-deictic, i.e. not anchored on the speech point. Comrie (1976) defines aspects as the ways of viewing the internal temporal constituency of a situation. Similarly, Kortman (1991) relates aspect to the fact that an event/situation, whether static or dynamic, telic or atelic, can be described as a completed whole or as something ongoing, in progress or simply existent for a given period of time. The fundamental aspectual distinction is the contrast between perfective and imperfective, with the latter including progressive, continuous and habitual (cf. Comrie 1976, Bertinetto 1997). Comrie (1976: 4) observes that 'perfective aspect looks at the situation from outside, without distinguishing any internal structure in the situation, whereas imperfective aspect looks at the situation from inside and as such is crucially concerned with the internal structure of the situation.' Thus, while the perfective aspect presents an event as an unanalyzable whole, the imperfect aspect views it as ongoing or habitually repeated. Some languages morphologically distinguish between two verb forms expressing the perfective and imperfective aspect (like in Moore, a Gur language, Hopi etc.) or periphrastically by means of auxiliaries, particles or clitics. In some West African languages, tone functions distinctively in the marking of aspect (cf. Anyanwu 1999). In some languages where temporal distinctions are less evident, the aspectual category assumes a more prominent role. This is often the case in many African languages where, for instance, the progressive coincides with the traditional present tense, as in English. In relation to time reference, there is a high tendency for perfective situations to indicate past events and for imperfective ones to indicate present events (typically progressive events). Within the domain of perfectivity, the perfect denotes a completed event, whose result still persists at a given point in time, often called reference time.

7.2 Etulo tense and aspect system

Evidence in Etulo indicates a tense distinction based on a future vs non-future opposition, and an aspectual distinction between perfective and imperfective. The situation is represented in the table below. VB stands for verbal base. The asterisk indicates some sort of restriction that characterizes the co-occurrence of the progressive and habitual morphemes with a subset of stative verbs. Perfective is expressed by the bare VB whenever the verb expresses past reference, as well as by the perfect and the future; imperfectivity is expressed by the bare VB in the relevant contexts (see Section 7.2.1 for details), and by the appropriate morphemes conveying the progressive, habitual/generic values.

Table 7.1 Tense-aspect distinctions

Markers	Time reference	Aspect value
bare VB	Past/present	Perfective/imperfective
ka + bare VB	Future	Perfective
le + bare VB*	Past/present progressive	Imperfective
ka + *le* + bare VB*	Future progressive	Imperfective
li + bare VB*	Habitual present	Imperfective
(*teji*) + *li* + bare VB*	Habitual past	Imperfective
li + bare VB	Generic	Imperfective
bare VB + *wa*	Present perfect	Perfective
(*teji*) + bare VB	Pluperfect	Perfective
bare verb + *wa*	Future perfect	Perfective

7.2.1 The non-future

The non-future in Etulo designates a situation or event that is anterior to or overlapping the utterance time. As is the case in other north-west African languages, the temporal interpretation of the bare verbal root is by and large a function of the eventive vs stative distinction: eventive predicates have a default past reference, while stative verbs have a default present reference. A similar situation is, for instance, recorded in some Benue Congo languages like Yala, an Idomoid language spoken in Nigeria (cf. Okoji 1986), Itsekiri (Omamor 1982), Igbo (Emenanjo 2015) etc. Needless to say, the context may override the default temporal interpretation of a predicate. Consider the following examples:

(1) a. àdì ǹdéɛ̆
       PN   be.tired
       'Adi is tired./Adi was tired.'
    b. àdì ǹdéɛ̆ èdédĕ
       PN   be.tired yesterday
       'Adi was tired yesterday.'
(2) a. àdì kíé éjî údzà kíé nū ǹgísè
       PN take 1PL:POSS money take give people
       'Adi takes our money and gives it to people.'
    b. àdì kíé ánî údzà kíé nū ìsèsé
       PN take 1SG:POSS money take give PN
       'Adi took my money and gave it to Isɛsɛ.'
(3) a. ánî tá ábû ámgbā
       1SG:SUBJ greet 2SG:OBJ greeting
       'I greet you.'
    b. ánî tá má ámgbā
       1SG:SUBJ greet 1PL:OBJ greeting
       'I greeted them.'

Sentence (1a) illustrates the stative event ǹdéɛ̆ 'be tired', which has a default present time reading but does not preclude past time interpretation. As a matter of fact, if one is tired now, she or he must have become tired at some time before now. This ambiguity is resolved in (1b) with the time adverbial èdédĕ 'yesterday', restricting its temporal reference to the past. A close study of bare verbs expressing dynamic events in context shows that they too are ambiguous between present and past time reading (2a and 2b). This is also true for the dynamic verb tá ámgbā 'greet' as shown in (3a) and (3b). Etulo does not mark temporal distance values in either past or future contexts time by means of morphological devices. The co-occurrence of time adverbials like 'yesterday' or 'now', with the bare verb, although not obligatory, may specify the time interpretation.

7.2.2 The future

The future denotes an event that will take place at an anticipated point in time after the utterance time. It is marked by the preverbal particle *ka* which directly precedes the verb and is characterized by tone polarity. In other words, the future marker has no inherent tone: its tonal value is determined by the tone of the immediately adjacent tone bearing unit (see Section 2.4.10 for more discussion on tone polarity). In examples (4a–b), the future marker occurs in declarative constructions directly preceding the verbs. It obligatorily co-occurs with modal markers in irrealis/modal constructions that express possibility, probability, ability or counterfactual (see 5a–b and Section 7.4 for further discussion on modality). As indicated in Table 7.1, the future tense interacts with other aspectual values, such as the progressive (see (7) in Section 7.3.1). As with the past reference, Etulo does not mark temporal distance values in the future. Below are some examples:

(4) a. ànwúntō ḿgbí ánî kà nwɔ́ɔ̄
cloth POSS 1SG FUT dry
'My clothes will dry.'

b. àdì kà bó íbɔ̄
PN FUT pray prayer
'Adi will pray.'

(5) a. ánî kà jágbá ʃì ìfúé
1SG:SUBJ FUT be.able dance dance
'I will be able to dance.'

b. ò kí kā ŋà
3SG:SUBJ MOD FUT surpass
'He would have won'

From the foregoing, it is reasonable to posit a future/non-future contrast for the Etulo tense system where the non-future is interpreted as preterite or present depending, first and foremost, on the default semantic class of the verb, but also on the context.

7.3 Aspectual distinction

Etulo makes, in most cases, a neat morphological distinction between perfective and imperfective aspect. The latter further distinguishes as the progressive and habitual (generic), while the former is explicitly marked in the perfect. The only area of ambiguity is that of the verb root, which can receive both interpretations in present- and past-referring situations depending on the predicate and on the specific context (see Section 7.2.1).

7.3.1 The progressive

The progressive expresses a continuous or ongoing situation which can be located in the past, present or future timeline. It is marked by a tonologically conditioned preverbal particle *le* which bears a high tone with inherently low tone verbs and a low tone with inherently high and mid tone verbs. It is thus a case of tonal polarity. It occasionally assumes a step tone when preceded by a high tone vowel such as the 3rd person plural subject. Given the Etulo future/non-future system, there is no morphological distinction between past and present progressive. The progressive form has a default present meaning but does not preclude a past reading, especially where time adverbs or temporal adverbial clauses are used. By contrast, the future progressive is expressed by a combination of the progressive and the future marker (7). From a cross-linguistic perspective, there is indication that the semantic class of the verb (dynamic vs stative) affects its compatibility with the progressive form. Comrie (1976) states that verbs tend to divide into two disjoint (non-overlapping) classes; those that appear in the progressive form (which roughly correspond to dynamic verbs) and those that cannot (which correspond to stative verbs). The extent to which this proposition applies to individual languages tends to vary. Bertinetto (1986) observes that different languages would be ranked differently in this respect. Languages like Italian (apart from some substandard varieties) disallow the co-occurrence of the progressive form with stative verbs while in languages like Portuguese and English the compatibility of the progressive form with many (non-permanent) statives results in the destativization of stative predicates. For instance, *Mary is being nasty* indicates that she is temporarily behaving in the stated way. Hence, languages like English tolerate, to an extent, the use of the progressive with some statives to suggest an idea of temporariness. Similarly, many Benue Congo languages like Yala, Itsekiri and Igbo exhibit a high level of compatibility of the progressive form with typical stative verbs (cf. Okoji 1986, Omamor 1982). In Etulo, the progressive marker is compatible with all dynamic verbs and with a substantial subset of stative verbs. However, a distinction should be made regarding the respective semantic interpretation. With dynamic verbs, the progressive aspect denotes an ongoing situation that is located in the past, present or future. In (6a), for instance, the progressive construction with the dynamic verb *ʃá* 'laugh' may be interpreted as either past or present (past progressive or present progressive), except in contexts where a temporal adverb or clause specifies the interpretation (6b). Likewise, the progressive morpheme *le* combines with the future marker *ka* to express the future progressive as illustrated in (7).

(6) a. ìsɛ̀sɛ́ lè ʃá ádī íʃá
PN PROG laugh PN laugh
'Isɛsɛ is laughing at Adi.'/'Isɛsɛ was laughing at Adi.'

b. ánî lè ʃá íʃá ɔ̀nɔ̀ nwí ó dí ánî mànì
1SG PROG laugh laugh time REL 3SG see 1SG:OBJ DET
'I was laughing when he saw me.'

(7) ń ká lè ná únâ ɔ̀nɔ̀ nwí ábû kà bá mànì
1SG FUT PROG sleep sleep time REL 2SG FUT come DET
'I will be sleeping when you (will) come.'

With a subset of stative verbs, the progressive aspect expresses a gradual change in state or the transition into a state. In other words, the co-occurrence of non-permanent statives with the progressive marker indicates the beginning or inception of a state, or else the gradual approximation to an ideal target. In examples (8a–d), the constructions *lè ǹdéē* 'getting tired', *lè kíē* 'getting old', *lè má* 'ripening', *lè jí ùjù* 'getting cold' imply a gradual change: from unripe to a ripe state, from hot to cold, from young to old etc. With respect to the beginning of a state, an alternative construction consists in using a periphrastic construction based on the verb *wítá* 'start' followed by the main verb.¹ Below is a list of stative verbs that are compatible with the progressive morpheme *le*:

(8) a. dí   'see'
     b. wɛ́   'remember'
     c. kìɔ̀ ìtíngā   'be angry'
     d. dɔ́ ótsē   'be sick'
     e. ǹdéē   'be tired'
     f. gbósá   'understand'
     g. nwɔ́ɔ̄   'be dry'
     h. m̀búò   'be full'
     i. kíē   'be old'
     j. má   'be ripe'
     k. jí ùjù   'be cold'
     l. kpā ìtúkwû   'love'
     m. dɔ́ èmbùà   'be hungry'

---

1   Etulo adopts a periphrastic means of expressing a variety of meanings, such as inceptive, conative and evolutive, using dedicated verbs: *wítá* 'start' (inceptive), *fìà* 'try' (conative) and *jé* 'become' (evolutive). For the inceptive meaning, however, native speakers indicate preference for the progressive construction (i) rather than the one based on the inceptive verb *wítá* 'start' (ii). Consider the following examples:

(i)	ánî	lè	wɛ́	àlí	ùnwɔ́	dúú	(inceptive)
	1SG	PROG	remember	every	thing	all	

*'I am remembering everything.'

(ii)	ánî	lè	wítá	ò-wɛ́	àlí	ùnwɔ́	dúú	(inceptive)
	1SG	PROG	start	PREF-remember	every	thing	all	

'I am starting to remember everything.'

(iii)	ánî	lé	fìà	ò-wɛ́	àlí	ùnwɔ́	dúú	(conative)
	1SG	PROG	try	PREF-remember	every	thing	all	

'I am trying to remember everything.'

(9) a. m̀tsà lè má
mango PROG be.ripe
'The mangoes are ripening.'

b. àdì lè kíē̄
PN PROG be.old
'Adi is getting/growing old.'

c. ùnwógīē nê lè jí ùjù
food this PROG be.cold cold
'This food is getting cold.'

d. ábû lè ṅdéē̄
2SG:SUBJ PROG tired
'You are getting tired.'

There are verbs like *wó* 'wear' and *tó* 'tie' which have stative and non stative uses. Both verbs receive a stative interpretation in (10a and 10b,) where they indicate that the subject is wearing a cloth or tying a wrapper for the time being. By contrast, they express a dynamic situation in (11a and 11b). Their occurrence with the progressive morpheme *le* implies that the subject is performing the act of putting on a cloth or tying the wrapper at the given moment. Other stative verbs, however, such as *dzè* 'live' and *ládzè* 'lay', are incompatible with the progressive morpheme. Their co-occurrence with the progressive morpheme results in ungrammatical or unnatural constructions (12a–b).

(10) a. àdì wó ànwúntò óndzúndzé
PN wear cloth white
'Adi is wearing a white cloth.'

b. ìɲànì tó ábídá
PN tie wrapper
'Inyani is tying a wrapper.'

(11) a. àdì lè wó ànwúntò óndzúndzé
PN PROG wear cloth white
'Adi is putting on a white cloth.'

b. ìɲànì lè tó ábídá
PN PROG tie wrapper
'Inyani is tying a wrapper.'

(12) a. *ìsèsé lé dzè àdì
PN PROG live PN
'Isese is living in Adi.'

b. *àdì lè ládzè mì ákwúló
PN PROG lie on bed
'Adi is lying on the bed.'

In addition to the progressive reading, the progressive marker may give rise to other interpretations: most notably, that of 'proximative', i.e. (imminent) future reading. This is frequently attested in other West African languages such as Moore (Bertinetto & Pacmogda 2013), and Tuwuli (Harley 2008). In Etulo, this seems to be lexically specific, i.e. the future reference expressed by the progressive is only possible with some verbs. For instance, in (13a), the motion verb *lú* co-occurs with the progressive marker to yield a future, rather than a progressive reading. Supposedly, this interpretation is triggered by the temporal adverb, since without it, a progressive interpretation is retained. In a sentence like *ánî lè lú ɔnɔ́ nwí ábû kwú ánî èlá mànî* 'I was leaving when you called me', the progressive marker clearly expresses progressivity. With a verb such as *dzè* 'stay', however, one has a future reading even without any futural adverb. In other words, (13b) may be rephrased as *ìsèsé ká dzè àdì* 'Isɛsɛ will stay in Adi'.[2] The occurrence of the progressive morpheme with a punctual verb like *kwɔ* 'cough' denotes repetition of the punctual event of coughing.

(13) a. àdì   lè   lúû   ékéká
        PN   PROG   go   tomorrow
        'Adi is leaving/going tomorrow.'

     b. ìsèsé   lé   dzè   àdì
        PN   PROG   stay   PN
        'Isɛsɛ is staying in Adi.'

     c. àdì   lè   kwɔ́   ókwô
        PN   PROG   cough   cough
        'Adi is coughing.'

7.3.2 The habitual

Bertinetto and Lenci (2012) classify habituals and other related categories as subtypes of gnomic imperfectivity. These categories have in common the ability to express generalizations of some kind. The habitual aspect characterizes a recurrent situation, i.e. an event that occurs repeatedly over a more or less extended period of time, featuring a characterization of a given referent or situation. It should be distinguished from iteratives and generics. In contrast with habituals, generics express a more law-like state of affairs which is considered to be timeless. The habitual tend to be morphologically marked more often than the generic (Dahl 1985), although both categories may be morphologically marked by the same means. Habituality interacts with the temporal domain: although mostly

---

2   The verb *dzè* realizes a variety of meanings in Etulo including 'be, have, live/stay' etc. In its function as a copula (be), or as a verb of possession (have), it is incompatible with the progressive morpheme.

referring to the past, it may have present value. According to Comrie (1976), the past habitual provides an implicature that the event in question no longer holds unless further assertion is made, as in 'He used to live there and still lives there'. In Etulo, the habitual is marked by the preverbal particle *lí* which bears a high tone. It equally marks the generic aspect (see 17). With respect to time reference, there appears to be no explicit distinction between past and present habitual; instead, the time adverbial *téjî* 'before' may be used to reinforce a past time reading as in (15a and 15b). When it co-occurs with the habitual form, it gives rise to the implicature that the situation no longer holds. This implicature is cancellable in contexts where the speaker expresses uncertainty about the present status of any past habitual event (see 16). The habitual form is compatible with dynamic verbs and a subset of stative verbs (contingent, i.e. non-permanent statives). The following examples are illustrative.

(14) a. ánî lí fó ákwɔ̀ ńgbí ábû àlí égbē dúú
       1SG:SUBJ HAB hear cry POSS 2SG every day all
       'I hear your cry every day.'
   b. ò lí ná únâ mì ákwúló
       3SG:SUBJ HAB sleep sleep on bed
       'She sleeps on the bed.'

(15) a. ó téjî lí ʃá íʃá jì éjî
       3SG:SUBJ before HAB laugh laugh with 1PL:OBJ
       'He used to laugh with us.'
   b. èkwɔ́ nê téjî lí nwɔ́ɔ̄
       tree this before HAB be.dry
       'This tree used to be dry.'

(16) àdì téjî lí lā ákwúló nánǐ kpàâ ònènê ánî jé bá
       PN before HAB lie bed that but now 1SG know NEG
       'Adi used to sleep/lie on that bed but now, I don't know...'

(17) ṁdà lí gíé óʃɛ̄
       cow HAB. eat grass
            GEN
       'Cows eat grasses.'

The habitual is compatible with frequency adverbials ('always', 'twice a day'). It is also compatible with iterative adverbials such as 'three times', in combination with a frequency adverbial. In (18a), for instance, the frequency adverbial 'everyday' has a wider scope over the iterative adverbial *akpo eta* 'three times'. Thus, the subject engages in the event at stake for the given number of times with the specified regularity. In the absence of a frequency adverbial, the habitual reading is retained, as illustrated in (18b), provided an appropriate frequency adverbial is presupposed by the speakers involved in a conversation. The NP subject regularly engages in an event for a specified number of times.

With the use of the appropriate time adverbials, the habitual may be referred to a specific interval of time in the past (see 18c).

(18) a. ánî lí kè ùmákáràntá àkpó ètá àlí égbē dúú
       1SG:SUBJ HAB go school time three every day all
       'I go to school three times every day.'

   b. ánî lí kè ùmákáràntá àkpó ètá
      1SG:SUBJ HAB go school time three
      'I go to school three times.'

   c. ònòvà nwí ɲé nâ iɲànì lí kɪ̀ɔ ùnwógīē àkpó ètá mì òfìâ
      year REL pass DEM PN HAB cook food time three in month
      'Last year, Adi used to cook three times monthly.'

Note that the adverbial *téjî* has a wide array of meaning/translations, including 'already', 'before' and 'first'. It is strictly analyzed as a time adverbial rather than a grammaticalized tense morpheme, partly because it realizes several semantic interpretations in different contexts, but also because it can be used interchangeably with similar temporal adverbials like *nósē* 'before' (19a–b). Its occurrence is optional in some contexts where it reinforces a past meaning.

(19) a. ánî téjí lí lélē
       1SG:SUBJ before HAB play
       'I used to play.'

   b. nósē ánî lí lélē
      before 1SG:SUBJ HAB play
      'I used to play.'

A situation may be viewed as being both habitual and progressive, by combining the habitual and the progressive marker. The event of singing, as illustrated in (20), receives a habitual and progressive interpretation with a kind of hyperbolic nuance ('He keeps V-ing all the time'). In other words, the event of singing occurs regularly and goes on for a while in each instance. While the combination of the progressive and habitual marker can be used with all dynamic verbs, native speakers consider it unnatural with some statives. [3]

---

3   Dynamic events are more likely to receive a habitual progressive reading. Native speakers consider the occurrence of some statives with habitual progressive morphemes unnatural. Example: *ábû lí lè ǹdéɛ̄ àlí ɔ̀nɔ́ dúú 'You are always getting tired'. They prefer the use of just the habitual marker in this context. They would rather say *ábû lí ǹdéɛ̄ àlí ɔ̀nɔ́ dúú* 'You are always tired'. Statives are mostly viewed as habitual without necessarily being viewed as progressive. This is probably one of the restrictions observed with the compatibility of the progressive with a subset of stative verbs in Etulo.

(20) ɪ̀ɲànì   lí   lè   ʃí   áʃí   àlí   ɔ̀nɔ́   dúú
     PN   HAB   PROG   sing   song   every   time   all
     'Inyani is always singing.'

7.3.3 The compatibility of statives with progressive and habitual markers

More generally, stative verbs differ in their compatibility with progressive and habitual markers. The table below shows the co-occurrence restrictions of a set of stative verbs with such markers. Verbs that express contingent states are more likely to occur with both morphemes. The habitual value is of course precluded for permanent stative verbs, as a permanent state cannot occur repeatedly. As for compatibility with the progressive marker, see the discussion in Section 7.3.1.

Table 7.2 Aspectual compatibility with stative verbs

Stative verbs	Gloss	Progressive - *le*	Habitual - *lì*
kíɛ̄	'be old'	+	-
kpā ìtúkwû	'love'	+	-
ǹdéɛ̄	'be tired'	+	+
nú òjèjè	'believe'	+	+
dɔ́ ótsē	'be sick'	+	+
jé	'know'	+	-
ládzè	'lie on'	-	+
gbósá	'understand'	+	+
dzè	'stay'	+	+
fó	'hear'	+	+

7.3.4 The perfectal

The present perfect is marked by the post-sentential morpheme *wà*. The perfect marker occurs with both dynamic and stative events. With the former ones, the perfect morpheme denotes a past situation with current relevance at the speech time. Its occurrence in sentence (21b), in contrast to (21a), describes the past and completed event of breaking one's leg, which is currently still broken. In other words, the effect of the event persists at the speech time. With some stative predicates, the perfect marker *wà* indicates a change of state which has current result, giving rise to a more emphatic present state. In perfect constructions with stative verbs like *ǹdéɛ̄* 'be tired', *m̀bùò* 'be full', *kíɛ̄* 'be old' etc., the perfect marker *wà* gives rise to a dynamic meaning indicating a change of state. In examples (22a and 22b), the use of the perfect morpheme with stative predicates implies a shift of X (the subject) from one state to another: i.e., X has left the state of being untired / young and is presently tired / aged. See also a predicate such as dɔ́ ótsē 'be sick', where again the perfect morpheme suggests entering into a resultant state. This inference is however less prominent with other stative predicates like wé 'remember' and fó 'hear' dɔ́ ótsē 'be sick', as shown in (23a and 23b), where one might merely perceive a past event, although the connection with the current moment is nevertheless present. In general, with dynamic verbs and a subset of stative verbs, my native informants intuitively assume that the perfect morpheme wà denotes a past event, but they reject this interpretation for other stative predicates like ǹdéɛ̄ 'be tired', m̀bùò 'be full', kíɛ̄ 'be old', which are interpreted as present-referring, since the result of the event persists at the speech time. Indeed, one is tired to the extent that she or he has become tired.[4]

The past perfect (pluperfect) is not grammaticalized but is rather expressed by a combination of the time adverbial téjî with the perfect morpheme wà and/or a time adverbial clause (see 24 and 25). In the absence of the adverbial clause in (24a), the construction ó téjî lúū wà could be reinterpreted as a present perfect with the translation 'He has already left'. Thus, the semantic reading of the forms téjî...wà as pluperfect is dependent on specific contexts (typically on the use of a time adverbial clause). Additionally, the English pluperfect construction 'At 5 o'clock Adi had left', may be loosely translated as àdì lúū dúúséè ògì èdá, literally 'Adi left before 5 o'clock', rather than as *àdì téjî lúū ògí èdá wà which is judged ungrammatical. Besides, example (24) shows that a kind of pluperfect reading can be obtained in the relevant context by means of the mere perfect, i.e. by contextual inference. This indicates that the tense structure of Etulo is organized on a relative, rather than deictic reference system. Because the pluperfect is not grammaticalized, Etulo uses a temporal adverbial to indicate that the event took place before a reference time located in the past.

For the future perfect, the preverbal future marker *ka* co-occurs with the bare verb and the perfect marker *wà* (see 26). The following examples are illustrative:

(21) a. ánî gbíkīē áfɔ́
       1SG:SUBJ break leg
       'I broke a leg.'

   b. ánî gbíkīē áfɔ́ wà
       1SG:SUBJ break leg PERF
       'I have broken a leg.'

---

4 With dynamic verbs and a subset of stative verbs, native speakers (my informants) intuitively assume that the perfect morpheme *wà* denotes a past event but they reject this interpretation for other stative predicates like ǹdéɛ̄ 'be tired', m̀bùò 'be full', kíɛ̄ 'be old'. Because English lacks adjectival predicates, their translation sometimes seems quite problematic. The closest equivalent involves the use of verbs like *become, get*.

(22) a. á ǹdéē̄ wà
3PL:SUBJ be.tired PERF
'They have become tired.'

b. àdì kíé wà
PN be.old PERF
'Adi has become old.'

(23) a. ìmgbàʃò wé má wà
god remember 3PL:OBJ PERF
'God has remembered them.'

b. ìmgbàʃò fó ákwô ḿgbī éjí wà
god hear cry POSS 1PL PERF
'God has heard our cry.'

(24) ɔ̀nɔ́ nwí ánî bā mà ó téjí lú wà
time REL 1SG come DET 3SG:SUBJ already go PERF
'When I came he had left.'

(25) ábû téjí nā únâ ɔ̀nɔ́ nwí ótsó éjî bá údé mànì
2SG already sleep sleep time REL father 1PL come home DET
'You had slept by the time our father came home.'

(26) àdì kà gíé ùnwógīē wà
PN FUT eat food PERF
'Adi will have eaten.'

7.4 Modality in Etulo

Traditionally, mood is viewed as a grammatical device that expresses different modal meanings. Modality is a type of illocutionary force that expresses the general intent of the speaker. In particular, it conveys the speaker's commitment to a proposition's obligatoriness, believability, desirability or possibility. Across languages, mood and modality are marked by verbal inflection, auxiliary verbs, adverbs and particles. Etulo expresses modality with the use of modal morphemes (adverbs, particles and modal verb). This section gives a description of the imperative (Section 7.4.1), hortative (Section 7.4.2) and other modal meanings such as the obligative (Section 7.4.3), counterfactual modality (Section 7.4.4), hypothetical modality (Section 7.4.5), potential/permissive (Section 7.4.6) and probability (Section 7.4.7).

7.4.1 The imperative

The imperative mood expresses command or prohibition of the actualization of an event or state. With the imperative mood, the addressee is in control of the future state of affairs. The Etulo verb is not morphologically marked for the imperative. A distinction is made between the affirmative imperative and the prohibitive (negative imperative) construction.[5] For the affirmative imperative, the verb retains its bare form. In contrast, in the negative imperative, the bare form is accompanied by the preverbal particle *ká* in addition to the standard negative particle *bá*. The Etulo imperative distinguishes between singular and plural addressee (see 27–29). When the speaker addresses a plural addressee, the plural marker/particle *náà* is introduced. This marker occurs in the clause final position of both the affirmative and negative imperative constructions. In speech, the imperative is marked by a high pitch. The subject may be covertly or overtly expressed. It is this high pitch that differentiates the imperative from the indicative construction when the subject is overtly expressed, as in (29).

(27) a. gíé
       'Eat!'
    b. gíé   náà
       eat   PL
       'Eat!'

(28) a. dúrú   ànwúntò   m̀gbí   ábû
       remove   cloth   POSS   cloth
       'Remove your cloth!'
    b. dúrú   ànwúntò   m̀gbí   émá   náà
       remove   cloth   POSS   2PL   PL
       'Remove your cloth!'

(29) àdì   ʃí   áshí
     2SG:SUBJ   sing   song
     'Adi, sing a song!'

7.4.2 The hortative

The hortative denotes an urge or invitation by the speaker to engage in an event. The Etulo hortative is expressed by the low tone marker *nì*. The use of the hortative marker is applicable to the 1st person singular/plural, 2nd person singular/plural and the 3rd person singular (30–32). The hortative marker is also used to embed an imperative clause (see 31).

---

5   The negative imperative (prohibitive) is discussed in Section 6.1.2. I repeat the examples below for clarity. It is marked by the high tone morpheme *ká*. The number distinction made for the imperative is applicable to both the affirmative imperative and the negative imperative as shown in the examples.

(i) ká   fá   ájàtù   bá   (ii) ká   fá   ájàtù   bá   náà
     PTCL   drive   car   NEG   PTCL   drive   car   NEG   PL
     'Don't drive the car!'   'Don't drive the car!'

(30) a. nì   ání   gìè   ùnwógīē
        HORT   1SG   eat   food
        'Let me eat food.'

    b. nì   éjí   gìè   ùnwógīē
        HORT   1PL   eat   food
        'Let us eat food.'

(31) a. nì   àdì   lúū
        HORT   PN   go
        'Let Adi go.'

    b. nì   emâ   gìè   ùnwógīē
        HORT   1PL   eat   food
        'Let you eat food.'

(32) a. àdì   gbɛ̌ɛ̄   nì   ábû   gìè   ùnwógīē
        PN   say   HORT   2SG   eat   food
        'Adi said you should eat food.'

    b. àdì   gbɛ̌ɛ̄   nì   éjî   gìè   ùnwógīē
        PN   say   HORT   1PL   eat   food
        'Adi said we should eat food.'

An alternative way of expressing the hortative meaning is by the use of the verb *nū* 'make'. The following examples are illustrative:

(33) a. nū   àdì   lúū
        make   PN   go
        'Let Adi go.'

    b. nū   má   gìè   ùnwógīē
        make   1PL   eat   food
        'Let them eat food.'

7.4.3 The obligative

The obligative (deontic) expresses the duty or obligation of the subject to perform an irrealis act expressed by the verb. Two different degrees of strength are identified in relation with the Etulo obligative. The higher degree of obligation is marked by the reduplicated adverb *kíémé kíémé* 'must/compulsory', while a lower degree of obligation is marked by two morphemes: *íwóʤɔ́* and *dzèmbísɔ̀*. Both morphemes are semantic equivalents of the English 'have to/ought to'. They are used interchangeably in constructions and occur in clause initial position (34–35). By contrast, the reduplicated marker *kíémé* occurs in clause final position, as illustrated in (36). These obligative markers are found in constructions that express irrealis events typically marked by the future morpheme *ka*. Consider the following examples:

(34) íwódʒɔ́   éjî   kà   gíé
    MOD   1PL:SUBJ   FUT   eat
    'We have to eat./We ought to eat.'

(35) dzèmbísɔ̀   éjî   kà   gíé
    MOD   1PL:SUBJ   FUT   eat
    'We have to eat./We ought to eat.'

(36) ábû   kà   gíá   ájàtù   nâ   àbúwò   ábû   kíɛ́mɛ   kíɛ́mɛ́
    2SG:SUBJ   FUT   buy   car   that   REFL   2SG   must   RED
    'You must buy that car yourself.'

7.4.4 The counterfactual modality

The *kí* marker expresses counterfactuality, namely the idea that something did not occur despite plausible expectations to the contrary (37). The context may indicate the particular set of circumstances under which an event may have happened (38). In the latter case, the *kí* marker co-occurs with the future morpheme *ka*: this suggests that in this context, *ka* should be regarded as an 'irrealis' marker, rather than an actual future marker.

(37) a. àdì   kí   dzè   údē
        PN   MOD   stay   home
        'Adi should have stayed at home.'

    b. ábû   kí   bɔ́   íbɔ̄   mì   ètùló
        2SG:SUBJ   MOD   pray   prayer   in   Etulo
        'You should have prayed in Etulo.'

(38) a. àdì   kí   kà   gìè   ùnwógīē   ní   ábû   kìɔ̀   ùnwógīē
        PN   MOD   FUT   eat   food   if   2SG:SUBJ   cook   food
        'Adi would have eaten if you had cooked.'

    b. ò   kí   kā   ŋà
        3SG:SUBJ   MOD   FUT   surpass
        'He would have won.'

7.4.5 The hypothetical modality

The hypothetical modality denotes non-factual situations or conditions upon which other events are dependent. The protasis is expressed by the complementizer *ní*, and the bare root plus the particle *jɔ́*. The apodosis is unmarked and there is no compulsory order of protasis and apodosis. The following examples are illustrative:

(39) a. ní   ábû   sɔ̀   èsé   jó   ábû   ká   gìè   ùnwógīē
         COND   2SG:SUBJ sit down PTCL   2SG:SUBJ FUT   eat   food
         'If you sit down, you will eat.'

    b.   éjî   kà   gíé   ní   á   bā   jɔ̄
         1PL:SUBJ FUT   eat   if   3PL:SUBJ come   PTCL
         'We will eat if they come.'

7.4.6 The potential/permissive modality

The potential modal meaning is expressed by the modal verb *jágbá* 'be able', which indicates the belief of the speaker in the ability of the subject to carry out an act (see 40). It also expresses permission from the speaker to the addressee to perform a given act (41). The potential modal marker directly precedes the main verb. The following examples are illustrative:

(40) a. ábû   kà   jágbá   gíá   ájàtù   nâ   àbúwò   ábû
         2SG:SUBJ FUT   be.able buy   car   that   REFL   2SG
         'You can buy that car yourself.'
         (Lit: 'You will be able to buy that car yourself.')

    b.   éjî   kà   jágbá   ʃì   ìfúé
         1PL:SUBJ FUT   be.able dance dance
         'We can dance very well.'

(41) a. àdì   kà   jágbá   lúū
         PN   FUT   be.able go
         'Adi can now go.'

    b.   á   kà   jágbá   ná   únâ
         3PL:SUBJ FUT   be.able sleep sleep
         'They can now sleep.'

7.4.7 The probability modality

The probability modal expresses the speaker's belief about the likelihood of the subject to perform or undergo an event expressed by the verb. In Etulo, this modal is marked by the morpheme *kábá*. It usually occurs in the sentence initial position but may be preceded by an adverbial morpheme like *ònènê* 'now'.

(42)   kábá   éjî   kà   gìè   ùnwógīē
         MOD   1PL   FUT   eat   food
         'We may eat food.'

(43) a. kábá   ìɲànì   lúū   ònèné   wà
         MOD   PN   go   now   PERF
         'Inyani might have left by now.'

   b.   ònènê kábá   ìɲànì lúū   wà
         now   MOD   PN   go   PERF
         'Inyani might have left by now.'

7.5 Conclusion

As far as temporal reference is concerned, Etulo adopts a two-way tense system: future vs non-future, where the non-future is realized as present or past essentially depending on the default actional value of the verb (dynamic vs stative). With the exception of the non-future tense, the aspectual values are explicitly marked by means of dedicated particles, as summarized in the Table 7.1.

Some of these morphemes have different combinatorial possibilities. The future marker *ka* (which may more properly be realized as an irrealis marker) can co-occur with the progressive morpheme *le* to realize a future progressive. The future marker may equally co-occur with modal morphemes like *jágbá* and *kí* (see 6a and 6b). When the progressive marker *le* accompanies the bare verb, it may have present or past time reference.

The morpheme *téjî* has been analyzed as a time adverbial rather than a grammaticalized tense marker. As a matter of fact, its occurrence is optional in some contexts where it merely reinforces a past meaning, and it can be substituted with other time adverbials yielding different contextual interpretations. The habitual marker *lí* describes a situation that is characteristic of an extended period of time and still holds. It equally denotes generic situations (timeless events). In combination with *téjî* or similar adverbs, *lí* gives rise to the implicature that the habitual situation no longer holds, although such implicature can be contextually cancelled. The perfect marker *wà* indicates a completed event whose result typically persists at the speech time. However, besides its default present perfect meaning, it may contextually have the value of the pluperfect even without the help of time adverbials.

Modality is expressed by means of modal morphemes such as *ní* to introduce a hypothetical clause, *nì* for the hortative, *kábá* for probability, *ká* for the imperative negative. For the expression of some modal meanings such as the obligative and the permissive/potential, the modal morphemes co-occur with the future/irrealis marker *ka*. Recall that the future marker *ka*, as opposed to the negative marker *ká*, is characterized by tonal polarity.

8. General Conclusion

This work has provided a grammatical description of the Etulo language. Etulo is a tone language, whose basic features are (amongst others): predominant SVO word order, non-inflectional morphology, prominent aspectual values, and verb serialization. It is predominantly isolating/analytic with some agglutinating features. Besides having no dedicated inflectional affixes, it apparently has only two derivational affixes, namely the hybrid prefix ò- (Section 3.2), and the extensional suffix -lu (Section 3.3). Seven word classes have been identified: noun, pronoun, verb, adjective (a small class), adverb, preposition and ideophones. There are instances of overlap in the function of some of these categories. In particular, the rich set of Etulo ideophonic words cuts across the adverbial and adjectival class. Etulo relies on specific strategies to make up for the paucity of some categories like prepositions, adverbs and adjectives.

Etulo shares grammatical similarities with not only Idomoid languages, but also with the languages of the larger subgroup of Benue Congo, especially with regard to the phonological structure of verbs and nouns. Armstrong (1983) notes that many Idomoid languages have the common 'Eastern Kwa' trait, that allows verbs to begin with a consonant and nouns to begin with a vowel. This observation holds in Etulo. The verb root typically begins with a consonant or syllabic nasal and is open ended, while the nouns begin with a vowel or syllabic nasal but rarely with a consonant. Etulo has an atypical vowel harmony system. Unlike typical West African languages such as Igbo, Yoruba and Ewe that have full vowel harmony systems where the harmonic value is spread leftward and rightward to affixes and pronouns, Etulo presents a partial system, based on advanced tongue root (ATR) values. Its scope is restricted, with some violations, to prosodic words and does not spread to affixes or pronouns.

Etulo adopts a two-way tense system: future vs non-future, where the non-future is realized as default present or past, depending on the verb. Aspectual distinctions are, in most cases, overtly expressed. Further investigation is required to establish the interplay of actional domain with time reference and aspect values, as well as the realization of tense-aspect values in modal contexts other than realis/indicative.

Etulo has a relatively complex verbal system, with two major distinctions: (i) obligatory complement verbs vs non-obligatory complement verbs, and (ii) simple vs complex predicates. From a typological viewpoint, the existence of complement verbs is not a peculiar feature of Etulo, because it is shared by many other West African languages like Ewe, Igbo, Yoruba and Idoma.

The present investigation is in no way conclusive. A number of observations require further investigation. For instance, in terms of lexical meaning, Etulo verbs may be characterized by a certain degree of idiomaticity, whereby a verb may have a core and an extended meaning. For instance, the verb *gbó àbɔ̂* 'clap hand' has the extended meaning 'beg'. The second meaning is probably drawn from the gestural attitude of a beggar. Additionally, in the discussion of multi-verb constructions, two relatively similar constructions were described: the serial verb and the consecutive construction. One needs to dig deeper to identify more formal means of differentiating them. Associated with serial verbs are various motion verbs, such as *lúū, ká, kɛ̀, wá, kì, jɛ̀/jɛ̀dɔ́, bā, lúbā,* for which further investigation is needed to ascertain their scope of usage. Furthermore, in the discussion of coordination, emphasis was on conjunctive markers and how they are assigned to specific constituents. However, a close analysis of Etulo narratives reveals the existence of other connective markers which require further analysis.

Appendix

Text 1. A story of the king, the hare and other animals

(1) ìtsúkwɔ́   ḿgbēnkɔ̄!   ìtsúkwɔ́   kê!
    story   (chants)   story   go

(2) ìtsúkwɔ́   kè   kpùrùrùrù   ká   tsà   jì   ùtɔ̀   béké
    story   go   IDEO   and   meet   with   king   join

    jì   ìʃàwé   jì   m̀búábā   ámgbéká.
    with   hare   with   animal   some

(3) égbé   òká   nê,   ùtɔ̀   lí   lè   gíé
    day   another   this   king   HAB   PROG   eat

    m̀búé   mi   ùdé   ḿgbán.
    meat   in   home   POSS.3SG

(4) m̀búé   wá   ńgīē   mî   ìbɔ̆lā   ḿgbī   ùtɔ̀.
    meat   come   finish   in   storage   of   king

(5) nétā   ùtɔ̀   dó   ésɔ́   kwū   ìʃàwé   òkàân   èlâ.
    then   king   send   message   call   hare   friend:3SG   voice

(6) ìʃàwé   nósē   lì   òmúkpē   kpàâ.
    hare   PST   COP   hunter   also

(7) ó   wá   ɲā   ìʃàwé   gbɛ̆ɛ̄   íʃáwē   íbúgé,   m̀búé   ḿgbí
    3SG:SUBJ   come   tell   hare   say   hare   dear   meat   POSS

    ánî   ǹgíé   mì   ìbólā,   lè   ké   égbé   ègín   dʒó.ānì.
    1SG   finish   in   storage   PROG   go   day   six   this

(8) lì   èdètû   jì   ándzílé   tā   nwí   ánî   lè   gíé
    COP   okra   and   vegetable   only   REL   1SG:SUBJ   PROG   eat

    ŋámâ   ánî   jé   òfè   òɲīī   nwí   ánî   ká   tū
    CONN   1SG:SUBJ   know   way   one   REL   1SG:SUBJ   FUT   get

    m̀búé   gíé   bá.
    meat   eat   NEG

(9) ògbí   kpàâ   ńgīē   mì   ùdé   ḿgbí   ánî   tsátsá.
    chicken   also   finish   in   home   POSS   1SG   completely

(10) néē   nwí   ìʃàwé   fó   ódzé   nê,   ìʃàwé   sí   ɲā
     CONN   when   hare   hear   talk   this   hare   then   tell

     kùtɔ̀   gběē   ítē   ùtɔ̀!   lì   ùnwɔ́   ábû   lè   pítá
     ing   say   oh   king   COP   thing   2SG:SUBJ PROG   find

     pítà   mà-dàà?
     RED   that-Q

(11) m̀búé   ònwí   gbé   èsé   nê.   ábû   jé   dàʃí   á
     meat   REL.P   full   ground this   2SG:SUBJ know   as   IMPRS

     kā   tù   m̀búé   lóò?
     FUT   get   mea   NEG.Q

(12) ání   kā   kwú   m̀búábā bā   m̀ménê   tsátsá dūū,   kpàâ
     1SG:SUBJ FUT   call   animal come   here   completely all   but

     mm̀búé   ání   jé   dí   ábû   só   ò-gíé-gīē jó   lì
     eat   1SG:SUBJ know   COMP   2SG:OBJ want   PREF.eat.RED PTCL COP

     m̀tsè.
     guinea.fowl

(13) ání   ká   bɔ́   émí   m̀tsè   òkwɔ̀   m̀gbí   ábû.
     1SG:SUBJ FUT   invite PL   guinea.fowl farm POSS   2SG

(14) tá   émí   m̀tsè   kà   téjî,   á   kā   lè   ʃí
     only   PL   guinea.fowl go   first   3PL:SUBJ FUT   PROG   sing

     áʃí,   á   kà   kíé   àngá   lè   gbó.
     song   3PL   FUT   take   drum   PROG   beat

(15) ání   ká   kìè   ámá   íjíkpâ.
     1SG:SUBJ FUT   come   3PL   back

(16) nwí   ánî   ká   kìè   ámá   ìjíkpâ nê,   ánî   kà
     as   1SG:SUBJ FUT   come   3PL   back   this   1SG:SUBJ FUT

     kíé   òkùtà   bí   ábô,   ánî   ká   ʃá   ígbē.
     take   staff   hold   hand   1SG:SUBJ FUT   hang   bag

(17) ánî   ká   lè   ʃí   áʃí   gběē   kíé   gbó-nwɔ́ kíé
     1SG:SUBJ FUT   PROG   sing   song   say   take   beat-kill take

     wō   ígbé   mân   ámgbéká ká   lè   gbélá   gběē
     put   bag   and   some   FUT   PROG   respond say

     [kpùn ká kpùn] chant: gbó-nwɔ́ kíé   wō   ígbé (three times)
     (IDEO: sound of stick/staff) beat-kill take   put   bag

(18) ní   ánî   gbó-nwɔ́ má   ŋátāā   mân   ánî   kà   gbé
     if   1SG:SUBJ beat-kill 3PL:OBJ until CONN   1SG:SUBJ FUT   pack

     má   wò   ígbé.
     3PL:OBJ put   bag

(19) ní   á   wá   m̀gbúò   ígbé   mân   ánî   kà   kíé
     if   3PL:SUBJ come   be.full bag   CONN   1SG:SUBJ FUT   take

     má   wá   nū   ábû.
     3PL:OBJ come   give   2SG:OBJ

(20) | tà | mân | lì | ìmbé | ábû | ká | tù | m̀búé | ʤo.álì. |
     | only | then | COP | place | 2SG | FUT | get | meat | that |

(21) | mân | ùtɔ̀ | sí | gbɛ̌ɛ̄ | kéì | ábókwé, | ání | jé | òdzè |
     | CONN | king | then | say | EXCL | friend | 1SG:SUBJ | know | talk.about |
     | ḿgbí | ábû. |
     | POSS | 2SG |

(22) | lì | ùnwɔ̂ | ònwí | kìɔ̀ | séè | nwí | ání | gbɔ̀ | gbɛ̌ɛ̄ |
     | COP | thing | REL.P | happen | before | REL | 1SG:SUBJ | talk | COMP |
     | lì | ábû | kìɔ̀ | ùnwɔ́ | nâ | kíémé | kíémé | mà-ʤó.àlî. |
     | COP | 2SG | do | thing | that | must | REDP | like-that |

(23) | ùnwɔ́ | ábû | gbɔ̀ | nâ | tíʃī. |
     | thing | 2SG | talk | that | be.good |

(24) | nwí | ùtɔ̀ | gbélá | jì | ìʃàwé | némáà, | `ʃàwé | kpàâ | sí |
     | as | king | agree | with | hare | CONN | hare | also | then |
     | jìdɔ́ | lú | ùdé. |
     | return | go | home |

(25) | mân | ìʃàwé | ká | kìè | ùnwɔ́ | kwɔ̄ | òndû | ìʃàwé | gbɛ̌ɛ̄ |
     | CONN | hare | go | take | thing | fix | mouth | hare | say |
     | èmí | m̀tsè | léè! |
     | PL | Guinea.fowl | EXCL |

(26) | m̀tsè | gbɛ̌ɛ̄ | éjí | tō | nálòò! | ìʃàwé | gbɛ̌ɛ̄ | èmá | kpá |
     | guinea.fowl | say | 1PL:SUBJ | COP.PL | EXCL | hare | say | 2PL:SUBJ | come |
     | pléplé | nâ! |
     | quick | EXCL |

(27) | lì | ùnwɔ̂ | káká | èwó | mì | ùdé | útɔ̄. |
     | COP | thing | enter | body | in | home | king |

(28) | mân | èmí | m̀tsè | sí | kwú | èwó | má | kwú | èwó |
     | CONN | PL | guinea.fowl | then | gather | REFL | 3PL | gather | REFL |
     | má | ámá | tō | òʃè, | ámá | tō | ùdé | dúú. |
     | 3PL | those | COP.PL | farm | those | COP.PL | home | all |

(29) | nósē | mà | m̀tsè | ŋàó | tō | ùdé. |
     | before | DET | guinea.fowl | surpass | COP.PL | home |

(30) | nwí | á | kwū | èwó | má, | nê-máà | á | sí | wá |
     | as | 3PL:SUBJ | call | REFL | 3PL | this-CONN | 3PL:SUBJ | then | come |
     | kwū | ákíè. |
     | gather | group |

(31) | ìʃàwé | ɲá | má | gbɛ̌ɛ̄ | nwí | émâ | dí | nénî, | ùtɔ̀ |
     | hare | tell | 2PL:OBJ | say | as | 2PL:SUBJ | see | this | king |
     | kíé | ádíʃí | óɲīī | kpàâ | wó | èsé | wàbá. |
     | take | yam.seedling | one | even | put | ground | NEG |

(32) émâ   ké   nì   éjî   kà   ʃí   ùtɔ̀   òkwɔ̀   nâ.
     2PL:SUBJ   go   MOD   1PL:SUBJ   CORD   plant   king   farm   that

(33) ùtɔ̀   gběē   nì   émâ   kà   ʃín   òkwɔ̀   ékéká.
     king   say   MOD   3PL:SUBJ   go   plant.3SG   farm   tomorrow

(34) ùnwɔ́   ḿgbī   ùtɔ̀   á   lí   lálā   bá.
     thing   of   king   3PL   HAB   delay   NEG

(35) mân   èmí   m̀tsè   dúú   sí   gbélâ.
     CONN   PL   guinea.fowl   all   then   agree

(36) mân   á   sí   lú   ùdé   ká   kíé-lū   ńlò   ḿgbí   ámá.
     CONN   3PL:SUBJ   then   go   home   go   take-SUFF   hoe   POSS   3PL

(37) tégbílīfàán   mì   ègbégbē   égbégbē   má   wá   tú   ìʃàwè   mì
     next.day   in   morning   REDP   3PL   come   meet   hare   in
     ùdé   útɔ̀.
     house   king

(38) ìʃàwé   gběē   nwí   ámá   kà   lú   òkwɔ̀   nê   ónwú
     hare   say   as   3PL   FUT   go   farm   this   3SG:SUBJ
     kā   tsò   má   àʃí   nâ.   nú   má   lè   ʃí
     FUT   sing   3PL:OBJ   song   that   make   3PL   PROG   sing
     áʃí   né   jɔ̄,   ǹgísè   óɲīī   kà   ǹdìné   ìjíkpá   lóò.
     song   this   PTCL   person   one   FUT   look   back   NEG
     ǹgísè   ńdìné   ìjíkpá   bajó   ónwú   kà   jěē   ódɔ̄   nâ.
     person   look   back   PTCL   3SG:SUBJ   FUT   become   soup   that

(39) mân   èmí   m̀tsè   dúú   sí   gbélâ.
     CONN   PL   guinea.fowl   all   then   agree

(40) mân   á   tō   òfè   lè   lúū,   mân   ìʃàwé   wítá
     CONN   3PL:SUBJ   COP   way   PROG   go   CONN   hare   start
     ʃí   áʃí   néní   gběē   kíé   gbó-nwɔ́   kíé   wókē   ígbé   [kpùn ká kpùn].
     sing   song   this   say   take   beat-kill   take   put   bag   IDEO

(41) mân   ìʃàwé   kíé   àngá,   kíé   ígbē   ʃà   gbé   òkùtà
     CONN   hare   take   drum   take   bag   hang   take   staff
     bí   ábɔ̂.   ìʃàwé   kìè   ìjíkpâ   lè   ʃí   áʃí   gběē
     hold   hand   hare   come   back   PROG   sing   song   say
     chant: kíé   gbó-nwɔ́   kíé   wō   ígbé   response: kpùn ká kpùn
            take   beat-kill   take   put   bag   IDEO

(42) ɔ̀nɔ̀   nwí   ìʃàwé   lè   ʃí   gbó-nwɔ́   kíé   wō   ígbé
     time   REL   hare   PROG   sing   beat-kill   take   put   bag,
     nê,   ìʃàwé   lè   gbó-nwɔ̄   m̀tsè   kíé   wó-kē   ígbé   [kpùn ká kpùn]...
     this   hare   PROG   beat-kill   guinea.fowl   take   put-go   bag   IDEO
     ò   lè   wó-kē   ígbé   gbó-nwɔ̄   m̀tsè   kíé   wó-kē   ígbé,
     3SG:SUBJ   PROG   put-go   bag   beat-kill   guinea.fowl   take   put-go   bag
     gbó-nwɔ̄   m̀tsè   kíé   wó-kē   igbe.
     beat-kill   guinea.fowl   take   put-go   bag

(43) m̀tsè   kpààˆ   á   wō   mā   òlâ   gbɛ̌ɛ̄   nù   má
    guinea.fowl ADV   IMPRS   put   3PL:OBJ law   COMP   make   3PL:OBJ

    ká   ǹdìné bā   ìjíkpá bá   lɔ̀ɔ̀.   m̀tsè   ǹdìné bā
    go   look   come   back   NEG   right.Q guinea.fowl look   come

    ìjíkpá bá   ŋátāā lú   òfɛ̀   òkwɔ̀ lè   kè.   ámá
    back   NEG   until go   way   farm   PROG go   3PL:SUBJ

    kpààˆ jé   nwí   òkwɔ̀ mà   dó   bá.
    ADV   know   REL   farm   the   end   NEG

(44) tàmáa á   sī   kìè   ŋátāā ùnwô   wá   wītā   ò-káká
    CONN   3PL:SUBJ then   come   until thing come start PREF-enter

    m̀tsè   ńtónê èwó   jó   áshí wá   lè   bɛ́   jì
    guinea.fowl these body PTCL   song come PROG draw.close with

    m̀tsè   kwékwé. m̀tsè   ámá-n   tō   ìyàyî àbábɔ̄ mànì
    guinea.fowl near   guinea.fowl they.REL COP.PL front first   the

    áshí wá   lè   bɛ́   jì   ámá kwékwé.
    song come PROG draw.close with   3PL near

(45) á   gbɛ̌ɛ̄   híí   dzíkán mà,   áshí nê   bɛ́   jì
    3PL:SUBJ say   EXCL   before the   song this draw.close with

    éjî   ŋá   ʤòò?   kíɔ́nè-sé shí   nê   lè   bɛ́   jì
    1PL:OBJ surpass so.Q   why   song this PROG draw.close with

    éjî   ŋàâ?
    1PL:OBJ surpass

(46) nwí m̀tsè   wá   ǹdìné bá   ìyíkpá jó,   á   dí
    AS   GUINEA.FOWL COME   LOOK   COME   BACK   PTCL   3PL:SUBJ SEE

    gbɛ̌ɛ̄ èmí ònwúnɔ́   ámán   tō   ìjíkpá mà,   á   kīē
    COMP PL   brother   they.REL COP.PL back   the   IMPRS take

    gbó-nwɔ́   má   wókē   ígbé wà.   á   sīsī   álɔ̄   èfà tá.
    beat-kill 3PL:OBJ put-go   bag   PERF   3PL:SUBJ remain   line   two only

(47) títá   ínɛ̌   nwí m̀tsè   ámgbéká bùlù tsíɲà   lú   óʃɛ̄.
    reason.why today REL guinea.fowl some   fly   run.race go   bush

    lì   ámán   tō   údɛ̄   nósē   mà   kà   tó   údɛ́.
    COP   those.REL COP   home   before DET   still COP.PL home

Translation

(1) Story! story! (2) This story is about the hare, the king and other animals. (3) Once upon a time, the king used to eat meat in his house. (4) Then, meat ran out in the king's storage. (5) The king sent a message to call his friend the hare. (6) He told the hare 'Dear hare, meat has run out in my storage for about six days now. (7) It is only okra and soup that I have been eating and I don't know how to find meat to eat. (9) Even chicken (meat) has completely run out in my house.'

(10) When the hare heard this, he then said to the king 'Oh king! Is that what you are looking for? (11) Meat that is everywhere, yet you don't know how to get meat? (12) I will call all the animals here but I know that the meat you like to eat is that of guinea fowl. (13) I will invite the guinea fowls to your farm. (14) The guinea fowls will go first. They will be singing and they will be drumming. (15) I will come behind them. (16) As I come behind them, I will hold a staff and hang a bag on it. (17) I will be singing a song saying "Kill and put in a bag," and some will respond saying "kpun ka kpun." (18) If I kill enough of them, then I will put them in a bag. (19) If the bag becomes full, I will give them (dead guinea fowls) to you. (20) This is how you will get meat.' (21) The king then said, 'My friend, I know you very well. (22) This was why I said that it is you that must do this. (23) What you said is good.' (24) As the king agreed with the hare, the hare then went home. (25) The hare went and took something (a voice amplifier, probably) and fixed it on his mouth and called out to the guinea fowls. (26) The guinea fowls replied 'We are here. (27) Something is wrong in the king's house.' (28) Then the guinea fowls gathered themselves, those in the farm/bush, those at home. (29) In the past, guinea fowls were more in the home (than in the bush). (30) As they called themselves, they then gathered together (31) The hare told them saying 'As you can see, the king has planted not even a single yam seedling (32) Let us go and farm for the king. (33) The king said that we should farm for him tomorrow. (34) Matters concerning the king require no delay.' (35) All the guinea fowls agreed. (36) They went home and took their hoes. (37) The next day, very early in the morning; they met the hare in the king's house. (38) The hare said that on their way to the farm, he will be singing a song for them. As they are singing that song, no one should look back. Anyone that looks back will become meat. (39) All the guinea fowls agreed. (40) On their way going, the hare began to sing this song that says 'Kill and put inside a bag.' (41) The hare then took a drum, hung a bag, and took a stick/staff. The hare was at the back singing and the guinea fowls were responding. (42) As the hare was singing this song, he was killing the guinea fowls and putting them inside a bag. (43) The guinea fowls were instructed not to look back right? So the guinea fowls did not look back until they were approaching the farm road. They did not even know the end (extent) of the farm. (44) They kept going until the guinea fowls in front became worried that the song was drawing closer to them. (45) They exclaimed 'Ah! Was this song very close to us before? Why is this song drawing closer to us?' (46) As they looked back, they saw that their brothers had been killed and put inside a bag. Those remaining were very few. (47) This the reason why today, some guinea fowls fly to the bush. It is those who were at home (those who did not go to the king's farm) that are still at home.

Text 2. How we plant yams

(1) òfè nwí éjî lí kíé ángwɔ́ kíé ńdzì jɔ́
    way REL 1PL:SUBJ HAB take yam take bury PTCL

    lì ònwú ʤɔ́.ànî.
    COP like this

(2) àbábɔ̂, ó lí ká kwɔ́ òʃé mì ímbé nwí
    first 2SG:SUBJ HAB go weed grass PREP place REL

    á téjî ʃí òkwɔ̀ bá.
    IMPRS before dig farm NEG

(3) ó kà nwá óʃé.
    2SG:SUBJ FUT weed grass

(4) ní ábû nwá óʃé ńgíē, ó ká ʃí òkwɔ̀.
    if 2SG:SUBJ weed grass finish 2SG:SUBJ go dig farm

(5) ó ʃí òkwɔ̀ ǹgíé, ó kà fé.
    2SG:SUBJ dig farm finish 2SG:SUBJ FUT wait

(6) ní ɔ̀nɔ̀ gíɔ́ ò-ndzì ìʃí, ó ká ǹdzì íʃì
    if time reach INF-bury yam.seedling 2SG:SUBJ go bury yam.seedling

    ḿgbí ábû.
    POSS 2SG:SUBJ

(7) ó ká ńdzî ìʃí nâ kíé òʃé túkwû ìkíèn.
    2SG:SUBJ go bury yam.seedling that take grass cover head.3SG:POSS

(8) ní ìʃì wá lū úmbí è tásê, ó kà wá
    if yam.seedling come sprout tendrils come.out 2SG:SUBJ FUT come

    kwùlú óʃḕ mì ìʃí nánǐ.
    open grass on yam.seedling that

(9) mân dúúséè nù ábû kwùlú óʃḕ mì ìʃí ná
    CONN before MOD 2SG:SUBJ open grass on yam.seedling that

    jɔ́ ònènê jɔ́ òtsé tɔ́ɔ̃́.
    PTCL now PTCL medicine be.out

(10) ó kwá kà kwó-wō ótsé.
     2SG:SUBJ then FUT inject-put medicine

(11) ní ó kwó-wō òtsè ɲéē̃, ó ká kwùlú óʃḕ.
     if 2SG:SUBJ inject-put medicine pass 2SG:SUBJ FUT remove grass

(12) ní ó kíé kwùlú óʃḕ mì ìʃí ó ká
     if 2SG:SUBJ take remove grass from yam,seedling 2SG:SUBJ FUT

     zǎntā mân kà wítá ò-kíǹdà ɲátáá lúū.
     leave.SG:OBJ CORD FUT start INF-flower until go

(13) ó ká wá kìè ìdájî ká wó òkwɔ́.
     2SG:SUBJ FUT come take fertilizer go put farm

(14) ìdájî wó òkwɔ̀ nâ, ó ká zǎntā ɲátāā bá
fertilizer put farm that 2SG:SUBJ FUT leave.3SG:OBJ until come

òfìà égīātā, òfìà égīànè.
month eight month nine

(15) mân ó kà wítá ò-tò-tô wá gīē.
CONN 2SG:SUBJ FUT start PREF-dig-REDP come eat

(16) lì ŋàâ éjî lí kìɔ̀ séé nwí éjî lí
COP how 1PL:SUBJ HAB do before REL 1PL:SUBJ HAB

dzè jì ángwɔ́ ʤó-àlì.
COP with yam like-that

Translation

(1) This is the way that we plant yams. (2) Firstly, you clear the grasses in a place that has not been farmed. (3) You will weed away the grasses. (4) If you finish weeding the grasses, you farm. (5) After farming, you wait. (6) If it is time to plant yam seedlings, you plant your yam seedling. (7) You plant the yam seedling and cover its head with grass. (8) If the yam seedling sprouts tendrils, you remove the grasses from the yam seedling. (9) Before you remove the grasses on that yam seedling, herbicides will be available (out). (10) You will then apply the herbicide. (11) After you apply the herbicide, you will remove the grasses. (12) If you remove the grasses from the yam seedling, you will leave it and it will start to produce flowers. (13) You will apply fertilizer on the farm. (14) The fertilizer you applied on that farm, you will leave it till the eighth or ninth month (August or September). (15) Then you will start to harvest and eat. (16) This is what we do to have yams.

Text 3. What I did yesterday

(1) èdědě ání k ìdúù.
yesterday 1SG:SUBJ go market

(2) ání dī mórò ḿgbī àkàɲà kíé ònwè òká dō
1SG:SUBJ see PN of PN carry child another on

àgwúgwù lè lúū.
bike PROG go

(3) ó kwúlésě̄ ò-ɲé ání gběē ékéká ʤúkwé kà bá.
3SG:SUBJ stop INF-tell 1SG:OBJ COMP tomorrow PN FUT come

(4) éjî kà ké kpájī únwɔ́ɔ̄.
1PL:SUBJ FUT go learn thing

(5) nwí   ó   ɲé   ánî   òdzè   nê   ńgīē   èdĕdĕ   mà
    when   3SG:SUBJ tell   1SG:OBJ talk   this   finish   yesterday   CONN

    ó   kìè   àgwúgwù   ḿgbán   ó   lúū.
    3SG:SUBJ take   bike   POSS.3SG 3SG:SUBJ go

(6) mâ   ánī   kpàâ   sí   lúū.
    CONN   1SG:SUBJ also   then   go

(7) ánî   ǹgíé   únwɔ́ɔ̄   mì   ìdúù
    1SG:SUBJ finish   thing   in   market

(8) nwí   ɔ̀nɔ̀   wá   gbò   èsé   nê,   ánî   jè   lú   ùdé
    when   sun   come   fall   ground   this   1SG:SUBJ   return   go   home

(9) mâ   ánî   kà   lá   èsé (lásé) mì   ùdé   ḿgbí   ánî
    CONN   1SG:SUBJ go   lay   down   in   home   POSS   1SG

Translation

(1) Yesterday I went to market. (2) I saw Moro Akanya (Akanya's Moro) with another child on a bike going along. (3) He stopped to tell me that tomorrow, Jukwe will come (4) That we will go and study. (5) After he told me this yesterday, he then carried his bike and he left. (5) I also left. (6) I finished my activities in the market. (7) When evening came, I went home. (9) Then I lay down in my house (and rested).

Text 4. What I do every day

(1) ùnwó   nwí   ání   lī   kìɔ̀   àlí   égbē   àlí   égbē
    thing   REL   1SG:SUBJ   HAB   do   every   day   every   day

    mì   òdzèdzé   ḿgbí   ánî   jɔ̄,   ègbè   òká   lí   ɲīnē
    in   PREF.be.RED of   1SG   PTCL   day   another   HAB   change

    kpàâ   ámá   nwí   ń   lī   ŋǎō   kíɔ́   má   kíémé
    but   3PL:OBJ   REL   1SG:SUBJ   HAB   pass   do   the   must

    kíémé   jɔ́   lì   ámá   ʤō-ánî.
    RED   PTCL   COP   3PL   these

(2) mì   ègbégbēè,   mì   èkéléfí   èdá,   án   lí   kìàtóō.   ánî
    in   morning   at   o'clock   five   1SG:SUBJ HAB   rise.up   1SG:SUBJ

    lí   sá   òndû   ánî   lí   lú   àdúà.
    HAB   wash   mouth   1SG:SUBJ   HAB   go   church

(3) àdúà   lí   wítá   mì   ògì   ègín   ŋátāā   fádá   ká
    church   HAB   start   from   o'clock   six   until   father   FUT

    kìɔ̀   àdúà.
    do   church/mass

(4) ánî   kà   gbé   èjí   éwōò   mì   ègbé   nánǐ
    1SG:SUBJ   FUT   collect blood   body   on   day   that

(5) ní   éjî   àdúà   wá   ńgīē,   ánî.   kà   tásê   jèdó
    1PL:SUBJ   blood   church   come   finish   1SG:SUBJ   FUT   come.out   return

    lú-bā   údé.   ánî.   kà   wá   ʃúwò.
    go-come   home   1SG:SUBJ FUT   come   bath.body

(6) nǒn   lì   ègbé   ídɔ́   nwí   ánî.   kà   jèdó   kéè
    if.3SG   COP   day   work   REL   1SG:SUBJ   FUT   return   go

    òpò   àdúà   jó,   ání   jè   ké   òpò   àdúà   kpàà
    thatch   church PTCL   1SG:SUBJ return   go   thatch   church   but

    nòn   lì   ègbé   ídɔ́,   ání   kà   kè   òpò   àdúà
    if.3SG   COP   day   work   1SG:SUBJ FUT   go   thatch   church

    bá.   ánî.   lí   lú   ókwɔ̀.
    NEG   1SG:SUBJ HAB   go   farm

(7) ání   kà   ʃí   òkwɔ   ŋátāā.
    1SG:SUBJ   FUT   farm   farm   until

(8) ní   ání   kà   kíéē   ókwɔ̀,   ń   ká   ʃùwó.   ní
    if   1SG:SUBJ go   close   farm   1SG:SUBJ   FUT   bath.body   if

    ání   ʃùwô,   ání   kà   giè   ùnwógīē,   ní   ání   giè
    1SG:SUBJ   bath.body 1SG:SUBJ FUT   eat   food   if   1SG:SUBJ   eat

    ùnwógīē,   ń   kà   tóɲā.
    food   1SG:SUBJ FUT   rest

(9) mân   ń   kà   wá   lú-bā   ìgbùdù   mì   àdì   nâ,   1ání
    CONN   1SG:SUBJ FUT   come   go-come main.road   in   PN   that   SG:SUBJ

    lí   lúū   *four o'clock.* ánî.   lí   lúū   *daily savings*   ńgbí   ánî.
    HAB   go   four o'clock   1SG:SUBJ HAB   go   daily savings   POSS   1SG

(10) *daily savings*   nâ   lí   wá   ńgīē   mì   ògí   ègín.   ní
     daily savings   that   HAB   come   finish   at   o'clock six   if

     éjî   ńgīē,   ánî   lí   sɔ̀   jì   èmí   òkà   ánî.
     1PL:SUBJ   finish 1SG:SUBJ HAB   sit   with   PL   friend   1SG

     ŋátāā   ègìàfà. mân   ání   lí   lú   údē.
     until   eight   CONN   1SG:SUB HAB   go   home

Translation

(1) The nature of my everyday activities changes but the ones that I must do every day are the following. (2) In the morning I rise up at five o'clock. I brush my teeth and I go to church. (3) Church service starts from six o'clock until the priest conducts mass. (4) I also take holy communion on that day. (5) If our church service ends, I go home and take a bath. (6) If it is a work day on which I have to return to church, I will go back to church (being a catechist) but if it is

not, I go to farm. (7) I will farm for a long time. (8) If I come back from the farm, I will take my bath and eat. If I eat, I rest. (9) Then, I will go to the main road located in Adi. I go at four o'clock. I go for my daily savings [daily contribution: a type of local banking which he runs]. (10) That activity of daily savings ends at six. If we finish, I sit with my friends until eight. Then, I go home.

Audio recordings

Audio Recording 1 A story of the king, the hare and other animals (Text 1) and What I did yesterday (Text 3). Featuring Mr. Ingyu Clement Agyo and Mr. Moro Akanya. http://hdl.handle.net/20.500.12434/fd138194

Audio Recording 2 How we plant yams (Text 2) and What I do everyday (Text 4). Featuring Mr. Ingyu Clement Agyo and Mr. Moro Akanya. http://hdl.handle.net/20.500.12434/af886b51

References

Aboh, Enoch, 2004. *The Morphosyntax of Complement-Head Sequences: Clause Structure and Word Order Patterns in Kwa,* Oxford: Oxford University Press. https://doi.org/10.1093/acprof:oso/9780195159905.001.0001

Adams, Inyani, 2012. *Tonal Features of Etulo,* MA thesis. Benue State University, Markurdi.

Adams, Maaki, 1975. *Unpublished Notes on Etulo: Let us Read in Etulo,* Nigerian Bible Translation Centre, Etulo Development Committee.

Agbedo, Christian U. & Kwambehar, S. T., 2013. 'Mainstreaming the ethnolinguistic vitality of the Etulo language of Benue State, Nigeria', *Research on Humanities and Social Sciences* 3, 44–52.

Aikhenvald, Alexandra Y., 2006. 'Serial Verb Construction in Typological Perspective', in Alexandra Y. Aikhenvald & R. M. W Dixon (eds.), *Serial Verb Constructions: A Cross Linguistic Typology,* Oxford: Oxford University Press, 1–60. https://doi.org/10.1093/oso/9780199279159.003.0001

Ameka, Felix K., 1999. 'Ideophones and the nature of the adjectives word class in Ewe', in F. K. E. Voeltz & C. Kilian-Hatz (eds.), *Ideophones,* Amsterdam: John Benjamins, 25–48.

Ameka, Felix K., 1999. 'The linguistic construction of space in Ewe', *Cognitive Linguistics* 6, 139–180. https://doi.org/10.1515/cogl.1995.6.2-3.139

Ameka, Felix K., 2001. 'Multiverb constructions in a West African areal typological perspective', in Dorothee Beermann & Lars Hellan (eds.), *Trondheim Summer School (TROSS) Online Proceedings,* Trondheim: NTNU, 1–24.

Ameka, Felix K., 2002. 'The adjective class in Ewe: its strata and emergent nature', paper given at the International Workshop on Adjective Classes, Research Centre for Linguistic Typology, La Trobe University, Melbourne, August.

Ameka, Felix, K., 2006. 'Ewe serial verb constructions in their grammatical context', in A. Y. Aikhenvald & R. M. W. Dixon (eds.), *Serial Verb Constructions: A Cross Linguistic Typology,* Oxford: Oxford University Press, 124–141. https://doi.org/10.1093/oso/9780199279159.003.0005

Anyanwu, Rose J., 2007. *Tone Systems in African languages,* Koln: Rüdiger Köppe.

Anyanwu, Rose J., 2008. *Fundamentals of Phonetics, Phonology and Tonology: With Specific African Sound Patterns,* Frankfurt: Peter Lang.

Anyanwu, Rose J., 2010. *Tense, Aspect, and Mood in Benue-Congo Languages,* Cologne: Rüdiger Köppe.

Armstrong, Robert G., 1955. *The Idoma People of the Niger Benue Confluence*, London: International African Institute.

Armstrong, Robert, G., 1964. 'Notes on Etulo', *Journal of West African Languages*, 1, 57–60.

Armstrong, Robert G., 1968. 'Yala (Ikom): A terraced level language with three tones', *Journal of West African Languages*, 5, 49–58.

Armstrong, Robert G., 1983. 'The Idomoid languages of the Benue and Cross-River Valleys', *Journal of West African Languages* 13, 91–147.

Armstrong, Robert, G., 1989. 'Idomoid', in John Bendor Samuel & Rhonda Hartel (eds.), *The Niger Congo Languages: A Classification And Description Of Africa's Largest Language Family*, Lanham: University Press of America, 323-336.

Azeb, Amha, 1999. 'Ideophones and compound verbs in Wolaitta', in F. K. Erhnard Voeltz & Christa Kilian-Hatz (eds.), *Ideophones*, Amsterdamn: John Benjamins, 49–64.

Baker, B. & Harvey, M., 2010. 'Complex predicate formation', in A. Mengistu, B. Baker & M. Harvey (eds.), *Complex Predicates: Cross-linguistic Perspectives on Event Structure*, Cambridge: Cambridge University Press, 13–47. https://doi.org/10.1017/cbo9780511712234.003

Baker, Mark C., 2003. *Lexical Categories: Verbs, Nouns and Adjectives*, Cambridge: Cambridge University Press. https://doi.org/10.1017/cbo9780511615047

BantuPsyn Project Members, 2010. 'Appendix: Relative Clause Questionnaires', in Laura Downing, Annie Rialland, Jean Marc Beltzung, Sophie Manus, Cédric Patin & Kristina Riedel (eds.), *ZASPiL 53: Papers from the Workshop on Bantu Relative Clauses*, Berlin: Zentrum für Allgemeine Sprachwissenschaft, 243–250.

Bauer, Laurie, 2003. *Introductory Linguistic Morphology*, Washington, D.C.: Georgetown University Press. https://doi.org/10.1515/9781474464284

Bertinetto, Pier Marco & Lenci, Alessandra, 2012. 'Habituality, pluractionality and imperfectivity', in Robert I. Binnick (ed.), *Oxford Handbook of Tense and Aspect*, Oxford: Oxford University Press, 852–880. https://doi.org/10.1093/oxfordhb/9780195381979.013.0030

Bertinetto, Pier Marco & Giucci, Luca, 2018. 'Non-prototypical derivation in Zamucoan', paper presented at the Workshop of the Austrian Academy of Sciences Zwischen Flexion und Derivation (Vienna, May 2018).

Bhat, D. N. S., 2004. *Pronouns*, Oxford: Oxford University Press.

Blench, Roger., 2008. 'The Central Delta languages: comparative word list and historical reconstructions', Ms., Kay Williamson Education Foundation, Cambridge.

Butt, Miriam, 2010. 'The light verb jungle: still hacking away', in A. Mengistu, B. Baker & M. Harvey (eds.), *Complex Predicates: Cross-Linguistic Perspectives on Event Structure*, Cambridge: Cambridge University Press, 48–78. https://doi.org/10.1017/cbo9780511712234.004

Cable, Seth, 2012. 'Distributive numerals in Tlingit: pluractionality and distributivity', paper presented at Semantics of Under-Represented Languages in the Americas (SULA) 7, Cornell University, May.

Childs, G. Tucker, 1999. 'Research on ideophones, whither hence? The need for a social theory of ideophones', in F. K. Erhard Voeltz & Christa Kilian-Hatz (eds.), *Ideophones*, Amsterdam: John Benjamins, 63–74.

Comrie, Bernard, 1975. *Aspect*, Cambridge: Cambridge University Press.

Comrie, Bernard, 1985. Tense, Cambridge: Cambridge University Press.

Comrie, Bernard, 1999. 'Haruai numerals and their implications for the history and typology of numeral systems', in Jadranka Grozdanovic (ed.), *Numeral Types and Changes Worldwide*, Berlin: Mouton de Gruyter, 95–111. https://doi.org/10.1515/9783110811193.81

Comrie, Bernard, 2013. 'Numeral bases', in Matthew S. Dryer & Martin Haspelmath (eds.), *The World Atlas of Language Structures*, Leipzig: Max Planck Institute for Evolutionary Anthropology.

Courtenay, Karen R., 1969. *A Generative Phonology of Yoruba*, Ph.D. dissertation. University of California, Los Angeles.

Croft, William, 2000. 'Parts of speech as language universals and as language-particular categories', in Petra Maria Vogel & Bernard Comrie (eds.), *Approaches to the Typology of Word Classes*, Berlin: Mouton de Gruyter, 65–102. https://doi.org/10.1515/9783110806120.65

Croft, William, 2005. 'Word classes, parts of speech and syntactic argumentation' [Commentary on Nicholas Evans and Toshiki Osada, 'Mundari: the myth of language without word classes'], *Linguistic Typology* 9, 1–141.

Crystal, David, 2003. *A Dictionary of Linguistics and Phonetics* (5th edition), Oxford: Blackwell.

Dahl, Osten, 1979. 'Typology of sentence negation', *Linguistics* 17, 79–106.

Dahl, Osten, 1985. Tense and Aspect Systems, Oxford: Blackwell.

de Clercq, Karen C., 2020. 'Types of negation', in Viviane Déprez and Teresa Espinal (eds.), *Oxford Handbook of Negation*, Oxford: Oxford University Press, 58–74. https://doi.org/10.1093/oxfordhb/9780198830528.013.2

Diessel, Holger, 1999. *Demonstrative Function and Grammaticalization*, Amsterdam: John Benjamins.

Dingemanse, Mark, 2011. 'Ideophones and the aesthetics of everyday language in West-Africa Society', *The Senses and Society* 6, 77–85. https://doi.org/10.2752/174589311x12893982233830

Dingemanse, Mark, 2011. *The Meaning and Use of ideophones in Siwu*. Ph.D. dissertation. Radboud University, Nijmegen.

Dixon, R. M. W., 2004. 'Adjective classes in a typological perspective', in R. M. W Dixon & Alexandra Y., Aikhenvald (eds.), *Adjective Classes: A Cross-linguistic Typology*, Oxford: Oxford University Press, 1–49. https://doi.org/10.1093/oso/9780199270934.003.0001

Dixon, R. M. W., 2010. *Basic Linguistic Theory*, Oxford: Oxford University Press.

Doke, C. M., 1935. *Bantu Linguistic Terminology*, London: Longman, Green & Co.

Dryer, Matthew S., 2005. 'Order of subject, object and verb', in Martin Haspelmath, Matthew Dryer, David Gil & Bernard Comrie (eds.), *The World Atlas of Language Structures Online*, Leipzig: Max Planck Institute for Evolutionary Anthropology.

Dryer, Matthew S., 2006. 'Word order', in Timothy Shopen (ed.), *Clause Structure, Language Typology and Syntactic Description*, Cambridge: Cambridge University Press, 61–131.

Dryer, Matthew S., 2013. 'Polar questions', in Martin Haspelmath, Matthew Dryer, David Gil and Bernard Comrie (eds.), *The World Atlas of Language Structures Online*, Leipzig: Max Planck Institute for Evolutionary Anthropology.

Egbokare, Francis O., 2001. 'Phonosemantic correspondences in Emai attributive ideophones', in F. K. Erhnard Voeltz & Christa Kilian-Hatz (eds.), *Ideophones*, Amsterdam: John Benjamins, 87–96. https://doi.org/10.1075/tsl.44.08egb

Emenanjo, Nolue E., 2015. *A Grammar of Contemporary Igbo: Constituents, Features and Processes*, Port Harcourt: M&J Grand Orbit Communications: .

Enfield, N. J., 2004. 'Adjectives in Lao', in R. M. W. Dixon & Alexandra. Y Aikhenvald (eds.), *Adjective Classes: A Cross-linguistic Typology*, Oxford: Oxford University Press, 323–347. https://doi.org/10.1093/oso/9780199270934.003.0014

Everett, Daniel L., 2005. 'Cultural constraints on grammar and cognition in Pirahã', *Current Anthropology* 46, 621–646. https://doi.org/10.1086/431525

Everett, Daniel L., 2009. 'Pirahã culture and grammar: A response to some criticisms', *Language* 85, 405– 442. https://doi.org/10.1353/lan.0.0104

Ezenwafor Chibunma, A. & Mmadike, Benjamin I., 2012. 'A study of the syllable structure and tone in Etulo', in O. Ndimele (ed.), *Language, Literature and Communication in a Dynamic World. A Festschrift for Chinyere Ohiri A*, Port Harcourt: LAN, 617–622.

Ezenwafor, Chikelu A., 2009. *Interaction of Tone with Syntax in Etulo*, M.A. thesis. Nnamdi Azikiwe University, Awka.

Ezenwafor, Chikelu I., 2012. *Negation in Etulo*, M.A. thesis. Nnamdi Azikiwe University, Awka.

Foley, William A., 2010. 'Events and serial verb constructions', in A. Mengistu, B. Baker & M. Harvey (eds.), *Complex Predicates: Cross-linguistic Perspectives on Event Structure*, Cambridge: Cambridge University Press, 79–109. https://doi.org/10.1017/cbo9780511712234.005

Gbor, J. W. T., 1974. *The Origin, Migration and Settlement of the Tiv in the Benue valley*, B.A. thesis. Ahmadu Bello University, Zaria.

Genetti, C. & Hilderbrandt, K. A., 2004. 'The two adjective classes in Manage', in R. M. W. Dixon & Alexandra Y. Aikhenvald (eds.), *Adjective Classes: A Cross-linguistic Perspective*, Oxford: Oxford University Press, 74–96. https://doi.org/10.1093/oso/9780199270934.003.0003

Gimba, Alhaji, M., 2000. *Bole Verb Morphology*, Ph.D. dissertation. University of California, Los Angeles.

Givon, Thomas, 1993. *English Grammar: A Functional Based Introduction*, Amsterdam: John Benjamins.

Eberhard, David M., Simons, Gary F., & Fennig, Charles D (eds), 2022. *Ethnologue: Languages of the World*, 25th edition, Dallas, Texas: SIL International.

Greenberg, Joseph H., 1963. *The Languages of Africa*, Bloomington, IN: Indiana University Press.

Greenberg, Joseph H., 1996. 'Some universals of grammar with particular reference to the order of meaningful elements', in Joseph H. Greenberg (ed.), *Universals of Language*, London: MIT Press, 73–113.

Hanlor, E. A., 1989. *Land Disputes in Tiv land: Mbagen vs Etulo Dommunities; a Case Study*, M.A. thesis. University of Jos.

Haspelmath, Martin, 2004. 'Coordinating constructions: an overview', in Martin Haspelmath (ed.), *Coordinating Constructions*, Amsterdam: John Benjamins, 3–39. https://doi.org/10.1075/tsl.58.03has

Haspelmath, Martin, 2008. 'Causatives and anticausatives: syntactic universals and usage Frequency', lecture delivered at the Leipzig Spring School on Linguistic Diversity (March 2008).

Haspelmath, Martin, 2009. 'An empirical test of the agglutination hypothesis', in Sergio Seause, Elisabetta Magni & Antonietta Biselto (eds.), *Universals of Language Today*, Dordrecht: Springer, 13–29. https://doi.org/10.1007/978-1-4020-8825-4_2

Heine, Bernd, 1976. *A Typology of African Languages*, Berlin: Dietrich Reimer.

Heine, Bernd, 2008. 'Contact-Induced word order change without word order change', in P. Siemund & N. Kintana (eds.), *Language Contact and Contact Languages*, Amsterdam: John Benjamins, 33–60. https://doi.org/10.1075/hsm.7.04hei

Hengeveld, Kees, 1992. 'Parts of Speech', in M. Fortescue, P. Harder & L. Kristoffersen (eds.), *Layered Structure and Reference in a Functional Perspective*, Amsterdam: John Benjamins, 29–56. https://doi.org/10.1075/pbns.23.04hen

Hengeveld, Kees, 2008. 'Prototypical and non-prototypical noun phrases in functional discourse grammar', in Daniel Garcia Velasco & Jan Rijkhoff (eds.), *The Noun Phrase in Functional Discourse Grammar,* Berlin, New York: De Gruyter Mouton, 43–62. https://doi.org/10.1515/9783110205374.43

Hengeveld, Kees, 2013. 'Parts of Speech as a basic typological determinant', in Jan Rijkhoff & Evan van Lier (eds.), *Flexible Word Classes: Typological Studies of Underspecified Parts of Speech*, Oxford: Oxford University Press, 31–55. https://doi.org/10.1093/acprof:oso/9780199668441.003.0002

Hellwig, Birgit, 2006. 'Serial verb construction in Goemai', in A. Y. Aikhenvald & R. M. W. Dixon (eds.), *Serial Verb Constructions: A Cross Linguistic Typology*, Oxford: Oxford University Press, 89–106.

Huddleston, R. & Pullum, G. K., 2002. *The Cambridge Grammar of the English Language*, Cambridge: Cambridge University Press. https://doi.org/10.1017/9781316423530

Hyman, Larry & Comrie, Bernard, 1981. 'Logophoric references in Gokona', *Journal of African Languages and Linguistics*, 3, 19–37. https://doi.org/10.1515/jall.1981.3.1.19

Hengeveld, K., Rijkhoff, J. & Siewierska, A., 2004. 'Parts of speech system and word orders', *Journal of Linguistics*, 40, 527–570. https://doi.org/10.1017/s0022226704002762

de John, Nicky, 1999. 'The ideophone in Didinga', in F. K. Erhnard Voeltz & Christa Kilian-Hatz (eds.), *Ideophones*, Amsterdam: John Benjamins, 121–138.

Kahrel, Peter, 1996. *Aspects of Negation*, Ph.D. dissertation, University of Amsterdam.

Klamer, Marian, 2000. 'Valency questionnaire', in 2000 East Nusantara Linguistics Workshop, Valency Workshop, Australian National University.

König, Ekkehard, & Siemund, Peter, 2007. 'Speech act distinctions in grammar', in Timothy Shopen (ed.), *Language Typology and Syntactic Description*, Vol. 1 (2nd edition), Cambridge: Cambridge University Press, 276–324. https://doi.org/10.1017/cbo9780511619427.005

König, E., Siemund P. & Topper, S., 2013. 'Intensifiers and reflexive pronouns', in Martin Haspelmath, Matthew Dryer, David Gil & Bernard Comrie (eds.), *The World Atlas of Language Structures Online*, Leipzig: Max Planck Institute for Evolutionary Anthropology.

Kortmann, Bernd, 1991. 'The triad, tense-aspect-aktionsart: problems and possible solutions', *Belgian Journal of Linguistics*, 6, 9–30.

Li, Charles, N. & Thompson, Sandra A., 1981. *Mandarin Chinese: A Functional Reference Grammar*, Berkeley, CA: University of California Press.

Lieber, Rochelle & Stekauer, Pavol, 2009. 'Status and definition of compounding', in R. Lieber & Pavol Stekauer (eds.), *Oxford Handbook of Compounding*, Oxford: Oxford University Press, 3–18.

Lord, Carol, 1975. 'Igbo verb compounds and the lexicon', *Studies in African Linguistics*, 6, 23–48.

Lord, Carol, 1993. *Historical Change in Serial Verb Constructions*, Amsterdam: John Benjamins.

Lyons, John, 1977. *Semantics*. Cambridge: Cambridge University Press.

Maduka, Durunze N., 1983. 'Igbo ideophones and the lexicon', *Journal of the Linguistic Association of Nigeria* 2, 22–29.

Marchese, Lynell, 1986. 'Tense/aspect and the development of auxiliaries in Kru languages', in Virgil L. Poulter & Desmond C. Derbyshire (eds.), *Summer Institute of Linguistics Publications in Linguistics*, Dallas, TX: Summer Institute of Linguistics, 1–274.

Martin, Samuel E., 1992. *A Reference Grammar of Korean*, Tokyo: The Charles Tuttle Company.

Matthew, Stephen, 2006. 'On serial verb constructions in Cantonese', in A. Y. Aikhenvald & R. M. W Dixon (eds.), *Serial Verb Construction: A Cross Linguistic Typology*, Oxford: Oxford University Press, 69–87. https://doi.org/10.1093/oso/9780199279159.003.0002

McLaughlin, Fiona M., 2004. 'Is there an adjective class in Wolof?', in R. M. W. Dixon & Alexandra Y. Aikhenvald (eds.), *Adjective Classes: A Cross-linguistic Perspective*, Oxford: Oxford University Press, 242–262. https://doi.org/10.1093/oso/9780199270934.003.0010

Meyase, S. M., 2021. 'Polarity in a four-level tone language: tone features in Tenyidie', *Phonology* 38, 123–146. https://doi.org/10.1017/s0952675721000063

Miestamo, Matti, 2005. *Standard Negation: The Negation of Declarative Verbal Main Clauses in a Typological Perspective*, Berlin: Mouton de Gruyter. https://doi.org/10.1515/9783110197631

Miller, Carol A., 1998. 'It takes two to tango: understanding and acquiring symmetrical verbs', *Journal of Psycholinguistic Research*, 27, 385–1411.

Nigerian Bible Translation Trust, 2012. *Reading and writing in Etulo*. Ms. (Unpublished draft)

Nebel, A., 1948. *Dinka Grammar (Rek-Malual dialect) with Texts and Vocabulary*, Verona: Missioni Africane.

Newman, Paul, 2000. *The Hausa Language. An Encyclopaedic Reference Grammar*, New Haven & London: Yale University Press.

Okoji, Oko R., 1986. 'Tense and aspect in Yala', *Journal of West African Languages*, 16, 37–52.

Okoye, Adaobi N., & Egenti, Martha C., 2015. 'On Etulo ideophones', IOSR *Journal of Humanities and Social Science*, 20, 56–59.

Okoye, Adaobi N., 2009. *A Preliminary Investigation into the Morphology and Syntax of Etulo*, M.A. thesis. Nnamdi Azikiwe University, Awka.

Omamor, Augusta P. E., 1982. 'Tense and aspect in Itsekiri', *Journal of West African Languages*, 12, 95–129.

Omoruyi, Thomas O., 1986. 'Adjectives and adjectivalisation processes in Edo', *Studies in African Linguistics*, 17, 283–302. https://doi.org/10.32473/sal.v17i3.107486

Payne, John R., 1985. 'Negation', in Timothy Shopen (ed.), *Language Typology and Syntactic Description*, vol. 1, Clause Structure, Cambridge: Cambridge University Press, 197–242.

Payne, Thomas E., 1997. *Describing Morpho-syntax: A Guide for Field Linguists*, Cambridge: Cambridge University Press.

Saint-Dizier, P., 2006. 'Introduction to the syntax and semantics of prepositions', in P. Saint-Dizier (ed.), *Syntax and Semantics of Prepositions*, Dordrecht: Springer, 1–26. https://doi.org/10.1007/1-4020-3873-9_1

Scalise, S., Fabregas, A. & Forza, F., 2009. 'Exocentricity in compounding', *Gengo Kenkyu* (Journal of the Linguistic Society of Japan), 135, 49–84.

Scalise, Sergio & Forza, Francesca, 2011. 'Compounding', *Linguistics*. https://doi.org/10.1093/obo/9780199772810-0060

Schachter, Paul & Shopen, Timothy, 2007. 'Parts of speech systems', in Timothy Shopen (ed.), *Language Typology and Syntactic Description*, vol. 1, Clause Structure, Cambridge: Cambridge University Press, 1–60. https://doi.org/10.1017/cbo9780511619427.001

Schuh, Russell G., 1998. *A Grammar of Miya*, Berkeley, CA: University of California Press.

Shain, R., 1988. 'Ethnologue 14 report for language code: utr', *Ethnologue: Languages of the World*, Dallas, TX: SIL International.

Stassen, Leon, 2000. 'AND-languages and WITH-languages', *Linguistic Typology*, 4, 1–154.

Stekauer, P., Valera, S. & Kortvelyessy, L., 2012. *Word Formation in the World's Languages: A Typological Survey*, Cambridge: Cambridge University Press, https://doi.org/10.1017/cbo9780511895005

Stolz, Thomas & Veselinova, Ljuba, 2005. 'Ordinal numerals', in Martin Haspelmath, Matthew Dryer, David Gil & Bernard Comrie (eds.), *The World Atlas of Language Structures Online*, Leipzig: Max Planck Institute for Evolutionary Anthropology.

Tabe, Sam, 2007. *A Brief History of the Etulo: An Introduction to Divine Kingship*, Makurdi: Aboki Publishers.

Thompson, Sandra A., 1973. 'Resultative verb compounds in Mandarin Chinese: a case for lexical rules', *Language*, 49, 361–379.

Trask, R. L., 1993. *A Dictionary of Grammatical Terms in Linguistics*, London: Routledge, https://doi.org/10.4324/9780203393369

Uchechukwu, Chiinedu, 2007. 'Subject-object switching and the Igbo lexicon', in Francisco José Ruiz de Mendoza Ibánez (ed.), *Annual Review of Cognitive Linguistics*, 5, 55–76. https://doi.org/10.1075/arcl.5.04uch

Welmers, William E., 1973. *African Language Structures*, Los Angeles, CA: University of California Press.

Willamson, Kay & Roger Blench. 2000. 'Niger-Congo', in Bernd Heine & Derek Nurse (eds.), *African Languages: An Introduction*, Cambridge: Cambridge University Press, 11–142.

Willamson, Kay, 1986. 'The Igbo associative and specific constructions', in Bogers Koen, Harry van der Hulst & Marten Mous (eds.), *The Phonological Representation of Suprasegmentals*, Dordrecht: Foris, 195–206. https://doi.org/10.1515/9783110866292-011

Willamson, Kay, 1986. 'Niger-Congo: SVO or SOV?', *Journal of West African Languages*, 16, 5–15.

Willamson, Kay, 1989. 'Benue-Congo Overview', in John Bendor-Samuel (ed.), *The Niger-Congo Languages*, Lanham, MD: University Press of America, 246–274.

Yeung, K., 2003. *Universal vs. Language Specific Properties of Grammaticalized Complementizers: Two Case Studies in Multi-Functionality*, M.Phil. thesis. University of Hong Kong.

Yu, Hyen-Kyeng, 1998. *A Study of Korean Adjectives*, Ph.D. dissertation. Yensei University, Seoul.

Zeller, Jochen, 2020. 'Syntax', in Rainer Vossen and Gerrit J. Dimmendal (eds.), *The Oxford Handbook of African Languages*, Oxford: Oxford University Press, 66–87. https://doi.org/10.1093/oxfordhb/9780199609895.013.67

Index

adjectives 37–38, 41, 43, 72–73, 75, 77–78, 80–81, 90, 92–96, 98–103, 111–112, 123, 127–129, 136, 172–173, 182, 186–187, 218, 243
adverbials 39, 68, 71, 103–104, 107–110, 112–113, 123, 129, 141, 159, 161–162, 167–169, 171, 176, 210, 224, 226, 228, 232–233, 235, 240–241, 243
adverbs 51, 103–108, 110–113, 120, 122, 127, 129, 146, 228, 231, 236, 238, 241, 243
  ideophonic adverbs 105–106, 113, 129
adversative marker 141, 153, 157–158, 171
adversative markers 157
affix 33–35, 37–38, 50, 68, 125, 128, 141, 146–147, 243
  hybrid affix 37–38, 50
  prefix 33–34, 37–39, 41, 50, 96, 98–101, 125, 127–128, 130, 142, 146, 172–173, 177, 221, 243
  suffix 33
affixation 7, 37–39, 50, 65, 128, 224
allophones 9, 15–17, 26, 35
anaphoric reference 64–65, 67, 72, 205
anticausatives 204, 206, 208
applicatives 195–197, 199, 201, 203, 207
argument structure 8, 189, 201
aspect
  imperfective 223–225, 227
    habitual 97, 108, 176, 180, 220, 224–225, 227, 231–234, 241
    progressive 23, 29, 84, 97, 128, 176, 180, 219–220, 224–225, 227–231, 233–234, 241
  perfective 144, 188, 223–225, 227
    perfectal 22, 108, 142, 234–235
assimilation 7, 9, 26–27, 29–30, 35, 45, 114, 118, 132, 138

associative construction 35, 47–48, 50, 72, 74, 79–81, 83

Benue (state) 1–5, 85, 131, 208, 225, 228, 243

causatives 201–202, 207, 212, 216, 218
coalescence. *See* vowel coalescence
complement clause 6, 93, 159–163, 172, 211
complementizers 159–163, 172, 211–212, 239
compounding 7, 37, 50, 131, 133, 139, 195
consecutive construction 208, 213, 218–219, 221–222, 244
consonant phonemes. *See* phonemes: consonant phonemes
constituent order 55, 78, 177–178, 182–183, 185–187, 218
coordinators 141, 153–157, 160
copula 38, 54, 59, 70, 72, 81, 93, 95–96, 99, 101, 114, 119–121, 128, 137–138, 141, 151, 172–177, 181, 187–188, 211–212, 231
  existential copula 114, 119–121, 172
  semi-copula 174–177
demonstratives 51, 64, 67–72, 75–78, 80–82, 96, 99, 107, 109, 128, 136, 166–167, 182, 184, 187
determiners 40, 51, 59, 61, 68–69, 71–72, 75–77, 80, 82–83, 99, 104, 107, 151–152, 166, 184
disjunction markers 141, 153, 157–158
double object construction 195–196

elision 7, 9, 27–29, 35, 50, 63, 86, 104, 195
Emai (language) 122
English (language) 4, 6, 10, 31–32, 59, 61–63, 65, 67, 71, 73–74, 92, 100, 104, 108, 111, 114–118, 126, 130–131, 137,

146, 148–149, 154, 157, 161, 168, 171, 174–175, 184–185, 189, 197, 200, 204, 206, 220, 223–224, 228, 235, 238
Etulo
  land 1–6
  people 1–5, 7
  religion 5
  speakers 2, 45, 107, 117, 131, 137, 169
Ewe (language) 35, 65, 85, 92, 103, 122–123, 126, 209, 218, 220, 243–244

fieldwork 1, 6, 10

genitives 44, 48, 77, 128, 141, 178, 185, 187
gerundive nominals 39–40, 43, 47, 50
glide formation 9, 27, 32, 35
grammaticalization 42, 44, 49, 63, 76, 121–122, 159–160, 172, 211–212, 223–224, 233, 235, 241

Hausa (ethnic group) 1
Hausa (language) 4, 31, 74, 93, 113, 131, 139
homorganicity 25–26, 30, 164

ideophones 7, 11–12, 37–38, 41, 43, 50–51, 92, 98–100, 103–105, 122–130, 141, 177, 243
ideophonic adverbs. *See* adverbs: ideophonic adverbs
Idoma (language) 4, 85, 244
Idomoid (languages) 1, 4, 7, 83, 225, 243
Igbo (language) 4, 33–35, 62–63, 79, 85, 90, 92, 103, 122, 130, 139, 142, 200, 218, 223, 225, 228, 243–244
Igede (language) 4
intensifiers 62–63, 72, 92, 102, 111, 123
International Phonetic Alphabet (IPA) 6
interrogatives 17, 22–23, 66, 70, 72, 75–77, 83, 104, 126, 141–142, 144, 147–149, 151–152, 154, 178–179, 187
isolating/analytic language 37, 50, 243

logophoric reference 52, 64–65, 72

minimal pairs 9, 11–12, 14, 21, 35
modality
  counterfactual 170, 227, 236, 239
  hortative 236–238, 241
  hypothetical 236, 239, 241
  imperative 126, 142–143, 220, 236–237, 241
  obligative 236, 238, 241
  potential/permissive 236, 240
  probability 227, 236, 240–241
multilingualism 4

nasalization 9–10, 15–17, 26, 29, 35, 52, 56, 62, 115, 118
nasalized vowel 15–17, 29
nasals 12, 14–17, 19, 24–27, 29–31, 38, 74, 82–84, 91, 96, 100, 164, 243
negation 7–8, 23, 71, 102, 126, 141–148, 209, 237, 241
Nigerian pidgin (language) 6
nominalization 28, 33–34, 37–39, 41, 47, 50, 96, 98–99, 101, 125, 127–128, 130, 173, 177
noun
  deverbal nouns 38
  noun compounds 23, 44–47, 50
  noun phrase 72, 76–77, 115, 118, 134, 136, 153, 156, 159, 172–173, 178, 181–182
  syllabic structure 26, 31
number marking 75
numeral system 51–52, 54, 58, 75, 77–78, 130–137, 139, 141, 182, 184
  cardinal numerals 131–132, 134, 136–137, 139
  distributive numerals 131, 137
  ordinal numerals 131, 134, 136, 139
object alternation/dative shift 197, 203
orthography 6–7

phonemes
  consonant phonemes 9–10, 12–13, 15
  vowel phonemes 9, 14, 35
phonology 2, 6–7, 9, 15, 17, 27–29, 31–32, 35, 44, 46, 52, 63, 72–74, 82–83, 86, 91, 93, 100, 103, 118, 122–124, 131–132, 135, 142, 148, 165, 195, 216, 243
phonotactics 9, 24, 31, 122
plural morpheme 51, 73, 75, 77, 82, 184
possessives 7, 40, 44, 47–48, 51, 59–62, 72, 75, 79–81, 99, 117–118, 141, 174, 177–178, 185
predicate 52, 61, 65, 73, 83, 85, 90–91, 93, 95–98, 100–101, 114, 119–121, 123, 130, 141, 145, 159, 161–162, 172, 175, 177, 179–181, 187–189, 191, 193, 195, 199, 201–204, 207–208, 210–211, 218, 225, 227–228, 234–235, 244

prepositions 29, 51, 55–56, 113–122, 137–139, 149, 162, 175, 178, 181, 185, 187–188, 191, 196–197, 199, 203, 216, 243
pronominals 17, 51–52, 56–57, 62, 64–65, 69, 72, 115, 165, 185, 193, 200, 204
pronoun
  free and bound pronouns 52, 56, 72
  interrogative pronouns 66, 72, 148
  object pronouns 51–52, 55–56, 62, 118
  personal pronouns 51–52, 59, 61–63, 72
  reflexive pronouns 51, 61–64, 72, 204, 207
  relative pronouns 51, 67, 72, 134, 164–166, 172
  subject pronouns 20, 23, 52–54
property concept 72, 81–82, 92–93, 96, 98, 100, 103, 126

qualificatives 51, 92, 96, 100, 102–103, 111, 123, 128, 139, 182, 188, 195

reciprocals 64, 204, 206, 208
reduplication 7, 37, 39–40, 43, 50, 69, 92–93, 98, 100–101, 104–105, 122–124, 130, 137, 238
reflexives. *See* pronoun: reflexive pronouns
relative clause 6, 67, 77, 96, 98, 101, 159, 164–168, 172, 178, 185, 187

SIL Comparative African Wordlist (SILCAWL) 6
switch function 218
syllable structure 7, 9, 24–27, 31, 124

Taraba (state) 1–2, 5
tense
  future tense 225–226
  non-future tense 106, 225, 227–228, 241, 243
tense, aspect and modality (TAM) 23–24, 83, 91, 97, 172, 177, 179, 188, 219–220, 222–223, 225
Tiv (ethnic group) 1, 3–4
Tiv (language) 4, 6, 74
tone polarity 23, 35, 91, 226
tonology 7, 84, 128, 227
typology 1, 37, 51, 68, 72, 92–93, 103, 153, 158, 177–178, 185–188, 208, 210, 223, 244

valence-decreasing operations 8, 189, 204–205
valence-increasing operations 8, 189, 195, 201, 203
verb
  ambitransitive verbs 189–190, 197, 201, 208
  ditransitive verbs 189–190, 195–196, 199, 201
  infinitive verb form 33, 38, 46, 50, 96, 160, 162, 172–173, 221
  intransitive verbs 189–191, 198, 201–203, 217
  non-obligatory complement verbs (NCVs) 85–86, 90–91, 190, 196, 201, 244
  obligatory complement verbs (OCVs) 85–88, 90–91, 189–194, 196, 201, 203, 244
  serial verbs 44, 48–50, 85, 90–91, 113, 117, 119, 121, 143, 180, 189, 196, 199, 203, 207–208, 210–211, 214, 216–217, 219, 221, 244
  speech verbs 160, 163, 211–212
  stative verbs 39–40, 92, 96, 100, 103, 176, 179, 212, 225, 228–230, 232–235
  symmetrical verbs 198, 200
  transitive verbs 189–190, 193, 195, 201, 204–206, 217
  verb classification 8, 85, 90
  verb compound 44, 48–50, 85, 90, 119, 202, 212
  verb phrase 105, 107, 111, 153, 155–157, 160, 178
  verb serialization 101, 119, 189, 208, 211, 243
vowel coalescence 31, 35
vowel harmony 9, 27, 33–35, 243
vowel insertion 31–32, 35
  epithetic 31–32
  prothetic 31–32
vowel lengthening 17, 22, 35, 122–124, 130, 142, 144, 147–148, 152
vowel phonemes. *See* phonemes: vowel phonemes

Wolaitta (language) 122–123
word order 8, 97, 141, 177–180, 185–187, 189, 196–198, 200, 243

Yoruba (language) 4, 35, 103, 122, 130, 139, 142, 223, 243–244

About the Team

Alessandra Tosi was the managing editor for this book.

Adèle Kreager proof-read this manuscript and compiled the index.

Jeevanjot Kaur Nagpal designed the cover. The cover was produced in InDesign using the Fontin font.

Annie Hine typeset the book in InDesign. The main font is Noto Serif.

Jeremy Bowman produced the PDF, paperback, and hardback editions and created the EPUB.

The conversion to the HTML edition was performed with epublius, an open-source software which is freely available on our GitHub page at https://github.com/OpenBookPublishers

Hannah Shakespeare was in charge of marketing.

This book was peer-reviewed by two anonymous referees. Experts in their field, these readers give their time freely to help ensure the academic rigour of our books. We are grateful for their generous and invaluable contributions.

This book need not end here...

Share

All our books — including the one you have just read — are free to access online so that students, researchers and members of the public who can't afford a printed edition will have access to the same ideas. This title will be accessed online by hundreds of readers each month across the globe: why not share the link so that someone you know is one of them?

This book and additional content is available at
https://doi.org/10.11647/OBP.0467

Donate

Open Book Publishers is an award-winning, scholar-led, not-for-profit press making knowledge freely available one book at a time. We don't charge authors to publish with us: instead, our work is supported by our library members and by donations from people who believe that research shouldn't be locked behind paywalls.

Join the effort to free knowledge by supporting us at
https://www.openbookpublishers.com/support-us

We invite you to connect with us on our socials!

BLUESKY	MASTODON	LINKEDIN
@openbookpublish.bsky.social	@OpenBookPublish @hcommons.social	open-book-publishers

Read more at the Open Book Publishers Blog
https://blogs.openbookpublishers.com

You may also be interested in:

Benjamin Franklin, Orthoepist and Phonetician
Insights into the Genesis of Colonial American-English Phonology

Gary D. German

https://doi.org/10.11647/OBP.0470

Morphosyntactic Variation and Contact
A Comparative View from Daco-Romance

Ștefania Costea

https://doi.org/10.11647/OBP.0494

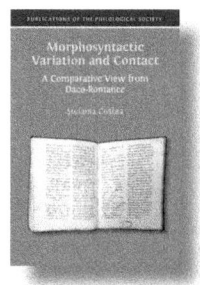

A Grammar of Jordanian Arabic
Bruno Herin and Enam Al-Wer

https://doi.org/10.11647/OBP.0410

www.ingramcontent.com/pod-product-compliance
Lightning Source LLC
Chambersburg PA
CBHW082019240426
43667CB00046B/2866